THE BLACK DEATH
IN EGYPT
AND ENGLAND

A Comparative Study

STUART J. BORSCH

UNIVERSITY OF TEXAS PRESS
AUSTIN

Copyright © 2005 by the University of Texas Press

All rights reserved
Printed in the United States of America

First edition, 2005

Requests for permission to reproduce material from this work should
be sent to Permissions, University of Texas Press, Box 7819, Austin, TX
78713-7819.

⊗The paper used in this book meets the minimum requirements
of ANSI/NISO Z39.48-1992 (R1997) (Permanence of Paper).

Library of Congress Cataloging-in-Publication Data

Borsch, Stuart J. (Stuart James), 1964–
The Black Death in Egypt and England :
a comparative study / Stuart J. Borsch
p.   cm.
Includes bibliographical references and index.
ISBN: 0292722133

1. Black Death—Egypt.   2. Black Death—England.   I. Title.
RC179.E3B67   2005
330.962'024—dc22

2004023691

— THE BLACK DEATH IN EGYPT AND ENGLAND —

This study is dedicated to my parents.

CONTENTS

A NOTE ON TRANSLITERATION

Diacritical marks are not used in the transliteration of words from Arabic. This was done on the reasoning that readers unfamiliar with Arabic would find them cumbersome whereas those with a knowledge of Arabic would not require them to recognize the words in question. The symbol ʿ is used to represent the Arabic letter ʿayn. The symbol ʾ is used for the letter hamza.

ACKNOWLEDGMENTS

The bulk of the research for this study was carried out in Egypt, and I would like to thank the Fulbright Organization and the Social Science Research Council for generous grants that made my two-year stay there possible. I am particularly grateful to friends and colleagues in Egypt who helped me navigate my way through Egyptian life. I owe a deep debt of gratitude to Ahmad ʿAbd al-ʿAziz Adam, my constant companion and friend in Cairo. My special thanks go to Muhammad Shishtawi, who assisted me in reading the endowment deeds (*waqfiyyat*) at the Ministry of Religious Endowments (*Wizarat al-Awqaf*).

I am immensely grateful to numerous scholars, friends, and family members who have helped me during my work as a student and researcher. I would like to express particularly strong appreciation for the efforts of Richard Bulliet, who inspired my interest in socioeconomic history and quantitative methodology. His guidance and assistance as my advisor over the years has been of immeasurable value. Joel Kaye was also immensely supportive, playing devil's advocate and helping me shape the focus of a comparison that constantly threatened to get out of control. If some elements of this comparison do indeed remain unwieldy, I can only say that I tried my best to internalize his wise, cautionary voice.

I would like to thank the other members of my committee who helped guide me through the final stages of my thesis, which preceded this work: Charles Tilly, Richard Nelson, and Neguin Yavari. Carl Petry assisted me with valuable advice on issues related to every facet of life in Mamluk Egypt. Remie Constable was extremely supportive with her suggestions and comments, particularly during the early stages of the research for this book. I would also like to thank the editors at the University of Texas

Press for their valuable help in the final stages of completing this work. I would finally like to express my warmest appreciation for some special people in my life who helped keep me going during the difficult final stages of finishing this study: Laura Straus, Erika Najinski, and my twin brother, Matthew.

ONE

INTRODUCTION
Plague and Methodology

We live in an age of steadily growing population and urban sprawl, with industrial growth continually encroaching on the few untouched pockets of our ecosystem, so it is hard for us to imagine our distant ancestors' fear of nature as an encroaching predator. It is harder still for us to conceive of the terror and shock they experienced as urban centers shrank and cultivated fields slowly reverted to their natural states. Yet this was the predominant mood that gripped the survivors of the Black Death. Their numbers had been devastated by a mysterious and horrifying disease that had come from "the East" and revisited generation after generation in waves of epidemics. Bewildered communities watched in dismay as nature took the place of humanity's civilized infrastructure. They drew together in fear as small hamlets disappeared from the map and villages dwindled to ghosts of their former selves. People fled in panic to the largest cities, only to find that the former epicenters of civilization were themselves shrinking, as once-crowded neighborhoods and bustling marketplaces fell into decay. Others held out in their familiar rural settings, helplessly trying to confront the powerful forces of nature as their small numbers grew too few to resist the oncoming wave of indigenous plants and forests that their ancestors had once cleared. The natural environment, aided by a small rod-shaped bacterium, had returned with a vengeance to reclaim its former dominance.

A ship arrived in Alexandria. Aboard it were thirty-two merchants and a total of three hundred people—among them traders and slaves. Nearly all of them had died. There was no one alive on the ship, save four of the traders, one slave, and about forty sailors. These [forty-five] survivors [soon] died in Alexandria.[1]

قدمت ماركب إلى الإسكندرية كان فيها اثنان و ثلاثون تاجراً و

ثلأمائة رجل ، ما بين تجار و عبيد ، فماتوا كلهوم، و لم يبق منهم

غير أربعة من التاجر و عبد واحد ، و نحو أربعين من البحارة،

وفماتوا جاميعاً بالثغر.

Account of a plague ship at Alexandria, 1347

This same story, often accompanied by a vivid account of a ship full of corpses drifting into port, was repeated in virtually every civilization of the Old World. A report of the Black Death's arrival at Bristol in England reads like the one from Alexandria. The death toll and symptoms were the same. The morbid story was reiterated in France, the Holy Roman Empire, the kingdoms of Spain, the Italian city-states, the Golden Horde in Russia, the Byzantine Empire, the principalities of North Africa, the al-Khanate sultanate in Persia, the kingdoms of India, and the Mongol Empire in China. This disease was "a random occurrence in history and almost unique."[2] So high and sudden was the mortality that some scholars maintain that its effects resembled those of a nuclear war more than those of a pandemic.[3] As Norman Cantor describes it, "It threatened the stability and viability of civilization. It was as if a neutron bomb had been detonated. Nothing like this has happened before or since in the recorded history of mankind, and the men and women of the fourteenth century would never be the same."[4]

"Black Death" is a term for the fourteenth-century manifestation of a plague caused by *Yersinia pestis*, a small rod-shaped bacterium (bacillus) that is usually carried by the rat flea, *Xenopsylla cheopis*.[5] In rodent colonies, the bacillus lives in the guts of the fleas and is transmitted back and forth between fleas and rodents.[6] The disease can remain endemic to rodent colonies indefinitely and does not need *Homo sapiens* to survive. When the disease does break out of its natural environment, it is usually, although not exclusively, spread by the joint action of fleas and the black rat, *Rattus rattus*.[7]

When a flea bites a plague-infected rodent, its esophagus becomes blocked with plague bacilli.[8] This blockage makes it impossible for the flea to eat. The flea eventually dies, but not before it vainly attempts to feed on the black rat or another warm-blooded host.[9] If the flea happens upon a human, it bites into the flesh, but rather than swallowing a small piece of human skin, it succeeds only in regurgitating massive amounts of plague bacilli into the superficial wound. The flea eventually dies, but not before it has had the opportunity to infect countless numbers of rats and humans.

When the flea regurgitates *Y. pestis* bacilli into a human host, they multiply in the victim's bloodstream. The lymph glands filter the bacilli out of the bloodstream, and the glands, typically those in the neck or groin area, subsequently become engorged with bacilli. This causes agonizing pain at the site of the lymph nodes, which first darken and then swell to form a "bubo" (hence "bubonic" plague). The buboes vary from almond- to orange-sized. The victim also suffers from flu-like symptoms, including a high fever (up to 107 degrees Fahrenheit). The bacilli then wreak widespread damage throughout the victim's body, attacking the lungs, heart, and kidneys. The bacilli also attack the nervous system, sometimes leading to the wild hysteria that gave rise to the phrase "the dance of death." In most cases, the victim then hemorrhages massive amounts of blood—which causes dark blotches to appear—before slipping into a coma and dying.[10]

The infection of the human host takes one of three clinical forms. The first of these is bubonic plague. This form of the disease arises as a result of a fleabite and cannot be transmitted directly from person to person. As described above, plague is spread through the lymphatic system. Symptoms generally appear within two to three days, and the disease is fatal in about seventy-five percent of the cases. The excruciatingly painful buboes discharge copious amounts of yellow pus if they burst open.[11] The damage to the nervous system adds to the agony caused by the swollen buboes, leaving the victim prostrate with pain. The victim frequently falls unconscious at this point. However, in many cases the victim stays awake, and the damage to the nervous system causes hallucinations and delirium. Although rendered nearly immobile by the pain, the patient will sometimes lash out in a mad assault at those around him. Other types of frenzied behavior in the midst of paralyzing pain are also recorded. An observer of the Black Death in the south of France reported that "a man climbed on to the roof of his house and threw down the tiles into the street. Another executed a mad, grotesque dance on the roof." [12] As the bacilli multiply in the victim's bloodstream, massive hemorrhages occur under the skin and in the body. Dark blotches often appear on the skin, and the intensely putrid odor caused by the disease is magnified as the patient vomits and discharges bloody urine and feces. At this point, the suffering patient lapses into a coma and dies, a week to twelve days after contracting the disease.

The second form of this disease is known as pneumonic plague. This secondary manifestation occurs when the bacilli settle in the lungs. The victim develops severe pneumonia and soon begins to cough up enormous amounts of bloody phlegm as the lungs hemorrhage. Pneumonic plague is nearly always fatal; death from asphyxiation occurs within two to four days. Not dependent on flea transmission, this form of plague is very infectious. The disease is spread by airborne droplets from the victim's cough and can infect an entire household within a matter of minutes.

The third and rarest form of plague is septicemic plague, which occurs when the bacilli manage to bypass the lymphatic system and enter the bloodstream directly. It is always fatal. Death occurs within hours, and there are often no accompanying symptoms.[13]

Y. pestis struck the Mediterranean with particular ferocity during the sixth-century reign of Justinian I. The disease remained endemic to this area for centuries thereafter.[14] It seems that the fourteenth-century plague originated in some part of Central Asia. Arab observers were well informed about the geography of the Old World at this time, and their accounts of the origin of the plague serve to confirm the hypothesis that it began somewhere in Central Asia.

Central Asia was the area that Ibn al-Wardi, a contemporary observer (and later victim) of the Black Death in Syria, described as the "land of darkness."[15] Other Arab observers, like their Western European counterparts, attested to its origins in the "East." In the account of al-Maqrizi, "It started in the land of al-Qan al-Kabir (the Mongol territory) . . . and this was in the year 742 (1341–1342) and news of this arrived from the land of the Uzbeks (in the Golden Horde) . . . and it spread throughout the Mongol lands (al-Qan) killing the il-Qan and his six children . . . and then it spread throughout the Eastern countries and the Bilad al-Uzbek, Istanbul, Qaysariyya, and Rum."[16]

Some contemporary Arab observers described how the eastern chain or gate that separated humanity from Gog and Magog had been broken, allowing this apocalyptic catastrophe to spread. The release of wild men from Gog and Magog appears in Islamic tradition as a harbinger of the end of the world. The word *ta'un* was used specifically for the Black Death. *Waba'* was used to describe the plague, but waba' embraces a wider scope. *Dummal* or *khiyara* was generally used to refer to the plague buboes. The root meaning of *ta'un* carries with it the specific notion of being pierced or transfixed by something. Some popular traditions associated this word with the notion that evil jinn, servants of Satan, were preparing plague arrows in the underworld, which they would then shoot into victims.[17] After the release of wild, mutant men from the great gate or chain that was used to confine them, the Antichrist (*al-Masih al-Dajjal*) would appear, and Jesus would return to the earth to defeat him.

That Central Asia was the starting point for the Black Death seems almost certain. As Don Nardo points out in the introduction to his book on the plague, "The earliest known appearance of the Black Death . . . was in a Christian [Nestorian] community just south of Lake Balkhash . . . archaeologists have found a cemetery with an unusually high number of graves dating to the years 1338–1339; three of the gravestones actually identify plague as the cause of death."[18] Other scholars have confirmed that Nestorian graves in Central Asia, dating from the early fourteenth century, identify the deceased as plague victims.[19] Dr. Pollitzer, a modern researcher of *Y. pestis*, has also concluded that early fourteenth-century Central Asia was the point of origin for the plague.[20]

Striking out from Central Asia, the Black Death, within a few decades, wrought havoc from China to Iceland. Some scholars have asked how this could have been *Y. pestis*. How can it have had a lethal impact that differed so fundamentally from that of known plague bacilli? Some historians have proposed that it was anthrax combined with *Y. pestis*.[21] But could these two disease vectors have operated in tandem over such a wide swath of territory? It seems unlikely. It seems probable that the fourteenth-century manifestation of the plague was something different from the *Y. pestis* that periodically afflicted populations in the Mediterranean.[22] When one looks at the wider scope of the plague, stretching from China through the Middle East to Western Europe, it becomes abundantly clear from the scale and scope of the mortality that there must have been something new, something that could strike with a universal impact over disparate regions of the Old World.[23]

What seems like a more logical hypothesis is that this strain of *Y. pestis* was a new and mutant strain of a previously encountered bacterium.[24] Lawrence Conrad, in his research on the early medieval plague of Justinian and the early Islamic caliphate, has concluded that "the plague bacillus spreading in the sixth century was an extremely virulent and toxic strain of *Pasteurella* [i.e., *Yersinia*] *pestis*."[25] He adds that "the *Pasteurella pestis* strains now found in northern Asia and central Africa are chemically related, yet distinct from that found in India and places to which the plague spread in the third [modern] pandemic."[26] Conrad also states that "with the victims succumbing quickly to bubonic infection, it appears that the strain of *P. pestis* responsible for the pandemic was much more toxic than it is today."[27] It must have been a mutation in the bacteria: how else could a disease endemic to the Mediterranean region suddenly cause an explosion of mortality that eclipsed almost all areas of the Old World?[28]

And how did this mutation take place? One plausible hypothesis might center on the blind evolutionary machinations of the disease and its dynamic interaction with its hosts. It is well known that successful diseases are those that can infect and live in their hosts without causing catastrophic damage to them. A successful disease is one that can evolve with its host, "tame" itself over generations, and become "friendly" enough to survive along with the host, even though it might cause some mortality along the way. The common cold is probably the best example: we suffer a bit, we sniffle, we cough, we spread the germs, but we almost inevitably get better after a short period of time. By contrast, any disease that kills most of its host population risks its own demise: it needs hosts in order to survive.

There are illustrative examples of the latter phenomenon to be found in history. This typically occurs when a disease has just made the jump from one species host to another: the more dissimilar the DNA, the more virulent the impact. Rinderpest, in 1891, decimated cattle in Africa, but then died out from a lack of host animals.[29]

A very cogent example is provided by the evolution of myxomatosis, a relative of smallpox. Myxomatosis, endemic among Brazilian rabbits, was introduced into Australia in an attempt to reduce the number of rabbits, which were breeding rapidly in the absence of predators and devouring pasturage intended for sheep. Australian rabbits, a separate genus from their Brazilian cousins, were nearly wiped out by the "Brazilian friendly" disease. What should be noted here is that the disease slowly acclimated itself to the Australian rabbit population. The disease was 99.8% fatal in the first year it was introduced to its new hosts. In the subsequent year, it was 90% fatal. By the seventh year, its rate of mortality had dropped to 25%. The disease, after having made the leap to a new breed of rabbits, was adapting in such a way that both host and virus could survive together, if not in symbiosis, then at least with an uneasy sort of truce.[30]

Y. pestis, in the pre–Black Death era, had established an uneasy sort of truce with its human and rodent hosts in the Mediterranean region. Plague outbreaks were at times severe, but nothing like the universal catastrophe of the Black Death. The bacteria, in regular contact with fleas, rats, and humans, had adapted to survive by becoming less lethal.[31] One could say the same for smallpox and measles, once highly virulent and fatal diseases that struck the Roman Empire in the second and third centuries CE, yet gradually became tamer and adapted to their human hosts over time.

So why might Y. *pestis* have suddenly appeared in a form that resulted in such dire mortality? A plausible hypothesis lies in the possibility that a strain of the bacterium had become isolated in a part of Central Asia where it had limited contact with humans and rats. An isolated human population in that part of Central Asia had developed taboos about rodent warrens, where the disease was endemic. The train of logic is then as follows. This isolated strain of plague, cut off from contact with humans and rats, evolved over time, adapting to live in a local species of rodents.[32] This species of rodent was not *Rattus rattus*, the black rat; more likely it was the Manchurian marmot.[33] The evolutionary history of this strain of plague was such that, lacking contact with both humans and the black rat, it was subject to divergent evolution.

What this means is that random mutations, occurring naturally over time, experienced no evolutionary pressure to maintain equilibrium with the either the black rat or human populations. These mutations, cut off from any incentives to survive in their former hosts, were likely to make the disease far more lethal than the Y. *pestis* that survived in the Mediterranean region (from the plague of Justinian I to the onset of the Black Death). What emerged in this isolated rodent population may have been a disease with a DNA structure that was simultaneously highly lethal, more easily transmissible, and yet similar enough to the unmutated strain to creep back into its former hosts, particularly the black rat.[34] That not all episodes of the Black Death were accompanied by an epizootic outbreak among rats may suggest that this strain was contagious among a wider range of animals, accounting for the death of livestock that some have attributed to anthrax. It is also possible that the disease could have been spread by the human flea, *Pulex irritans*, which would have provided for easier transmission. It should also be noted, in light of the rapid spread of the disease over such a wide area, that the rat flea can live for several months without feeding.[35]

We still need an explanation for how humans made contact with this isolated rodent population and then spread this strain of Y. *pestis*. According to William McNeill, the Mongols established new trade routes that passed through the area. From there, traders and their potentially flea-infested cargoes carried the infection east, to China, and west, to the Mediterranean and Europe.[36]

It seems quite possible that the mutant strain of Y. *pestis* was capable of being transmitted far more easily than earlier or modern strains of the disease. Perhaps the bacteria had even evolved to spread from human to human, not just in the form of the highly contagious pneumonic plague, but also as a bacillus that could be spread by the human flea.[37] (This does not seem to be the case with the modern version of the plague and *Pulex irritans*.)[38] This might also help explain why the disease spread to areas where shipborne rats were not widely found. It would certainly help explain why the disease was suddenly and universally lethal in the Old World.

It should also be noted that there are a variety of other flea species that may have influenced the course of the Black Death, especially if that particular strain of *Y. pestis* varied from the modern one. *Xenopsylla cheopis* is not the only culprit that may have been involved. There are other fleas that can act as disease vectors, with varying levels of efficaciousness, among them *Ceratophyllus fasciatus* (another European rat flea), *Nosopsyllus fasciatus* (the northern rat flea), *Xenopsylla astia* (a Southeast Asian rat flea), *Xenopsylla vexabilis* (another Southeast Asian rat flea), and *Stivalius cognatus*.[39]

It should also be noted that *Rattus rattus* is certainly not the only disease host that is associated with plague-infected fleas. Other rat species, such as *Rattus norvegicus*, are also quite capable of acting as a source of transmission. Even flies can act as vectors for the transmission of *Y. pestis*, as Alexander Yersin noted in his work in East Asia.[40] These factors should be considered by historians attempting to explain the extremely high virulence of the fourteenth-century pandemic, especially if *Y. pestis* was prevalent in a mutant form.

Since rat fleas can survive for up to six months without feeding, they can carry plague bacteria over long distances, independent of rats.[41] It would account for the appearance of plague in such isolated areas as Iceland and Greenland. It might account for the appearance of the plague in areas such as the Khymer Empire in Cambodia, an irrigation society that collapsed at the time of the Black Death.

This remains hypothetical, but any discussion of the impact of this civilizational disaster should include some explanation of its lethality. Whatever its origins were, it devastated China in the 1330s, overwhelmed the Golden Horde in Russia, and swept on through the Mediterranean basin. However tenable the above hypothesis might be, we know that the impact of the plague on disparate regions, such as the Middle East, was horrifically traumatic.

The Black Death followed trade routes as it rapidly spread from Central Asia into the Middle East. Fleas in bundles of grain or other produce could have easily been transported across the long distances between

Mongol trade stations to the Crimea. From there it spread to Constantinople and thence to Syria, Egypt, North Africa, and Spain (as well as Southern Europe). It seems likely that it also followed an overland trade route to Iraq.[42]

The grand scope of this pandemic cries out for further studies, particularly ones that focus on non-Western areas of the Old World, and, as I will argue, studies that use Western Europe, or parts of Western Europe, as focal points for comparison. The critical question posed by this work concerns the survivors. How were their civilizations and economies changed by the pandemic? How did the survivors adapt, or fail to adapt, to dramatic depopulation?

In many regions, survivors were unable to adapt to the traumatic changes in their surroundings and died from numerous manifestations of "secondary death." In other areas, survivors were able to adapt, finding new ways to manipulate the environment that allowed them to recover and even flourish. Yet all of the survivors, from the walking dead to those fortunate enough to adjust, knew that their culture, their religion, their economy, and their social structure would never be the same.

This study tells the story of those survivors. It asks why people in one region fell prey to a secondary death while those in another adapted and recovered from the trauma of the pandemic. The question is answered through a comparison of Egypt and England, and the dramatic divergence in outcomes illustrates just how profound a role the Black Death played in the history of world civilizations.

Comparing late-medieval Egypt and England is obviously not an easy task from any standpoint, linguistic, cultural, structural, or methodological. As I will detail below, many of the dissimilarities that appeared daunting at first could be reduced within the framework of an economic model. However, finding balancing sets of data posed an arduous task. Since viable statistics on any medieval or ancient economy can be hard to find, locating matching quantitative sets and then juxtaposing them in a methodologically sound framework is challenging.

Economic data for late-medieval England is widely available. By contrast, the number of published sources and studies for Egypt is minuscule. This is especially true for Islamic Egypt, which has received far less attention than pharaonic, Ptolemaic, Roman, or Byzantine Egypt. Medieval Arabic chronicles are available, but they are mostly devoted to political events; in many cases, only a few valuable economic figures can be found in the midst of thousands of pages. Any economic historian working on medieval Egypt must be able to quickly scan these chronicles, reading with enough accuracy to pick out economic details that can be used either qualitatively or quantitatively. As I worked to reach this reading speed, a two-year research trip to Egypt provided me with the opportunity to attain fluency in colloquial Egyptian, a mandatory task for anyone who embarks on an in-depth exploration of the resources available in Cairo.

Not surprisingly, it was in Cairo that most of the data was collected and compiled. It was there that I was able to reevaluate the source material I had already been using and to explore new avenues of research. I was subsequently able to find the documents that I needed to match the sources for late-medieval England.

Some of my most crucial discoveries came from the unpublished archives of Egypt's Ministry of Religious Endowments. These archives contain a large number of unpublished endowment deeds (*waqfiyyat*). The waqfiyyat and accompanying endowed institutions (*waqf*) are analogous to mortmain in Europe. The waqf contain full records of the pious endowments through which a donor would bestow assets (e.g., agricultural land, urban real estate) to support an institution that served a public good.[43]

On a grand scale, endowed institutions could be as vast as the enormous mosque-madrasa complex of Sultan Hasan, ruler of Egypt in the mid-fourteenth century. This towering structure encompasses a mosque, a tomb intended for the reigning sultan, and a vast maze of classrooms, separated into four sections, each one spiraling upward for some ten stories. Students were trained here in secular as well as religious subjects. Parts of this school were exclusively devoted to scientific education, embracing areas such as astronomy and medicine, fields in which, before the plagues, Islamic science still surpassed that of Western Europe. Other endowed institutions were on a far smaller scale, ranging from local mosques to public fountains.

The waqf are also divided into *khayri* (philanthropic) and *ahli* (family) endowments. The revenues of the former were immediately invested in the charitable institutions, whereas the revenues of family waqf were divided in such a fashion that some or all of the revenue went to the family of the donor until the last descendants of the family had died, at which point the entire revenue would be transferred to the eleemosynary institution.

The waqf were endowed in perpetuity, a boon to historians and archaeologists, as both the properties and the original records were much more likely to survive the six centuries of urban transformation in Cairo that left so few of the fourteenth- and fifteenth-century palaces and grandiose residential structures intact. The deeds for these endowments contain a wealth of information, from the details of the endowed structure and its administration to the sources of revenue and revenue extraction. The value of these archives for historians of Egypt cannot be understated. They proved invaluable for this project; without them many of the intricacies of the Egyptian economic system would have remained impossible to analyze.

Although the endowments deeds were vital for my research, the bulk of the information for this project nevertheless came from sources, such as narrative chronicles, more familiar to most Islamic historians. Each historian approaches these sources with his or her own agenda, and given the relative paucity of scholars in the field of medieval Islam, there remains a vast amount of information that has not been scrutinized in detail. The narrative chronicles are supplemented by other valuable resources. Chancery manuals are one example. Written as handbooks for state officials to use as a reference for the complexities of state administration, these resemble encyclopedias and contain valuable information covering a vast array of subjects. For the purposes of this research project, they were particularly useful for analyzing the landholding system. Many other sources from the fourteenth and fifteenth century were also used in this study, and all of this material was supplemented with secondary studies by Egyptian and foreign scholars.

In the process of collecting data, I solved a number of mysteries and answered several unresolved questions about the economic history of Egypt. A few of these findings are worth mentioning at the outset. I was able to discover the exact value of the *dinar jayshi* (a unit of account) and, consequently, to extract solid quantitative statistics from Egypt's 1315 land survey in order to determine Egypt's land revenue before the plagues. I then analyzed an informative Ottoman survey of Egypt conducted in 1596–1597. This made it possible for me to establish reliable approximations for the value of Egypt's agrarian revenue after the plagues. Most importantly, I studied the Mamluk landholding structure in detail, mapping out a complicated system that had not been accurately synthesized by previous scholars.

The first two of these research findings, the value of the dinar jayshi and an in-depth analysis of the Ottoman land survey, formed a crucial part of the quantitative aspect of this study. One of the most important elements of my research was to determine, within a reasonable degree of certainty, how Egypt's economic output had been changed by the plagues. Because the vast bulk of Egypt's gross domestic product (GDP) was composed of agricultural commodities, the initial efforts of this study were aimed at ascertaining the direction and extent of change in the agrarian economy.

At first, I thought that the 1350–1500 decline in Egypt's agrarian output had been analyzed and quantified by previous scholarly investigation. However, it soon became clear to me that the figures used by historians had not been carefully examined. The direction and extent of change in Egypt's agrarian economy had been based on two data points, one before the onset of the plagues (1315) and one well after the Egyptian population had reached its nadir (1522). Yet both of these data points had been established only as approximate guesses, leaving one uncertain not only about the extent of Egypt's economic decline, but even whether such a decline had actually occurred. This was the situation I faced five years ago, at the start of my work on this project.

The first of these data points, a 1315 land survey, is a highly promising source of detailed quantitative information, yet its utility for scholars has been handicapped by several elements of uncertainty. The most important of these was the ambiguity surrounding the dinar jayshi. Historians have previously used only rough approximations or guesses for the value of this currency. Because the value of the dinar jayshi remained a mystery to scholars, the exact value of the 1315 survey, upon which it was based, remained a mystery as well.[44]

This study provides a definitive value for the dinar jayshi. Chapter 5 will show precisely how much the dinar jayshi was worth and, equally important, exactly how its value was manipulated by the upper-caste Mamluks of Egypt and the bureaucrats who carried out their policies in the rural arena. By examining the origins of the dinar jayshi in the Ayyubid period (1169–1250) and analyzing its development through the Mamluk period down to the Ottoman period, I was able to demonstrate *how* the dinar jayshi really worked. It was a unit of account that operated on two different levels, a "dual usage" currency that functioned both for extracting revenue and for making payments to soldiers.

Having discovered the exact value of the dinar jayshi, I was then able to use the 1315 land survey to full effect. The revenue values of the 1315 survey can be translated into precious-metal currencies or a fixed "basket" of agricultural goods. Hence, the first data point, 1315, is no longer a source of ambiguity: it can now be used as an exact measure of Egypt's agricultural wealth before the onset of the plagues.

Finding an approximate value for the second data point (Egypt's post-plague land revenue), involved less original-source research than in-depth analysis of published sources that had not been combed for their full potential. In 1968, Stanford Shaw translated a late sixteenth-century Ottoman survey of Egyptian land revenue from Turkish into English.[45] This survey gave revenue figures for each province in Egypt. Using this source to double-check the figures from 1522 and fix a value for Egypt's agrarian output posed many challenges. Most difficult was trying to ascertain the level of surplus-extraction (rent) gathered by the Ottoman officials. Without this information, the revenue could not be converted into a figure for agrarian output. Shaw's extensive study of the Ottoman administrative and financial system, though valuable in many respects, was riddled with quantitative errors. After a long process of analyzing and comparing sources for Ottoman Egypt, I was able to correct Shaw's errors and determine a range of values for land rent.[46] Once this was done, the Ottoman survey became comprehensible from a macroeconomic standpoint. The Ottoman survey, combined with the second data point, gave a figure for Egypt's post-plague economic output. Within a reasonable margin of error, this figure is a reliable and precise indicator of the state of Egypt's post-plague economy. When this sixteenth-century data was combined with the definitive value of the 1315 survey, the dramatic decline in Egypt's economic output became quantifiable. These data points could also be used on an absolute scale to make comparisons with England.

This study also presents a structured picture of the functioning of Egypt's landholding system. The intricacies of this landholding system have frustrated many historians who have tried to sketch out a clear pattern of its structure. Some historians have argued that it was a decentralized system in which individual landholders operated freely and were directly involved in the management of their estates. Others have labeled it as a simple model of an agro-managerial economy, along the lines of one of Wittfogel's oriental despotic states.[47] The truth lies somewhere between the two, and the lack of archival records has made it difficult for scholars to put a clear picture together.

Yet scrutiny of primary and secondary sources made it clear that there were enough bits and pieces in the historical records to outline a basic structure for the system. With the help of previous scholars who have toiled in this area and some recent studies that outline certain features of the system, I was able to assemble many of the pieces of this puzzle.

However, some large gaps remain, and it was impossible to construct a working macroeconomic model for this system with these pieces still missing. The chronicles are full of telling clues, but the lacunae left by contemporary urban historians are often too large to fill by reading more narrative sources. Encyclopedias and manuals of statecraft were useful, but they too were silent where some vital connecting links were needed. Critically lacking were the fundamental archival sources: the records of the *Diwan al-Jaysh* (the department of the military, partially in charge of landholding assignments). These would probably provide all the answers a historian could ever hope for, but they have been lost for centuries.

Fortunately, the serendipitous nature of ongoing research eventually provided a solution to this problem. In the midst of combing the endowment archives for information about wages, I realized that mortmain functioned along the same lines as the much more prevalent military prebends. An examination of the endowment deeds, cross-checked by comparison with the chronicles, showed that the workings of the landholding system for endowed land mirrored the landholding system as a whole. The waqfiyyat in the Ministry of Religious Endowments thus provided a cognate archive that could be used to fill in the remaining gaps in the historical record.

Egypt's landholding structure is indeed a complex one, and yet a structured outline of this detailed canvas does emerge; Chapter 2 models the system on a macroeconomic level. Without this model, it would have been impossible to carry out a comparative study, and as the reader will see, without a comparative study it would have been impossible to determine exactly *why* Egypt's economy was so devastated by plague depopulation.

Before venturing into this comparison and the underlying causes for economic change, I must include a few words about the place of this study in the wider scholarly debates surrounding the Black Death and its impact on late-medieval society. The impact of the plagues remains a subject of controversy. This has long been the case for historians of Western Europe. One can only hope it will soon be the same in other parts of the world that were equally affected by this pandemic.

The scholars who study the late-medieval period of Western Europe have long debated, and will doubtlessly continue to debate, the many possible changes caused by depopulation in the fourteenth and fifteenth centuries. This is as true in the arena of economic history as it is in the history of religion, art, science, and culture in general. Disputes over the economic implications of the plague have ranged back and forth between those who emphasize its positive effects and those who see it as a setback for the economies in this area of the late-medieval world. It has alternately been viewed as either a turning point in history or a marginal event in the economic development of Europe. The subject has also been a source of conflict for rival schools of economic thought, pitting Marxist economic historians against more "commercially" oriented historians.[48]

In spite of the disputes over many significant issues, scholars agree about certain aspects of the outcome in Western Europe, particularly northwestern Europe.[49] In many areas, urban and rural wages rose, land rents declined, grain prices dropped, agricultural output became more diversified, and unemployment levels decreased. Furthermore, the percentage decrease of agrarian and total output was less than that of the population, and per capita incomes rose. Overall economic recovery was largely completed by the year 1500. Landholding systems were transformed, and the manorial system, which was on the wane in some areas, collapsed in many parts of Western Europe, and was replaced by tenant farming or small peasant landholdings. Where these conclusions are accepted, they are often accepted as an axiomatic response to the relative scarcity of labor and the abundance of land that accompanied depopulation. The concessions that landlords made to peasants also seem to be an obvious consequence of the relative scarcity of rural labor.

Yet if we look beyond Western Europe, many of these economic responses, which, on the surface, seem to be natural responses to plague depopulation, did not occur.[50] Nowhere is this truer than in Egypt, the epicenter of the Mamluk sultanate that dominated the eastern Mediterranean between 1250 and 1517. Plague depopulation, both urban and rural, was at least as severe in Egypt as in the more heavily stricken areas of Western Europe. Over the course of a century, Egypt lost roughly half of its total population, taking into account the initial Black Death and subsequent plague outbreaks. Yet, as will be shown in this study, the consequences of this depopulation in Egypt were profoundly different from those that prevailed in much of Western Europe. Wages dropped precipitously, land rents increased, grain prices rose, agricultural output became less diversified, and unemployment levels increased. The percentage decrease in agrarian and total output was greater than that of the population, and per capita incomes plummeted. The landholding system did not undergo a radical transformation, and the aristocracy was able to successfully contest the demands of scarce rural labor. Furthermore, economic recovery was nowhere in sight by 1500; the agrarian system lay in ruins, and agricultural output had declined by approximately sixty-eight percent.

The economic decline of Egypt did not conform to the pattern of post-plague transformations witnessed in Western Europe. Neither was Egypt's demise in any way adumbrated by the economic trajectory of the Mamluk regime itself. Before the plagues, Egypt had enjoyed a robust and growing agrarian sector that contributed the vast bulk of wealth to its overall economy. Egypt's rulers had expanded arable land by some fifty percent in the years before the Black Death. Egypt had a wealth of diversified crops, a crop rotation system that was at least the equal of the best in Western Europe, and high levels of soil fertility that were due not only to the Nile flood, but also to the intensive use of root crops, such as clover, that were not widely utilized in Western Europe until the nineteenth century.[51] Many of the vast number of winter and summer crops, such as flax, sugar, and cotton, fed into the production of high quality textiles and proto-industrial "factory" wares that could easily rival Europe's best manufactured goods. Leaving aside the numerous accomplishments of Egypt's urban economy, the agrarian economy alone seemed to be set on a course of robust and promising growth and development.

And yet almost all of this came to an end with the plagues. The same disease that left many of Western Europe's survivors in a better economic position devastated Egypt and left the remainder of its populace in desperate economic straits. Despite some historical work on the Black Death, the fundamental reasons for Egypt's demise in this period remain unknown. Why was Egypt devastated when many areas of Western Europe not only survived, but also underwent agrarian transformations that were polar opposites of those that took place in Egypt?

This study will explore this question by using England as the comparative example. England's economy epitomized the most positive economic transformations that took place in Western Europe in the wake of the plagues. The scarcity of labor in England destroyed the remnants of the manorial system, which was replaced by tenant farming. Wages rose, rents and grain prices dropped, unemployment decreased, per capita incomes rose, and the economy fully recovered by the year 1500. The impact of the plague in England was the antithesis of that in Egypt. In this sense, England represents the best test case for comparison with Egypt and the best model for examining the sources of Western European recovery and the causal factors behind Egypt's demise.

Despite the obvious social and cultural differences between England and Egypt, and the seemingly vast differences in geography, England represents an excellent standard for comparison with Egypt. Although no area of Western Europe can serve as a perfect match for Egypt, England is a far more appropriate model for comparison than France, the kingdoms of Spain, the principalities of the Holy Roman Empire, or the Italian city-states. Both England and Egypt were exceptionally centralized compared to other regimes in Western Europe and the Middle East. Both countries were ruled by monarchs whose authority was circumscribed by a landholding aristocracy. Both countries had roughly equivalent levels of population before and after the plagues. Agriculture was the mainstay of the economy in both countries, and urban commerce, industry, and long-distance trade, though greater in Egypt, formed a relatively small percentage of the two countries' GDPs. Both countries were islands: England lit-

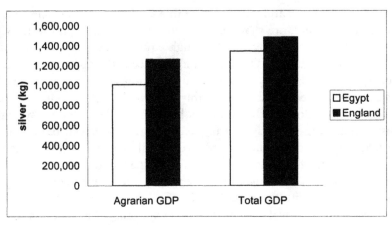

GDP (agrarian and total) of Egypt and England before the plague

erally so and Egypt functionally so (since it was enveloped on three sides by desert and on one by sea). Furthermore, the pre-plague levels of total and agrarian GDP were roughly equivalent, as illustrated here.[52]

Although Egypt and England shared a number of important similarities on a superficial level, it may seem to the reader that certain differences make a comparison unmanageable. England was part of Western Christendom and shared the legacy of Western Europe's political, economic, and legal development. Egypt had its own unique history and was part of the Islamic world, with legal and cultural institutions that it shared only with other Muslim countries. England lay at the northern extremity of Europe and had strong ties to France and the Low Countries. Egypt bordered the Mediterranean and had strong trading ties to southern Europe and India. England was ruled by a hereditary aristocracy that had dropped many of its former cultural and linguistic ties to northern France. Egypt was ruled by a nonhereditary aristocracy (the Mamluks) that imported slave children from Central Asia and the Caucasus to serve in its military. England's area of arable and pastoral land was far larger than Egypt's thin strip of arable land in the Nile Valley and Delta. England's agrarian system was rain-fed; Egypt's was a basin-irrigation system. This is just a short list of the obvious contrasts between the two countries. Other differences, such as those in the landholding system, will be spelled out in Chapter 2.

The entire array of differences may be divided into three categories. In the first category are those differences that appear to be vast in scope, but are, in fact, far less striking when viewed more closely. For example, although the surface area of Egypt's arable land was smaller than that in England, this was more than compensated for by the higher fertility of Egypt's soil (thus allowing for the rough equivalence in population and overall agrarian output). Of greater importance is the apparent difficulty in comparing a rain-fed system with an irrigation system. The contrast in this case would seem to be ineluctably governed by geographical determinism, overshadowing the contrasts between the landholding systems. This seeming gap is partly due to the influence of the old paradigm of "Oriental despotism." The theory of Oriental despotism holds that the geography of irrigation systems dictates the nature of the political and cultural structure. An irrigation system calls for a large administrative network to deal with the complexities of its management. According to this theory, the political system is of necessity one of "agro-managerial" despotism.[53]

Not only have more recent studies discredited many aspects of this theory, but it is clear that for Egypt, in particular, nothing could have been further from the truth. Egypt's irrigation system was originally built up from local zones of irrigation control called nomes. These nomes gradually merged to form a larger regime that eventually encompassed Egypt as a whole.[54] Whatever degree of centralization that emerged was a product of cultural development, not environmental determinism. This can be most clearly seen in the course of Egypt's history. Control of the irrigation system moved back and forth from centralized to local control, and the nomes never disappeared.

One particular historical example is very pertinent to this study. Roman Egypt had a localized system of irrigation control. The landholding system in Roman Egypt, far from being a model of Oriental despotism, was more akin to that of England in the High Middle Ages. Landowners in small towns or villages controlled segments of the irrigation system that corresponded to nomes. Landholding was hereditary, and landowners had close ties to their estates, which were near at hand.[55] What makes this example especially instructive is the fact that Roman Egypt suffered a massive epidemic in the late second century CE during the reign of Marcus Aurelius.[56] The economic outcome of this epidemic was, in many ways, strikingly similar to the outcome of the plagues in late-medieval England. Depopulation was severe, eliminating perhaps one-third of the tax-paying population.[57] However, the fall in agrarian output was less severe than the decline in population, as was the case with late-medieval England. Furthermore, landowners reduced the rents for peasants on the land as they competed with one another in an attempt to keep peasants on their local estates.[58] Agrarian wages rose with the fall in population, indicating that the per capita income of the local stratum of the population rose.[59] Finally, Roman Egypt recovered relatively quickly from the devastation caused by the plagues. All of these features resemble the effects of the plagues in late-medieval England rather than in late-medieval Egypt.

The salient point here is that the landholding system, not geography alone, determined the outcome for Egypt's agrarian economy. If fourteenth-century Egypt had had a landholding system like that of Roman Egypt (similar to the one that predominated in late-medieval England), Egypt would have weathered the plagues just as well as England did in the fourteenth and fifteenth centuries. Had Egypt's landholding system been under local control, as it was in many periods of its history, Egypt would have been in a position to respond to depopulation in the same way that England did after the Black Death. The prime importance of landholding will be discussed in greater depth in the chapters that follow, but the example here suggests that differences in geography were not the predominant factor in determining the differential outcomes from the plagues in the fourteenth and fifteenth century.

The geographical location of Egypt and England is also less important than it seems at first glance. Although Egypt bordered the Mediterranean, it did not have a Mediterranean economy. Unlike the Italian city-states and other small Mediterranean countries that relied heavily upon long-distance trade, Egypt derived almost all of its GNP from agrarian revenue. Total annual exports to the northern Mediterranean accounted for less than two percent of Egypt's GDP.[60] With the long-distance trade between Egypt and countries farther east added in, Egypt's ratio of long-distance trade to GDP is relatively close to that of England.[61] Thus, the apparent contrast in geographical location along trading routes is also not as great as it first appears.

As will be further discussed below, an important observation in this study is that Egypt had a robust and flourishing domestic economy and, within the realm of the Mamluk sultanate, a vibrant local trade that was fully capable of standing on its own. This cuts against the grain of characterizations of Egypt (and other parts of the Middle East) as trading centers that simply passed goods back and forth from the Far East to Western Europe. Egypt's economic prosperity and decline were largely dictated by changes within its agrarian regime. Long-distance trade played a subordinate role in the overall development of Egypt's economy.

Implicit in this comparison of Egypt and England is a denial that their cultures cannot be compared on an economic level. This study analyzes Egypt's economy from a nonessentializing approach. Nowhere is this more important than in the arena of religion, so often the source of sweeping generalizations that attribute positive economic developments to Christianity and negative cultural and economic factors to Islamic culture. Even if the comparisons spare Islamic culture from castigation, it is often depicted as an alien "other" that needs to be examined through the lens of a supposedly all-embracing religious culture that sets it apart from Western Europe. One of the purposes of this study is to try to escape from this Orientalist trap and view the socioeconomic outcome in a more objective fashion. As will become clear in this study, Islamic culture played a marginal role in the differential outcomes from the plagues.

Therefore, the third set of differences is of primary importance. Here, the picture that has emerged from this study gives pride of place to the differences in the landholding system. As the case of Roman Egypt indicates, had the landholding system been in a phase of localized nome control during the later Middle Ages, the repercussions of plague depopulation would probably have been quite similar in Egypt and England. As will be shown, the different structures of the landholding systems were the key element that determined the final outcome in the two countries.

One final obstacle to this comparison is worth mentioning here. The historical trajectory of England is often seen by historians as exceptional and thus not representative of Western Europe as a whole. England's geographical location as an island allowed for a greater degree of royal authority and centralized control. England's system of feudalism and manorialism did not correspond to the supposed "classic" case on the continent. England's success in dismantling the manorial system and replacing it with the tenant farming that eventually led to agrarian capitalism is also seen as a paramount feature setting it apart from the continent. England's early development of rural proto-industry is also at times viewed as a special feature of its economy. Finally, the fact that England was the first economy in the world to industrialize is taken as a sign that its development must have been strikingly different at an earlier period of history. All of these are part of the commonplace label of "English exceptionalism."

Although England's feudal and manorial systems were never exactly like those on the continent, one would be very hard-pressed to come up with a "classic" case of feudalism or manorialism, if indeed such an entity ever existed for any appreciable length of time in Western Europe. Every part of the continent exhibited its own variations on the feudal-manorial model, and no one area could really serve as a model during the changing climate of the late Middle Ages. It is true that England was an early leader in the development of tenant farming, agrarian capitalism, and rural proto-industry, but it was a leader, not an exception. Developments along these lines were taking place throughout Western Europe at different times in the late Middle Ages and the early modern period; England embodied only the most intensive mix of these features. England's geographical setting as an island, and its attendant features of royal control and a higher degree of economic centralization, might indeed be seen as features of so-called exceptionalism; but centralization and royal authority were equally (if not more) powerful in Egypt, making a comparison with England all the more worthwhile.

Finally, it should be added that if England was somewhat exceptional for Western Europe, Egypt was equally so for the Islamic world. Egypt was an island in the Middle East and was also—before the plagues—a leader in economic development in the region. And just as there is no classic prototype for development for Western Europe, so too is there none for the Islamic Middle East. The purpose of this study is to find two economies with similar parameters (e.g., population, levels of GDP, predominance of agriculture, percentage of long-distance trade in the economy, royal control, etc.) so that a comparison of agricultural regimes can be carried out with a degree of normative control. England and Egypt fit this requirement quite well, much better than any other two regions in Western Europe and the Middle East. If one is to do a cross-regional, cross-cultural comparison, England and Egypt are the ideal choices.

This brings us to the subject of why a cross-regional, cross-cultural comparison of this nature is so important and so long overdue. On a very broad level, many scholars have argued that the late Middle Ages were a crucial period of divergence between East and West, a period when Western Europe leapt ahead of the Middle East and other ancient civilizations. These arguments have come from several different schools of thought. Many historians assert that the Black Death set the stage for a critical surge in agrarian progress and technological innovation in Western Europe. To take one example, David Herlihy, in his posthumously published *The Black Death and the Transformation of the West*, emphasized the numerous "positive" sides of the plagues' impact on Western Europe.[62] He argued that the plagues initiated a transition to more diversified economies, raised the standard of living for the majority of the population, and spurred innovations in technology (particularly in areas where differential factor endowments allowed for the substitution of capital for labor).[63]

At the same time, some historians have argued that the Middle East, and other parts of the non-Western world, fell into intellectual and cultural stagnation during this period.[64] Still others contend that no such dramatic transition occurred at this time, and that the civilizations of Western Europe, the Middle East, China, and India remained roughly equal in terms of economic development prior to 1500 (or even later).[65]

Quite a few scholars have called for more studies of non-European areas during the plague years, both as a plea for more comparative work and in the hope of resolving some aspects of the debate surrounding developments in Western Europe at this time. Samuel Cohn, in his introduction to Herlihy's book on the plagues, points out that in the face of conflicting sets of evidence, "Herlihy's sweeping analyses for Western Europe cry out for comparative investigations. Were the social, political and psychological consequences of the Black Death as uniform throughout Western Europe as Herlihy's essays imply? And how do we account for the sharp differences between eastern and western Europe in economic and social developments set off by the plague or, even more profoundly, between *the West and the Middle East*, where the plague was as virulent as if not more so than in the West?"[66]

J. M. Blaut, in a critique of Brenner's localization of the birth of capitalism in rural England in the late Middle Ages, comments that "Brenner is mistaken in searching for fundamental transformations in northern Europe: he should search also in Fujian, Vijayanagar, Kilwa, the Nile Valley, the upper Niger valley, and so on."[67] Blaut also adds a telling comment on world development that is a plea for more comparative work: "A number of writers, Marxists and non-Marxists, have argued that . . . processes of change out of something like a feudal or tributary mode of production and toward something like capitalism were occurring in many world regions during the Middle Ages."[68] It is a testament to the gulf that divides generalists or global historians and specialists in the history of the Middle East that Blaut can make these assertions and certain prominent historians of the Middle East can dismiss them out of hand. One eminent historian of the Middle East, by no means alone in his views, has asserted that the failure of the Middle East to advance on material grounds was a foregone conclusion. He also suggests that these questions are not worth exploring and that the larger comparative issues "[a]re probably best left to the more up-market writers of science fiction."[69]

In no way does this study pretend to be an attempt to resolve the grand contentious issues of macrohistory that broadly compare Western Europe's successful economic development with the rest of the world's. Rather, it seeks to narrow the focus of the comparison so that sweeping generalizations can be avoided and more specific questions can be answered with greater certainty. Comparative studies of East and West have tended to be so grand and all encompassing in scope that they allow too much room for loose generalizations.[70] It is time for cross-regional comparative studies to assume the dimensions of more limited and focused analyses that can minimize generalizations and concentrate on differential sociological and economic factors in a smaller and more manageable sphere of inquiry. This study, limited to a relatively short time frame, largely focused upon rural development, and centered on a disease that respected no regional demarcations or cultural boundaries set down by modern historians, will give generalists and world historians a base upon which to build theories of wider scope.

Nowhere is this more called-for than in the area of economic comparisons between Western Europe and the Middle East (which are still in their infancy). And nowhere is it more needed than in the almost nonexistent area of comparative East-West studies of rural development, the "prime mover" of preindustrial Europe according to many economists. For too long the few comparative studies of Western Europe and the Middle East have been focused on the subject of long-distance trade. It is time for comparisons that focus on agrarian systems, rural industry, and interregional trade.

This study is divided into six chapters. Chapter 1 provides an introduction to the nature of the plague and the methodological issues in the book. Chapter 2 briefly analyzes the demographic impact of the plague in England and Egypt and then examines the nature of Egypt's landholding system and agrarian economy. Chapter 3 offers a detailed description of the economic impact of the plague outbreaks on the rural economy of Egypt. Chapter 4 evaluates the economic impact of the plague in England. Chapter 5 compares the total agrarian output ("agrarian GDP") of Egypt and England, using new research that allows us to estimate the value of the dinar jayshi and the cadastral surveys of Egypt. Chapter 6 examines prices and wages in Egypt's pre- and post-plague economy and then compares these price scissors with England's. An appendix gives a detailed mathematical and graphical analysis of the way that the marginal, average, and total products of labor are used in this study.

TWO

MORTALITY, IRRIGATION, AND LANDHOLDERS IN MAMLUK EGYPT

A discussion of the plague's mortality in England is unnecessary here since numerous studies have analyzed the demographic impact of the plague in that region. Although scholars have long debated the level of population decline, recent studies seem to agree that roughly half the population of England succumbed to repeated outbreaks of *Yersinia pestis*.[1] England had a population of roughly six million before the Black Death, and repeated series of plague outbreaks lowered the population level to three million or less by the late fifteenth century. England's population did not reach six million again until the early seventeenth century.

Far less is known about the Black Death's mortality in Egypt. Michael Dols, in his pioneering study of the Black Death, has estimated through various accounts (funeral orations, coffin counts, and inheritance taxes) that at least a third of the population perished in the initial outbreak of the plague.[2] Dols's figures for the major plague outbreak in 1429–1430 are particularly meticulous, and his calculated figure of over 90,000 dead in Cairo alone seems quite accurate. (Dols's calculated mortality figure actually coincides with the estimate given by Ibn Taghri-Birdi, a contemporary observer of the 1429–1430 outbreak.)[3] Contemporary observers, both Egyptians and foreign travelers, give accounts of the initial plague and subsequent outbreaks that leave no doubt that it was viewed as a disease of uniquely devastating virulence, in both the cities and the countryside.[4]

It seems likely that the plague was every bit as catastrophic in rural areas as in urban ones. Contemporary witnesses report an extremely high mortality rate in the countryside, sometimes providing numbers that seem quite accurate, given the likely level of population in certain provinces.[5] More importantly for the purposes of estimating rural mortality, the geography of Egypt suggests that the rural population would have been extremely susceptible to *Y. pestis*. Areas of Europe that were near coastal areas, rivers, or canals were extremely hard-hit by the Black Death. The layout of Egypt's rural areas suggests that no better candidate could be found for a vulnerable countryside. Egypt's Nile Valley is a thin strip of arable land, bounded by desert, hugging the Nile River at all points. Egypt's delta was crisscrossed with canals and inland waterways that were used for transporting grain on small ships, a perfect system for transmitting plague-bearing rats and fleas. The annual Nile flood inundated the fields surrounding the villages, forcing rats to seek shelter in human habitation located on higher ground. Given all of these factors, it seems certain that the reports of massive death tolls in the countryside were no exaggeration.

Thus England and Egypt, which had roughly equivalent levels of population before the plague, found themselves with a similar level of depopulation after the plagues.[6] The social structures that determined the countries' different economic responses to the plague will be the next subject of this chapter.

THE EGYPTIAN LANDHOLDING SYSTEM

From 1250 to 1517, Egypt was ruled by a group of specialized warriors known as Mamluks.[7] They were a class of "slave soldiers," Christian or pagan children who had been purchased via Italian intermediaries from the Caucasus.[8] Carefully selected for their physical attributes, they were brought to Cairo, converted to Islam, and trained in a specialized style of warfare that Egypt had adopted from Seljuk and Mongol techniques of combat. Upon completion of their training, they were manumitted and placed in the service of amirs (as amiral Mamluks) or the sultan (as sultanic Mamluks). According to merit, they were given the opportunity to advance in rank, from amir of ten (i.e., leading ten Mamluks), to amir of forty, to amir of one hundred (commander of 1,000 on campaign), and, finally, to the ultimate prize of ruling sultan.

The sultan held the highest rank, yet intermediate bodies tempered his authority.[9] More importantly, he was constantly threatened by shifting factions among the upper ranks of the amirs. Thus, although Egypt had a centralized monarchy, the ruler was often in a vulnerable position. This was as true in fifteenth-century Egypt as it was in fifteenth-century England. Factions of Mamluk soldiers, led by amirs, formed coalitions that continually battled over control of Egypt and vied for the coveted position of sultan. Emblazoned insignia decorated the armor, urban palaces, and other possessions of the amirs, dramatically announcing their distinctive identity.[10] The factional strife between these amirs echoed the contemporaneous struggles of Lancaster and York during England's War of the Roses.[11]

This elite caste, the Mamluks, the amirs, and the ruling sultan, formed the preponderant body of landholders in Egypt.[12] The most striking feature that characterized their system was the ephemeral nature of land tenure. Landholding was nonhereditary, short-term, and constantly subject to the winds of political and military fortune. The Mamluk caste was unique in the medieval world for its devotion to the principle of nonhereditary succession: only newly imported slave children were allowed to enter the military landholding aristocracy. Children of Mamluks, amirs, and even the sultan were downgraded to a lower caste as *awlad an-nas* ("children of the people [of Egypt]"). Landed estates were not passed along from father to son.[13]

Furthermore, even for the individual landholder, tenure was subject to rapid turnover.[14] The individual *iqta'* holding changed hands frequently due to military promotion, demotion, transfer, and death. These features were the result of rapid shifts in the winds of fortune, part and parcel of the fighting between military factions that characterized this period. Victory of one faction over another was followed by massive turnovers in military office holdings and military ranks, and hence entailed the transfer of the underlying iqta' holding attached to that office and rank.[15]

In the urban arena, a prominent feature of this instability was the hiding, hoarding, and eventual seizure of currency and other assets.[16] Demotion from office was often followed by imprisonment and the use of torture in the search for hidden assets.[17] Less prominently mentioned in the sources, but equally important, was the far simpler process of seizing landed estates, a rather difficult asset to hide. The obvious difference between cash that could be carefully dispersed and estates that were easy targets of any political-military power transfer put significant pressure on any large landholder to convert rural revenue to currency as expediently as possible. This in turn created pressure to maximize short-term profits from the estate. And this pressure was doubled by the need for a constant source of liquidity: payments of cash and kind for one's civilian and military retinue. These payments were needed to ensure the loyalty of one's followers, for without them an amir's urban power base would vanish and he would risk demotion or death.

The short-term nature of land tenure and its vulnerability to seizure meant that a landholder typically had a very short-term financial horizon vis-à-vis his estate. Financial expenditure or other costly measures taken by a landholder to safeguard the agrarian health of his estate, even in a five- to ten-year time frame, would be tactically disastrous in the context of factional fighting. The instability of tenure had a deep and dramatic impact on the behavior of landholders who had the means to invest in the upkeep of agrarian estates.

Additionally, the landholders (both amirs and Mamluks) were geographically concentrated in urban areas (particularly Cairo), and usually lived far from their estates. This geographical separation was compounded by the scattering of estates: not only were landholders distant from their estates, but their lands were usually divided into many separate pieces, even small parts of villages, in widely separated regions of Egypt.[18] Furthermore, the distance between the landholder and his estate was in a sense as much cultural and psychological as it was geographical. Mamluk military culture was largely urban culture, and the Mamluks remained a caste apart from the civilian population, speaking their own language (generally a Turkish dialect, but a Circassian dialect was spoken as well) and embodying the norms of their own culture.[19] Though this was not universally the case in the urban milieu, it was certainly so for the rural domain. A vast gulf separated the Mamluk warrior-landholder from the Egyptian peasant. A barracks-trained Turkish- or Circassian-speaking Mamluk and a village peasant were probably as foreign to each other as Egyptians and Europeans. This psychological and cultural distance is important because it helps explain why the landholding system worked the way it did. Contacts between Mamluks and peasants were brief, rare, and usually violent.

An equally salient feature of this divide between peasant and landholder was the role played by Egypt's civilian bureaucracy (*mubashirun*, as they were called when referred to as a general body). This class of civil servants played the crucial role of transforming Egypt's annual agricultural harvest into urban revenue flows for sultans, amirs, and Mamluks. This amorphous body of native Egyptian civil servants stretched from financial accountants and treasurers in the cities down to the level of local overseers who interacted with peasant leaders in managing the affairs of annual irrigation control, crop rotation, and schedules of agrarian tax payment. As such, they served as both a filter and a conduit between the distinctive urban culture of the Mamluk military class and the local norms of the peasant community. They were the ones who communicated with the local village leaders (*shaykhs*), local irrigation experts (*khawlis*), village guards (*khafirs*), and local overseers (*mutadarrikin*). They were the ones who balanced the account books for the sultans and amirs and were held responsible for translating this agrarian system into a positive flow of resources for the military.[20]

The bureaucrats often served individual patrons (sultans and amirs), sometimes forming a secure and long-lasting tie that bonded master and servant closely together. But they were also a fluid body of civil servants, moving from amiral diwan to sultanic diwan and from one master to another.[21] Like the Mamluk soldiers, they were often torn between loyalty to their master and the opportunities offered by the shifting winds of political fortune. Like the Mamluk who broke ties with his *ustadh* (manumitter) or *khushdash* (barracks companion), a bureaucrat too could switch loyalties when changes in factional alliances offered the opportunity for rapid advancement. If disaster struck, the overzealous follower was threatened with the ruin of his fallen master.[22]

And just as bureaucrats' loyalties could be altered by urban political events, their allegiance could also be divided by the practice of multiple office holding. Furthermore, the boundaries of different diwans (administrative departments) were quite amorphous. An amiral diwan could intersect with one of the sultanic bureaucracies. And the functions of several diwans within the sultanic bureaucracy could overlap.[23] Thus, for the landholders the bureaucrats represented a set of resources that could grow or dwindle over time.

Though the civilian bureaucrats did not change hands as quickly or capriciously as the agrarian estates themselves, they were not a fixed asset that could always be counted on. These human resources, the bureaucrats, were as valuable for the military landholder as any other asset at his disposal. They were the keys to the wealth of the land; they were the ones who turned the theoretical yield of an estate into real cash and produce. And so, from the landholders' perspective, they were the resources (along with military muscle) that could turn urban political power into quantifiable assets from Egypt's rich lands. It may sound strange, but in the day-to-day context of Mamluk competition within the urban scene, the bureaucrats, and not the land itself, were the focal point of competition for agrarian revenue.

The functioning of the landholding system and the central role of the bureaucrats are illustrated in the charts that follow. The notes and key to the chart show the symbols used for the flow of rent extraction and payments. The first chart shows the flow of revenue and payments from one village to numerous diwans, illustrating how bureaucracies served as a focal point of competition as they channeled payments to different landholders. The second chart shows the flow of payments from multiple vil-

Notes and Key to Landholding Charts

Note: Mubashirun

The term "mubashirun" is used here to refer to bureaucrats attached to the civilian bureaus and specifically involved in rural revenue collection. They usually include, among others, the following officials:

na'ib (viceroy of the bureau)
nazir (controller)
shadd (superintendant)
katib (scribe)
nasikh (copier)
mu'in (clerk)
mustawfi (accountant)
masih (surveyor)
dalil (working partner of the masih)
'amil (intendant)
jahbad (collector)
khazin (treasurer)

Revenue Collection and Payment Flows

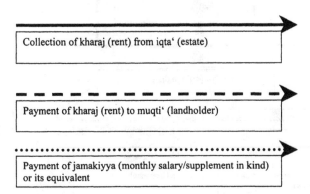

Collection of kharaj (rent) from iqta' (estate)

Payment of kharaj (rent) to muqti' (landholder)

Payment of jamakiyya (monthly salary/supplement in kind) or its equivalent

Key for landholding flowcharts

lages in different parts of Egypt (the provinces of Gharbiyya, Sharqiyya, Asyutiyya, and Qusiyya). The second chart also demonstrates how the scattering of estates and multiple holdings in one village complicated the picture for the individual landlord. It was the urban-rural bureaucracy that served as the linchpin for putting these revenue flows together into a logical stream of payments to landholders.

But none of this is to suggest that the bureaucrats were the true power behind the scene. They were the linchpins of the agrarian system, but they were not a collective power that could actively oppose the rule of their

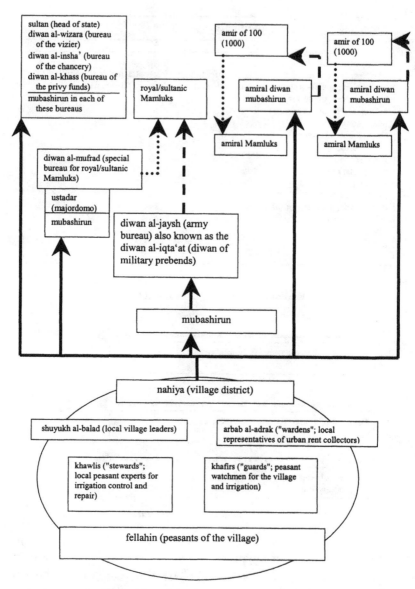

Landholding flowchart for Egypt as a whole

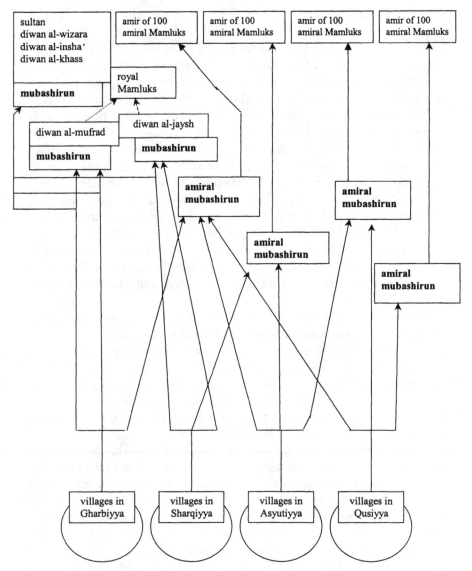

Landholding flowchart for selected Eqyptian provinces

Mamluk military masters. Nor were they even considered the cream of the civilian society in their time. As Carl Petry has suggested, the class of bureaucrats can be visualized as the lowest point in the triangle of three civilian elite categories. Compared to the other two broad groups, jurist-scholars and religious functionaries, the bureaucrats were often the butts of ridicule and scapegoats for the abuses of the Mamluk military class.[24]

Nor should the role played by the bureaucrats suggest that Mamluk soldiers were never to be seen in the rural provinces and on agrarian estates. The Mamluks did indeed play a vital role in the rural system, but it was not as local land managers. In addition to being the ultimate recipients of agrarian income, the Mamluks were, for the rural system, the policemen of last resort. When we look beyond the regular seasonal management of rural estates and witness the eruption of crises in the countryside, the Mamluks were there. When the local village guards or even local garrisons were not capable of handling a really serious problem, natural catastrophe, Bedouin raid, or local insurrection, the Mamluks and amirs appeared on the scene in a large and usually invincible army of enforcers.

The appearance of Mamluks and amirs in rural areas thus took place not in an orderly sequence of annual visits to individual estates, but rather as a collective body of urban military power suppressing rural turmoil, regardless of whom the land in question actually belonged to. Estates were scattered. Military expeditions were sent to troubled regions. Typically, the area in question would include the estates of many different landholders. Thus, military expeditions were collective, not targeted to the interests of any individual landholder.[25]

In this context, it is important to consider again what an agrarian estate really represented for a member of the Mamluk military caste. An iqta' holding was a temporary deed to land. It was a written entitlement (*mithal* or *manshur*) to the revenue of a specific plot of land from the Army Bureau (*Diwan al-Jaysh*). However, the actual income and power of control for the iqta' holder hinged upon one's military rank. To a soldier at the bottom of the chain of command, whether he was an amiral Mamluk or one of the sultan's Mamluks, this deed really amounted to nothing more than a stipend, and as such can be viewed as the equivalent of a monthly salary (*jamakiyya*).[26] For a Mamluk soldier in the ranks, it literally made no difference. Whether he held an iqta' deed or was paid via monthly stipend, his actual revenue was determined by his commanding amir. But as one rose higher in military rank, this iqta' deed took on a very different meaning. Coupled with the military muscle of a Mamluk retinue and the expertise of bureaucratic followers, this same deed (manshur) gave the amir the preponderant authority over this land and the ability to control the land via his own bureaucrats.[27]

So the true value of an iqta' holding was largely a function of the urban resources at the landholder's disposal. Yet at the same time, the higher one's standing on the military ladder, the more deeply one would become involved with the frenetic activities of urban politics and factional military alliances. So the power to actually control the land brought with it a commensurate need to focus on urban politics. Thus, as one rose in rank and gained the accompanying power to actually control and manage agrarian land, the need to maintain one's urban power base became an overwhelming distraction. Paradoxically, during the intense urban factional struggles of the fifteenth century, when a soldier finally rose to the rank of amir of 100 (when he would have sufficient urban resources, i.e., bureaucrats, to manage his estates) he no longer had the time or incentives to manage them.

All of this brings us to a recognition of what iqta' specifically was not. It was not the management of a rural estate by a small landholder who had the inclination, expertise, and, most importantly, the financial time horizon to focus on the affairs of his agrarian estate. The importance of this "antonym" will become clear below, when we turn to the dynamics of the system under the impact of the plagues.[28]

These features, taken together, meant that landholders had tremendous collective power vis-à-vis the peasantry. Rather than forming a loose group of individual landholders closely associated with their estates and the local village communities, Mamluk landholders formed a unified body that would often act together to support their interests in the rural scene, regardless of whose estate or revenue was involved. As we will see, this collective power and its orientation to the center had vital implications for the dynamics of the system in crisis (i.e., under the exogenous impact of depopulation).

Yet at the same time, this collective and cohesive power seems to be contradicted by the instability and decentralization within the urban milieu. This seeming contradiction, however, only strengthened the collective power of landholders facing challenges from the outside. The point has been aptly summed up by Robert Irwin:

> Paradoxically and less obviously, their fights among themselves had cohesive results . . . education, patronage, and, above all, the organization of factions, all conduced to lead the thoughts of the ambitious and the able toward the center. Though it was always possible for a rebellious emir to increase his following by recruiting Balabakki archers or bedouin and

Turkoman tribesmen, in the end he was dependent on the size of his Mamluk retinue to enforce his demands. For the Mamluks so overwhelmingly excelled their subjects in the arts of war, and Mamluks were, in the main, purchased, trained, and garrisoned in Cairo ... factional strife, however accidentally it had originated, operated in the interests of central authority. Those who appeared to challenge the central authority did not wish to destroy it, but rather to invest themselves with it.[29]

THE IRRIGATION SYSTEM

The dynamics of this sociopolitical system worked within the milieu of Egypt's agrarian geography: a vast complex of canals and dikes that provided and trapped water for the winter harvest (the summer harvest utilized lift irrigation). It is important to reiterate here that the specific nature of Egypt's landholding system was not necessarily a product of geographical determinism. There had been numerous periods (in both pharaonic and Greco-Roman Egypt) when the irrigation system was controlled on a local (provincial or nome) level. Nor was short-term landholding the only system. There were long periods when not only was Egypt governed nome by nome, but local members of the aristocracy owned its lands (in the full legal sense).[30] The origins of the irrigation management system itself are beyond the bounds of this study; suffice it to say that there were many factors, cultural, religious, and historical, that shaped its peculiar form in the Mamluk period.

The flow from the White Nile is relatively constant and is fed by rains from equatorial Africa, but the flow of the Blue Nile varies dramatically. The annual monsoon system in the Indian Ocean brings heavy summer rains to Ethiopia. These rains flood the Blue Nile, which in turn produced the flooding of the Nile in Egypt (before the construction of modern dams). The annual flooding of the Nile resulted in a fourteen-fold increase in the rate of volumetric discharge (as measured at Cairo) that reached its peak around the end of September.[31]

The annual cutting and blocking of dikes, carefully coordinated with the timing and the level of the annual flood, allowed each basin to be watered for a set period of time (roughly forty days).[32] This was a timing sequence that had been slowly developed over thousands of years, and was organized in such a way that each basin received the correct amount of water and alluvial fertilizer before the sowing of the winter crop.

On the local level, the level of the individual village community, this network was replicated on a smaller scale to allow for the distribution

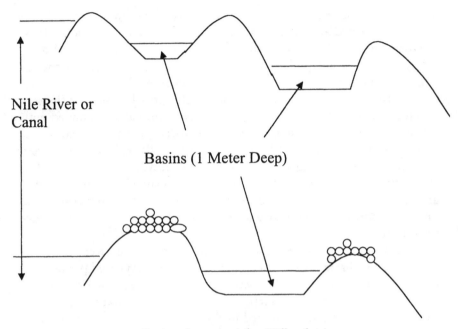

Nile River or
Canal

Basins (1 Meter Deep)

Basin schematics (after Willcocks)

of water into smaller basins via village dikes (*jisr* or *jusur*, called baladi dikes) and smaller irrigation channels (sometimes called *tur'a*).

But the smooth functioning of this network depended not only on the exactness of its timing, but also on a substantial input of labor and raw materials for its annual maintenance. For the same annual flood that Egypt's agriculture depended upon could also be its worst enemy. The same alluvium that so richly fertilized the soil every year would also deposit thick layers of silt at the bottom of the canals, inhibiting the distribution of water. The same flood that watered the land every year would also wear away at the dikes, threatening to disrupt the control of flooding and the timing of the harvest. All of this was compounded by fickle variations in the level of the Nile flood; years of exceptionally high water could bring heavy damage to the system, requiring massive amounts of rural labor to restore its condition.[33] And if maintenance of the system were ever neglected, the potential devastation of a high flood would be compounded many times over. Egypt's blessing could become Egypt's curse, an unfortunate by-product of variable floods in the best of times, but a devastating famine if the system itself were to break down.

How, then, was this intricate system maintained? Under ordinary conditions annual repairs were technically much simpler than the management of the flood itself. However, the quantity of men, animals, and materials represented an imposing annual struggle, even in the best of times. The basic process began with the dredging of the canal. Teams of oxen led by laborers would pull dredging instruments along the floor of the canal, removing the built up layer of silt and alluvium.[34] The canal channel flowing freely again, the dredged mud would often be used for the second major task, dike repair. The mud, shaped into balls and mixed with straw, would be used to build up weakened areas of the dikes or construct new ones in areas that had been damaged by a flood.[35] So the process itself, although requiring substantial manpower, was simple enough. But if the canal-and-dike system were neglected for a sufficient period of time, and then hit by a substantial overflood, the required repairs could take on the proportions of a massive investment of labor in a vast reconstruction effort.

During the early fourteenth century, irrigation repairs were managed according to a basic division that dated back to the Ayyubid period, and probably much earlier.[36] This was the divide between two categories: sultanic irrigation and baladi irrigation. Although the dikes, and not the canals, are more often mentioned in this division, it is clear from other sources that these administrative categories embraced the canals as well.[37] The terms "sultanic" and "baladi" were meant to indicate the scale and scope of the component (i.e., sultanic irrigation being large in size and serving vast areas, baladi being local and smaller).[38]

But it is probably more accurate to think of a division between public and private goods. Although the boundaries of public and private were sometimes blurred in this system, I use the term "public" here simply to illustrate an economic concept.

The sultanic irrigation network functioned as a public good. The larger networks of canals and dikes served general areas (or even whole provinces, 'iqlim) and benefited a multiplicity of landholdings rather than any particular estate.[39] So in this sense it served the public good of all the landholders rather than of any specific individual. It also was a public good in the sense that it usually tied together the smaller (baladi) networks, and so served the rural community as a whole rather than any specific village.

The baladi irrigation networks were, to use this same economic reference point, private goods in the sense that they were usually inside the domains of specific iqta' estates and belonged to particular village communities. The management and maintenance of the baladi irrigation networks were under the jurisdiction of the specific *muqti'* whose iqta' farmland they served. What this means is that they were managed and repaired by the specific village community that they served, supervised by the urban and rural bureaucracies of that iqta'.[40] The local, private character of the baladi network, mediated by the urban landholding apparatus, remained essentially the same throughout the Mamluk period.

However, the same cannot be said of the sultanic irrigation network. The collection of general taxes (usually called *muqarrar al-jusur*) and their expenditure on sultanic irrigation changed over time. At some point in the fourteenth century the management of this network changed hands, an event that was to have momentous consequences for the system in the long term. Al-Maqrizi recounts that they were once managed by employees (*mustakhdimun*) of the central bureaucracy, but then, sometime well before the reign of Sultan al-Nasir Faraj (i.e., before 801/1399), the great amirs took over the system (*a'yan al-'umara' al-dawla*).[41]

And it is clear from later references that the great amirs (i.e., usually amirs of 100) continued to manage this system during the period of this study. As al-Zahiri describes the system of the mid-fifteenth century, inspectors of earthworks or irrigation (*kushaf al-turab*) were appointed annually for each province. Usually an amir of 100, the inspector was responsible for collecting the money and assembling the labor for dredging major canals and building up the sultanic dikes. But the baladi jusur were outside the jurisdiction of these inspectors: they were the responsibility of the iqta' holders (*arbab al-qurya*) and their subordinates.[42]

This shift in the management of the sultanic irrigation system (from the sultanic diwans to the amirs of 100 and their diwans) intensified some of the principal flaws in the Mamluk landholding system, flaws that became apparent only under the impact of plague depopulation. To understand the nature of this particular defect, let us return to the concept of a public good. In economic terms, any good that serves the general public and whose benefit is not specific to a private individual is a public good. The sultanic irrigation system was, by this definition, a public good of the Egyptian landholding system. And the same economic logic that defines the concept of a public good also lays out its structural weakness vis-à-vis the private marketplace of individual interests.

This is the familiar economic "free rider" problem. It means that faced with the necessity of spending money on any good that serves the general public, some individuals will choose to favor their personal financial horizon over that of the general welfare (regardless of the long-term cost, which is obviously not an impediment to most "rational" short-term thinkers). When these individuals stop spending on this public good, they become free riders on the backs of those that continue to do their duty. If the public good is truly national and indivisible (the example par excel-

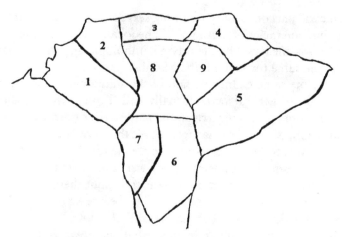

Nomes in the Nile Delta in the 14th and 15th centuries.
1 = Buhayra 2 = Fuwwa 3 = Nastrawiyya 4 = Dumyat
5 = Sharqiyya 6 = Qalyubiya 7 = Minufiyya 8 = Gharbiyya
9 = Daqhaliyya

lence in modern economics is national defense), the rest of the spenders, burdened by the additional costs of paying for free riders, will follow in their footsteps, leading to the collapse of the system.

Did the sultanic irrigation network, under the management of the great amirs, face this free-rider problem from the inception of this change? Not necessarily. Assuming an average of twenty-four amirs of 100 (their number fluctuated over time) and a central government that still had a substantial say in appointments, the system would not have collapsed.

In fact, references to Sultan Muhammad al-Nasir's supervision of amirs of 100, specifically in the context of their management of fourteenth-century irrigation projects, shows that the early fourteenth-century system worked as efficiently as ever. The record of irrigation works in the late thirteenth and early fourteenth centuries is impressive, and shows that the system, both before and after this change, could produce impressive results. The irrigation system of Egypt was greatly extended during the period that preceded the onset of the plagues. From the twelfth century to the fourteenth century, and particularly during the early Mamluk period (circa 1260–1341), the central government directed enormous projects, such as digging large canals, restoring damaged irrigation channels, erecting new dikes, and enlarging and restoring existing dikes.[43]

The remarkable features of these projects were not only their size, but also the way in which the sultan and the central government acted to organize these ventures and deter the use of corvée in the construction works, choosing instead to pay the locally recruited peasantry.[44] Among the many prominent examples of irrigation construction and restoration in this period are the excavation of the Tayriya Canal (682/1283), which greatly extended the agricultural area of al-Bahayra Province, and the repair of the Alexandria Canal in 710/1311, which also added to the cultivable area of al-Buhayra.[45] The latter project involved the employment of some 40,000 workers and was said to have increased the area of grain agriculture by 100,000 feddans (i.e., about 150,000 acres).[46] Sato's research in this area lists over twenty-five reconstruction projects, major and minor, that were undertaken during the early Mamluk period, involving sultanic canals such as Ushmun-Tannah and Sardus, as well as the work on the Tayriya and Alexandria Canals.[47] As a result of these projects, the agrarian land of Egypt increased by some fifty percent during the early Mamluk period.[48]

THREE

THE IMPACT OF THE PLAGUES
ON THE RURAL ECONOMY
OF EGYPT

As the repeated plague epidemics moved from village to village, rural de-population began to take its toll.[1] Many areas were left with insufficient labor to keep the local (baladi) dikes in working order.[2] When these dikes decayed, the Nile flood became harder to control, which in turn led to episodic parching or waterlogging of the village soil. These villages thus suffered from a substantial decline in the average yield per acre. And though yields declined, rents initially remained at the same level.[3] There-fore, many peasants faced an increase in the rate of surplus-extraction on a local level. At the same time, the peasants in severely depopulated villages had to work much harder just to keep the local irrigation sys-tem running at minimal efficiency. These two factors together, increased surplus-extraction from crops and more intensive irrigation work, led to an effective increase in rent in the absence of any overt increases in rent rates.

Yet how did the landlords respond to the drop in rural revenue and rural labor supply? Did they lower rents? Here we need to return to the dynamics of the landholding system. The Mamluk landholding system had characteristic features of both centralization and decentralization. It was centralized in terms of its relative power vis-à-vis rural labor. The Circassian, urban culture of the Mamluks, the filter provided by their bureaucracies, the lack of regular managerial contact between landholder and estate, and, most particularly, the expeditionary nature of military responses to rural rent arrears or rural rebellion, all meant that Mamluk landholders presented a united front in the face of rural labor demands. In this sense, the economic status of landholders can be viewed as a form of "collective bargaining" vis-à-vis peasant communities. Although cohe-sive village units might have presented a united front against landholder extractions, their relative power was minimal in the face of this urban military apparatus. The system, seen in the light of relative bargaining power, might lead one to expect that a noneconomic response would have prevailed; indeed, one might expect that rents would have been maintained at their previous levels.

Nevertheless, the Mamluk landholding system was also decentralized. Urban political competition and factional strife acted to inhibit centralized planning by the landholders. As I have argued above, this decentralization was expressed within the urban arena by competition over military and bureaucratic resources. It did not (for the most part) entail competition between landlords in rural areas. Yet, in theory, it could have led to some form of economic competition for scarce tenants between urban landlords and their bureaucrats.

It should be noted that decentralization in the 1347–1468 period contrasts with the much stronger central control that prevailed before the plagues. The epidemics ushered in a period of elite infighting over scarce resources.[4] This explains why the iqta' system worked so well before the plagues, and it was one of the reasons why it functioned so poorly after the plagues. The same phenomenon took place in England in the wake of depopulation.[5]

How did this urban decentralization affect rural rents? For the most part, the loss of revenue engendered by plague depopulation prompted landholders to demand restitution via the urban-rural bureaucracy. Egyptian bureaucrats and other agents within the rural milieu responded not by competing with one another but rather by diverting payments and resources intended for local (baladi) irrigation repair.[6] Obviously, this worsened an already precarious situation within some of the villages. Not only were the problems of irrigation maintenance and declining yields afflicting many villages, but now they were no longer supported by external payments and resources traditionally expected as a proportional return from their rental payments. The decay of local canal systems and the ensuing decline in arable productivity was augmented by this diversion of local irrigation resources. This, in turn, led to a further increase in the rate of surplus-extraction from the peasantry.

An even more serious problem arose from the decay of the larger system of canals that connected village irrigation systems to the Nile or natural branches of the Nile. The upkeep and repair of these sultanic canals and dikes were the responsibility of high-ranking amirs known as *Kashif al-Jusur*. During most of this period, there was one amir responsible for each of the fourteen provinces of Upper and Lower Egypt. Since the assignment of kashif rotated and the amirs' estates were widely scattered throughout Egypt, those responsible had little self-interest in undertaking repair work.[7] During times of plenty and under the hand of a strong ruling sultan, this system worked efficiently. But as the sultan's authority declined in the late fourteenth century and amiral land revenue shrank, this system was beset by the free-rider problem. As was the case with village irrigation systems, money collected from rural provinces for the maintenance of this larger network was diverted to the pockets of amirs serving as kashifs. As portions of the larger system began to decay, repairs became increasingly expensive. From the standpoint of the individual amir, there was less and less incentive to try to solve the problem. It was no longer simply a question of rediverting provincial taxes: additional funds and resources above and beyond the traditional sources were now required. Few if any amirs who faced this situation were willing to take the additional steps necessary to launch an increasingly daunting repair effort. The lack of self-interest inherent in this system was its undoing.[8]

The decline of the larger interconnecting irrigation network (in the provinces where the decay was the worst) caused more serious and widespread problems for Egypt's agrarian systems. The loss of flood basins in Upper Egypt led to unprecedented annual increases in the level of the Nile and to an early drop in the annual flood. However, this was only part of the problem created by the decay of the irrigation system. In addition to the loss of the Upper Egyptian basins, the larger sultanic system as a whole was in crisis.

Of all the Mamluk historians, al-Maqrizi is the most unambiguous and direct about the decay of the irrigation system and its effects on the agrarian economy. Yet, as we shall see, he is by no means alone in voicing these complaints. It seems to have been the most obvious problem in Egypt's 1350–1450 agrarian system, catching the attention of even the most urban-centered scholar.

Al-Maqrizi dates the decline of the sultanic irrigation system to the traumatic famine of 806/1403–1404. This is hardly surprising, but it is not necessarily a reliable starting point, since he dates almost every problem in Egypt to the disasters (*hawadith*) of this year.[9] But he insists that it is the system of amiral supervision that was to blame. After 806/1403–1404, the amirs were no longer paying laborers with the irrigation tax money. Rather they were bringing the irrigation tax back to Cairo and forcing peasants to work on irrigation projects as corvée labor.[10]

Al-Maqrizi can be a dubious source at times, and his observations need to be taken in context. There is good reason to be suspicious about generalized statements made in his famine treatise (*Ighathat al-ummah bi-kashf al-ghummah*) and figures that he offers from centuries before his time. Some of his estimates (like the total number of feddans under cultivation, the number of villages in Fatimid Egypt, or even the height of the Royal Striped Palace on the citadel, the *Qasr al-'Ablaq*) are obviously given without any basis for realistic measurement.[11] These numbers are also suspiciously rounded off.

Al-Maqrizi was the market inspector (*muhtasib*) of Cairo on three separate occasions from 801/1399 to 807/1405 and was adept at mathematics, as can be clearly seen in his extensive calculation of currency exchange rates and values. But whenever he rounds off a number, it is a clear sign for the historian to take care. His ability to work with economic data was not, however, limited to coinage. There are numerous cases where he gives figures for other quantities, even land area, that match perfectly well with other sources and with geographical data. See, for example, his estimate of a special tax imposed upon the province of Giza in 822/1419, where his totals and tax rates per feddan match exactly the area of the land in question.[12]

An appropriate methodology for discrimination between quantitative data in the literary sources needs further refinement. The archival data for the Mamluk period is simply too scarce to serve as a substitute for numbers in the chronicles.[13] Hence, a better technique for cross-checking numbers within the literary sources is needed. The proper use of such a methodology can produce reliable numbers, even estimates suitable for long-term macroeconomic history. This approach needs more emphasis if the chronicles are to be used to their full economic potential and previous mistakes avoided. For example, Eliyahu Ashtor was highly selective in his use of statistics, using only those that served his argument. Boaz Shoshan used a centuries-old, rounded-off number for land area, when far better information was available in the contemporary sources.[14]

On issues that have an internal logic and are regularly presented within the context of other events, al-Maqrizi's observations should be given due credit. This connection of cause and effect to repeated observation occurs in his annual chronicle of political and economic events, *Kitab al-suluk li-ma'rifa duwal al-muluk*. Written over the course of several decades (after his famine treatise), *Suluk* takes note of a systematic decay of the irrigation system and links this problem, again and again, to corruption (*fasad*) in its administration. Al-Maqrizi singles out for blame the amirs (particularly amirs of 100) who keep the irrigation tax for themselves rather than spending it on its intended purpose. Starting in the early 1420s and becoming steadily more pronounced, his observations record the breakdown in the system of both dikes and canals and its devastating impact on agriculture.[15]

Al-Maqrizi's annual record provides the most extensive details of the breakdown in the system, but he is by no means alone in giving this problem special emphasis. On the contrary, nearly every major historian of the period dwells on this growing crisis. Al-'Asadi, writing in the middle of the fifteenth century, vividly describes the collapse of the irrigation system and links it to a crisis in the supervision of irrigation maintenance. He contrasts the moderate regulations of earlier times with the harsh corvée labor of the fifteenth century.[16] Al-Qalqashandi also emphasizes the scale of the problem and notes that the breakdown is especially pronounced in the sultanic irrigation network (as opposed to the baladi network).[17] Ibn Taghri-Birdi points to the slow decay of the basin irrigation system and links it to the neglect of annual repairs.[18] And Ibn Iyas provides abundant evidence of a decline in the system and perhaps gives an indication of when the problem first became noticeable. He describes the silting up of the Alexandria Canal in 770/1369 and then the futile attempt at its restoration in 826/1423.[19] In his own annual chronicle, *Bada'i' al-zuhur fi waqa'i' al-duhur*, Ibn Iyas details the lack of maintenance in the late fifteenth century and the recurrent problems of breakdown in the irrigation system.[20] Carl Petry made extensive use of Ibn Iyas and other late-Mamluk sources in his study of the reigns of Sultan Qaytbay (872/1468, 901/1496) and Sultan Ghawri (906/1501, 922/1516).[21]

Petry's analysis of economic conditions in late fifteenth-century and early sixteenth-century Egypt takes note of nearly all of the problems mentioned above: the use of corvée labor and ad hoc taxes to finance irrigation repairs, dike ruptures, the silting up of canals, the scarcity of successful restoration efforts, and other details that strongly indicate a system that continued to decay up to the end of the Mamluk period.[22] Particularly important for this study is Petry's observation that repairs were generally delayed until disaster struck, and then involved such a burdensome outlay of expenses that they were rarely carried out.[23]

So our fifteenth-century sources make this more than a matter of economic logic. The problem is clearly laid out and culprits are named. Both match the cause and effect of the model above. What then are the specific effects of this breakdown in the agrarian economy?

Flood maxima and minima were measured in cubits (about half a meter) and fingers (twenty-four fingers equaling one cubit) at the Cairo Nilometer, a square well with channels that let Nile water into the well.[24] The Nilometer was reconstructed from an earlier version in the eighth century. It was in continuous use until dams and barrages were built in the nineteenth century.

In 835/1432, a year in which the flood maximum, as measured at the Cairo Nilometer, was 20.5 cubits (20 cubits and 12 fingers), al-Maqrizi reports that although some lands were flooded beyond capacity—the basins too waterlogged to bear crops and the barns ruined by rising waters—other lands were parched from lack of water. He lays the blame for this confluence of tragedies squarely on the decay of the irrigation system and the failure to spend irrigation taxes on its upkeep.[25] He reports the same confluence of flood and drought in the year 838/1435.[26]

What happened to the range of safety in the Nile floods? Although the acceptable level of variation in flood maxima was never that great, there seems to have been a margin of at least 3–4 cubits within which the maximum could waver without causing undue damage.[27] Now it seems either that this range had been reduced to less than one cubit or that there was no range: 20.5 cubits meant both flood and drought at the same time.

And the flood variations in this period were normal compared to those from earlier periods in Egypt's history.[28] The Nile, once again, does not seem to have been the culprit. And it seems clear that blaming the irrigation system was justified. Though some parts of the system may have broken down altogether (e.g., particularly in those areas taken over by Bedouins), the system in the rest of the agrarian lands underwent a slow decay. The dikes broke down: not so much that the water swept at random through the basins, but enough that the flood was no longer under dependable control. The canals silted up: not so much that the water was completely blocked, but more than enough to make the supply of water dangerously unreliable.

Most significant in this regard were the numerous years in which it was said that floods were "too short" or had "receded too quickly" or that the fall of the Nile occurred "too soon." Al-Maqrizi makes numerous references to this trend in the 1420s and 1430s, often during years in which the Nile maximum, as measured at the Cairo Nilometer, was between nineteen and twenty cubits.[29]

Petry quotes a suggestive account from Ibn Iyas in 916/1510, when a woman's dream about the coming flood was widely reported in Cairo: "It was said that she beheld in a vision two angels descending from Heaven. They proceeded to the river, and after one of them touched its surface with his foot, it sank rapidly. The angel then addressed his companion: 'Truly, God the All-High did order the Nile to reach a level of twenty cubits. But when tyranny prevailed in Egypt, he caused its sinkage after only eighteen!' Upon the woman's awakening the next morning, the Nile had indeed fallen over the night by the foretold measure."[30]

Nineteenth-century geologists' observations are of help here, since they give us a potential key to understanding this puzzling behavior of the Nile. Although the flood usually reached its maximum level in September, the length of that maximum, or the maintenance of a level that was close to the peak, was largely under the control of the irrigation system itself. As the water was led from the Nile through the large canals and smaller irrigation channels into the basins, it was subsequently drained out again after the moisture had settled into the millions of feddans of fields designated for winter crops. The backflow from this water, draining into the Nile, kept the flood at a high level, not necessarily the maximum, but a level far above average through the month of October.[31]

The dynamics of this process suggest that the fifteenth-century irrigation system was no longer working this way. Since dikes and canals had been allowed to slowly decay, the Nile flood entered basins and stayed on the soil, and the drainage canals were either no longer manned or else functioned so poorly that drainage was ineffective. These basins were probably those in which flooding was reported, while other lands were left dry. In other areas, where the Nile water failed to reach the basins at all, the soil was also left dry.

Historical accounts also confirm that the duration of the Nile flood was dependent upon the condition and control of the irrigation system. For example, al-Maqrizi describes how neglected sections of the system did not drain properly.[32] 'Abd al-Latif al-Baghdadi's observations for a much earlier period are also revealing. After the disastrously low flood of 1200, when the Nile was so low that peasants fled the lands in large numbers, he reports that the floods washed in and out of unmanned and uncontrolled irrigation channels, leading to another short and disastrous flood, though the level should have been more than enough to water all of the agricultural lands.[33]

Again, in the fifteenth century nature does not seem to have been the culprit. The evidence seems to point to general, widespread dysfunction in the irrigation system. In most areas, this decay did not lead to the complete collapse of the irrigation network, but rather to a slowly growing loss of control and a dwindling margin of safety for agriculture.

This process, this generalized decay affecting most of the agrarian lands, seems to account for the quantitative data and narrative descriptions regarding the functioning of agriculture in the fifteenth-century climate, as well as the physical features of the vast network itself. And if this picture is correct, it leads us to consider again the state of agrarian output in fifteenth-century Egypt.

Villages within afflicted provinces, even those spared heavy plague deaths and so able to keep their local irrigation networks intact, were now beset by episodic but potentially catastrophic damage from a basin flood system out of control. Well-maintained and ordered local systems now collapsed suddenly during years when decay led either to severe flooding or to equally devastating droughts caused by breaches in the larger network of dikes and canals. These random disasters occasionally wiped out villages, but more generally caused a serious decline in overall agrarian productivity. As was the case with the decay of local irrigation, declining productivity coupled with static or rising rents led to a further increase in the rate of surplus-extraction. Exacerbating the situation, sporadic efforts at repairs of the larger network were attempted by pressing peasants into corvée labor, increasing the burden on the peasantry and the tensions in rural areas.

As suggested above, agrarian rents in Egypt, on average, remained either static or increased. But the local situation over short time periods was far more complex and burdensome, especially from the viewpoint of the uninformed peasant. Dramatic changes in currency took place after the Black Death, partly from the decline in agrarian revenue. The silver coin, the dirham, was debased, and silver currency largely disappeared, in part because of the silver famine in Europe.[34] The dirham was largely replaced by copper currency (*fulus*). As copper moved from being a tertiary to a secondary currency, a money of account was created, called the *dirham min al-fulus* (somewhat of an oxymoron, since this could be translated as "the silver coin made of copper").[35] The copper coin was in turn debased with even lesser metals, and for a time its value relative to gold dropped accordingly.[36] These dramatic changes in currency were well understood by most urban merchants; however, for the peasant in the countryside they were confusing and destabilizing. Although prices in gold remained relatively stable, prices in copper and the copper money of account appeared to rise precipitously. As gold currency remained largely outside the realm of the peasant economy, the inflation in copper prices also appeared, from the peasants' point of view, as a dramatic rise in rents.[37] So even when real rents remained stable, many peasants felt they were being afflicted with yet another burden from the landholders.

Furthermore, in most cases this burden was indeed more than just an illusion. The rapid changes in currency, coinage values, and pricing systems naturally led to destabilization in rural market centers. It also led to a shift to a barter system and to rental payments in kind.[38] Most of these changes appeared highly unfavorable to the ruling urban landholders, which led to further tensions and panic in the countryside.

Peasant fears of rent increases were justified. High-ranking amirs competing for power within the urban milieu sporadically resorted to rack-renting in order to curry favor with their troops and bureaucrats and to increase the size of their entourage.[39] These individual increases in real rent rates were not only episodic but also geographically unpredictable, since landed estates changed hands rapidly under the iqta' system. Indeed, at times amirs faced with a lack of trusted bureaucratic resources to connect them with their estates would resort to tax farming.[40] For the peasant, it was a confusing and usually threatening situation. Above all, it inhibited interrural mobility, since incentives and disincentives caused by local circumstances were almost impossible to predict at any given time and place—at least as far as rents were concerned. The overall situation simply appeared as an increasingly burdensome life for agrarian labor.

The centralized government of Mamluk Egypt played a critical role in this situation. Landlord authority was reinforced by legal action on the part of the ruling authorities. Just as the English landlords had attempted to act collectively through Parliament, the sultan and the high-ranking landlords in the Majlis al-Mashura passed a series of laws that reinforced the power of the amirs and the bureaucracy. But whereas collective legal action failed in England, it triumphed in Egypt.

From the late fourteenth century to the mid-fifteenth century, the state passed one decree after another raising the official rent rates that landholders could impose on the peasantry. And although some of these decrees were simply adjustments for the debasement and changes of currency, they ultimately aimed at increasing real rent rates. Contemporaries recorded the passage of these decrees and commented on their deleterious effects on the economy. For example, al-Maqrizi's five-thousand-page chronicle, *Kitab al-suluk li-ma'rifa duwal al-muluk*, largely devoted to the late fourteenth- and early fifteenth-century events, documents the later decrees, i.e., those that increased the rents in real, as opposed to nominal, terms. A record of events for 1416 informs us that "during this time, a decree was issued raising the official rent level by 200 dirhams [of fulus] per feddan [a feddan was equal to roughly 1.4 acres at this time]. The rent thus rose to a total of 600 dirhams of fulus per feddan after having been 400 dirhams (of fulus) . . . and only the sultan and amirs benefited from this situation"; this increase represented a twenty percent rise in real rent rates from the time of the Black Death's arrival in Egypt.[41] Thus although English landlords were unable to maintain the status quo,

Egyptian landholders managed to go beyond it and raise the financial burdens on the peasantry.

For the historian, peasant reactions to this web of problems are often difficult to glean from the sources. The problems were complicated and usually interrelated with a web of dilemmas emerging from the plague years: the worsening situation in the countryside and the role of Egyptian landholders in this process. Some peasant responses were incremental and subtle, taking place over a very long time. Others were sporadic, taking the form of sudden eruptions of outrage and panic.

Moreover, as in England these statutes and ordinances governing laborers created tensions and conflicts between landlord and peasant. No mass uprising on the scale of the Wat Tyler rebellion took place in Egypt, but peasant resistance emerged in fits and starts in both Upper and Lower Egypt. In many cases, uprisings were intermingled with Bedouin incursions into agricultural areas.[42] Peasant collusion with Bedouin tribes, whether real or suspected, was dealt with harshly by Mamluk soldiers. As in England, armed peasant resistance was met with heavily armed violence, and was defeated. And as in England, actions were taken to disarm the peasantry. However, in Egypt this disarmament was far more extensive and successful over the long term. Shortly after the onset of the plagues, Mamluk expeditions forcibly disarmed the rural villages. Swords and horses were confiscated in many villages throughout the delta and Upper Egypt. Only the local *mutadarriks* (local enforcers of the landlord-bureaucracy apparatus) were allowed to retain their weapons and horses.[43]

One of the more gradual but significant peasant reactions was rural-to-urban flight. Unlike their counterparts in England, Egyptian peasants had far less incentive to relocate within the rural milieu. Although there were fluctuations in rents from village to village and different levels of decay in irrigation from one area to another, they were almost impossible for even the most well-informed peasants to predict. As villages and provinces changed hands and as different segments of the irrigation system decayed or collapsed according to flood levels and landholder conduct (whether on a village or provincial level), interrural mobility became a chancy and hazardous proposition.[44] From the peasants' perspective, which was not entirely inaccurate, conditions in the countryside as a whole were becoming steadily more burdensome. Under these circumstances, urban centers—particularly Cairo—appeared to be a far more attractive and reliable alternative.

Michael Dols argues that in addition to the increasing burdens of agrarian conditions, plague outbreaks themselves drove peasants to urban centers. The random nature of plague outbreaks, sparing a village for one cycle and striking with full force during the next, instilled a panic that drove peasants to what they believed, rightly or wrongly, was the safer haven of the city. For the peasant, Dols argues, "the cities offered organized religious services, access to physicians, exorcists, and pharmacists, and large food reserves."[45] William Tucker's work on the psychological impact of plague outbreaks reinforces this view. The most extreme plague outbreaks served to uproot communities from their familiar network of protective social customs.[46] A sense of alienation and detachment from a reliable, if burdensome, existence was instilled by the more virulent plagues. The resources of the city offered a haven of refuge, a new and alternative source of social and psychological support.[47]

At least as important, and more obvious from an economic point of view, was the impetus provided by urban grain reserves. As surplus-extraction grew more onerous in rural areas, urban demand for public grain distribution rose in tandem, and scholars have argued that urban famine relief was an essential focus of Mamluk policy and social tension.[48] This moral economy was without doubt a magnet for peasant communities in times of extremis.[49] Ira Lapidus argues that "taxation, requisitions, and forced sales could transfer grain to the cities in spite of shortages in rural areas. Thus, in time of famine, peasants actually came to Cairo in search of food rather than the reverse."[50]

Just as often, self-protection on the part of the village community took on the character of a retreat into autarchy. Since wheat, barley, broad beans, and other crops served as obvious targets for urban rent collectors, peasants turned to other sources of sustenance. Particularly important in this regard were small plots of dhurra and sorghum. Peasants would grow these as flood crops in subdivided sections of the basins during the early part of the Nile's rise in August. Not only did this strategy provide the peasants with a source of sustenance outside the purview of rent collectors, but these crops were also well suited to the harsh conditions arising from the gradual decay of the irrigation system. Easier to grow and more resistant to flooding, drying, and salinization, they could provide food for villagers in areas where irrigation was functioning poorly.[51] Peasants also supplemented dhurra and sorghum with waterfowl, pigeons, and salted fish—again, sources of nutrition that were less prone to seizure on the part of landholding agents. When relations between the village and the city became strained beyond endurance, peasant communities attempted to maximize these alternative, autarchic sources of sustenance.

Contemporary chroniclers give us occasional glimpses of this process as it emerged during times of economic hardship.[52] The peasants' strong identification with the local village community, along with their protective set of resources to fall back upon, had further effects on the character of rural flight. Social structure and the landholding system inhibited interrural mobility. The nature of the system encouraged the peasant communities to stick to the autarchic, marginal resources of their local village, favoring the devil they knew. As times became more difficult and the yoke of urban extraction more burdensome, they stayed put within the familiar setting they knew, trying to ride out the bad times with their own hidden sources of sustenance. Under these circumstances, rural-to-urban flight took on the nature of a punctuated equilibrium. Long periods of endurance were followed by sudden outbreaks of panic, whether from the plague itself, the burden of rising surplus-extraction, or a catastrophic failure of irrigation—followed by mass exodus from a village.

An equally significant factor contributing to rural depopulation was increasing pressure from the Bedouin takeover of rural areas. The Bedouin tribes were a perpetual source of economic turbulence for the complex basin system of Egypt's agriculture. During times of state weakness, Bedouin tribes waxed in power and moved inward from the desert fringes. But in the plague years of the fourteenth and fifteenth centuries, this phenomenon came to play a role of major significance, dwarfing Bedouin incursions of the past.[53] To begin with, many agrarian villages, already underpopulated and left defenseless both by Mamluk policies of disarmament and by their distance from Mamluk power centers, were ill prepared to resist the raids of Bedouin tribes.

But other factors played an equal or more important role in the process of bedouinization. Whereas dhurra and sorghum were the by-products of an irrigation system in decay, a broad spectrum of weedy plants known as *khirs* were the by-product of an irrigation system that had fallen into utter ruin. As parts of the irrigation system fell apart, the Nile floods washed in and out of basins, leaving khirs as the only species suited to the altered soil and water ecology. For agriculturists, silted canals, collapsed dikes, and weed-clogged basins were uninhabitable ruins, beyond salvaging by even the hardiest autarchic peasant communities. Yet for the Bedouin, these areas were a perfect ecological niche, a niche where they could feed their sheep and goats and where their power and numbers could blossom. Bedouins not only profited from rural depopulation and the gradual decay of the irrigation system, they also actively participated in it, cutting dikes and ruining basins to intentionally foster their own expansion.[54]

Massive military expeditions against the Bedouin were frequently launched, and the chronicles are full of stories of Bedouins captured, tortured, and executed in Cairo. Yet because the state lacked an economic base to sustain its agrarian power in ruined and outlying areas, the advantage of time lay on the side of the Bedouin. To worsen matters, many of the expeditions against the Bedouin were also directed against the peasantry suspected of collaborating with them, further exacerbating the problems in the countryside by weakening the armed potential of peasant communities. Finally, the collaboration was not merely the product of paranoid imagination. Peasants in the most severely affected areas resorted to joining the Bedouin tribes. This process of peasant-Bedouin crossover was yet one more reaction by villages trapped in a landholding system that was ill equipped to deal with the onset of the plagues.

All of these outcomes—action and reaction on the part of landholders and peasants in an increasingly hostile environment—tended to move in a vicious circle. As waves of epidemics struck, landholders successfully implemented their own short-term solutions to complex long-term problems. In response to rural depopulation and declining rural revenue, they increased the rate of surplus-extraction, abetted the decay of the local and provincial irrigation systems, and promoted the collapse of a standardized monetary system of rural rents. Peasants reacted by sporadically attempting resistance, fleeing to urban areas, resorting to autarchic means of survival, and retreating from the monetized system of rural exchange, causing depopulation and rural revenue to drop further, prompting landlords to respond in kind, and furthering another cycle of active-reactive agrarian decay. By the mid-fifteenth century, Egypt's agrarian system had been badly damaged. The irrigation system was functioning poorly in many areas and lay in ruins in other areas. Badly damaged systems were overrun by Bedouin tribes: large sections of Upper Egypt and the eastern and western sections of the delta lay in Bedouin hands.

If we look more broadly at the dynamics of Egypt's declining agrarian system, we find a dramatic contrast with the economic dynamics of England's underpopulated countryside. Prior to the onset of the plagues, England's average product and marginal product of agrarian labor were beyond the point of diminishing returns because of overcrowding (given the prevailing level of technology) and the extension of grain crops to soils of marginal fertility (see the appendix for a review of the economic concepts of the marginal, average, and total products of labor). The returns to labor thus resembled the typical function of a variable factor (labor) applied beyond the point of diminishing returns to a fixed factor (land). Subsequent plague depopulation led to a retreat from lands of lower arable potential, diminished overcrowding, and a shift to crop diversification and the expansion of pasture. Thus although the total product of agriculture dropped, the average and marginal products of labor increased, and per capita income from agriculture rose.

The matrix of factors described above drove the outcome in Egypt. Two of these factors were of particular significance for the subsequent change in the average and marginal products of labor. The first was the diversion of two variable factors, labor and materials, away from the larger network of canals that connected the individual villages to the Nile and natural Nile branches. This system (the sultanic canal system), when functioning properly, produced large returns to labor and material according to the economy of scale. The input of labor and materials (such as the construction projects of the earlier Mamluk period) thus generated upward-sloping average and marginal products, essentially the reverse of the agrarian labor function for England (see the appendix for a review of these economic concepts). Therefore, when labor and materials were withdrawn from the system, causing sections of it to decay and collapse, the average and marginal products decreased, and the fall in total product was precipitous: per capita income from agriculture declined. It is impossible to measure the exact magnitude of this phenomenon, but the descriptions of irrigation decay, the dynamics of the irrigation system, and the resultant plunge in total product suggest that it played an important role.

Equally or more important was the retreat of rural labor from lands occupied by the Bedouin tribes. In the delta, areas abandoned to the Bedouin were largely (but not exclusively, by any means) located in the provinces of Buhayra, bordering the western desert, and Sharqiyya, bordering the eastern desert. Although one might be tempted to think that these areas were less fertile than the central provinces of the delta, the agrarian geography of Egypt suggests otherwise. Thus the retreat of agriculture from these lands entailed little, if any, increase in average and marginal products.[55]

Although the delta itself was of relatively uniform soil fertility, the same cannot be said of Egypt as a whole. Upper Egypt had significantly greater soil fertility. This is an obvious geographical feature of lands situated upstream on the Nile. Closer to the source of nutrient-rich Ethiopian topsoil from the Blue Nile and the Atabara River, Upper Egypt received a proportionately greater layer of alluvial deposit during the flood season.[56] Following the plagues, Upper Egypt, more than any other part of the country, was completely overrun by the Bedouin tribes.[57] The resulting effect was again a significant drop in the average and marginal products and a decrease in per capita income from agriculture.

Given the available source material, we can only hazard a guess as to which of these factors, the sultanic canal breakdown or the Bedouin in-cursions, had a greater impact. Yet together they provide a likely explana-tion for the extreme decline in the total agricultural product witnessed by Egypt during this period. Additionally, as these two factors drove down agrarian revenue, they also contributed to the vicious circle of landholder reaction described above. The ruin of Egypt's agricultural system was thus the product of an exogenous shock (plague depopulation) applied to a socioeconomic system of landholding that was disastrously unable to deal with this kind of crisis.

To clarify this further, let us pose a counterfactual possibility of a dif-ferent landholding structure in Egypt. A localized and proprietary land-holding system would have responded very differently to the plagues' impact. Hereditary landowners, as opposed to temporary landholders, would have felt the gradual impact of rural labor's supply and demand and would eventually have responded to its economic pull. They would have been exposed to the economic effects of local irrigation decay and, given time, would have responded accordingly. Bedouin predation on outlying estates would still have been a problem, but localized leadership would have made an enormous difference in this struggle. The collapse of the larger sultanic irrigation system could have been prevented by a permanent system of provincial control by larger landholders. There was certainly a precedent for this. Egypt's basin irrigation system had itself been constructed province by province. Furthermore, during earlier pe-riods, both pharaonic and Greco-Roman, not only had the system been governed locally, but permanent, local, and hereditary landowning (as opposed to landholding) had been the norm.[58] Under a different land-holding system, Egypt's economy could have survived and rebounded from plague depopulation.

FOUR

THE IMPACT OF THE PLAGUES
ON THE RURAL ECONOMY
OF ENGLAND

THE ENGLISH LANDHOLDING SYSTEM
IN COMPARISON WITH THE EGYPTIAN

In contrast to their Egyptian counterparts, English landholders had a much more direct economic interest in the welfare and management of their estates. This was due to several key structural differences. England's landholders retained their estates on a long-term basis, usually hereditarily, and therefore had a much longer financial time horizon, even if that horizon might seem short and inefficient by modern standards. Planning for the future revenue of their lands, even two or three years down the road, was long-term for Egyptians of the time. England's landholders were far more involved in the economic management of their estates. Granted, there was an intermediate body of reeves, bailiffs, and other stewards. Yet the estate managers and cultural filters in England formed a much thinner barrier than that faced by the Mamluk or amir in Egypt.

English landholders were far more likely to live in their manor houses or, failing that, they would at least visit their rural estates. Many of the Mamluk landholders by contrast had never even seen their estates. The notion of a rural manor did not exist in medieval Egypt. Estates in England were more geographically concentrated than those in Egypt. Again, there were exceptions, where several English landlords shared control of a village area. But on a relative scale, these exceptions were not significant.[1] This geographical concentration allowed England's landlords easier access to, and control of, their landed domains. The scattering of estates in Egypt (carried out by Sultan Muhammad al-Nasir in 1315) was specifically intended to prevent local landed power from establishing bases from which to foment rebellion. All of these factors meant that English landholders were far more attuned to the economics of rural labor's supply and demand and to its effect on their individual revenues. This was to play a critical role in the wake of plague depopulation.

Finally a word is needed here on "bargaining" between lord and peasant on a comparative scale. In the manorial economy of England and the Mamluk landholding system of Egypt, economic negotiations were mediated within the intersecting spheres of class relations and demographic-market forces. Negotiations for the terms of rent, tenure of usufruct, and the vast array of *consuetudines non taxatas* (*mudafat* and *diyafa* in Egypt) were carried out within both countries. In certain periods of medieval English history (e.g., the eleventh, early twelfth, late fourteenth, and early fifteenth centuries), class relations and the recourse to violence clearly played the dominant role in relation to market forces and demography. Between two periods of labor scarcity in England (the eleventh century and the fifteenth century) there was a critical shift in the structure of the rural economy: the development of factor markets for land and labor. England's landholding system in 1086 was shaped by the dynamics of an economy dominated by a commodity market. Within this restricted domain, "the lord was able to enforce this one-sided contract on his dependent workforce, despite the fact that labor rather than land was the scarce factor of production, because of his military monopoly and a tacit monopsony arrangement (an exclusive purchasing agreement) with his fellow barons and knights . . . the only alternative to the threat of force, both military and ecclesiastical, by manorial lords was competition between them. The latter, which would have increased the return to labor and reduced the manorial surplus, would not have been a rational undertaking by manorial lords within the economic circumstances of the late eleventh century."[2] The most important change that took place in the intervening period (1086–1300) was the emergence of land and labor markets and the capital markets and credit facilities that provided them with services.

Yet it should be noted that labor markets (and, to a lesser extent, land markets) existed in Egypt long before they had developed in England.[3] As we will see, it was the structure of the landholding system itself that played the crucial role in the wake of plague depopulation. Egyptian landholders were effectively unified and able to bargain collectively with rural labor. England's landholders, by comparison, were eventually driven to individual bargaining arrangements with their tenants. This was to be of momentous consequence for the subsequent history of the two economies.

THE ECONOMIC IMPACT OF DEPOPULATION

As the Black Death and the following plague outbreaks swept through England, the scarcity of rural labor exacerbated tensions between landlords and peasants.[4] Rural labor had been an abundant resource for so long that many landlords had become accustomed to relying on market forces as much as extra-economic compulsion to secure profits from their estates.[5] After this extensive period of demographic expansion, landlords now faced an environment of labor shortage like the one their Norman forebears had dealt with long ago. Servile tenants and leaseholders were seeking to have their rents reduced, and wageworkers on demesnes were demanding higher pay.

In a sense, fourteenth-century landlords tried to revert back to a previous era, an era when seigniorial authority had played the paramount role in surplus-extraction, when the Norman and early Plantagenet landlords had tightened the reins of serfdom during a time of relative labor scarcity.[6] Yet England in the late fourteenth century was a far different environment from the England of William the Conqueror or Henry II. The two periods of labor scarcity were separated by an unbridgeable gap of profound socioeconomic changes. Many of these changes had had a dramatic impact on the mentality and assertiveness of peasant communities.

The economy had become much more commercialized following the development and expansion of markets, regional and long-distance trade, credit mechanisms, and urban centers. The rule of law, in the framework of an increasingly centralized monarchy, had expanded. The legal proceedings of royal courts and, more importantly, manorial courts had become more standardized (as written records replaced oral records); they had also become more familiar to the peasantry. Estate management had improved. Coinage had largely replaced payments in kind. Labor dues had, for the most part, been replaced by cash payments from villeins and hired workers on the demesnes. The calculus of exploitation and customary restraints was now easier for the peasant to understand.[7]

It is worth noting that all these changes had taken place in Egypt long before: Fatimid Egypt in the tenth century was as commercialized as England in the early fourteenth century. Commercialization, centralization, and the development of legal institutions were all-important precursors to the economic outcome of the plagues in England. Yet these elements were equally present in Egypt and were not the central cause of the contrasting economic reactions to the plagues.[8]

Despite its impressive record of economic progress, England in the early fourteenth century was a country facing a number of problems. England was overpopulated, given the existing level of agrarian management and technology. As will be detailed below, this caused a host of problems that troubled the agrarian economy. It should also be noted here that overpopulation limited the scope for further economic specialization and the growth of rural industry. Christopher Dyer has argued that there was a limited demand for manufactured goods and that

> English industry was underdeveloped in relation to that of the continent; in particular English cloth-making seems to have been stagnating or even in retreat until the early fourteenth century . . . as a consequence of the large pool of labor, rates of pay were very low at the end of the thirteenth century, with unskilled workers often earning no more than 1d. per day, and full-time *famuli* commonly received annually 2s. to 5s. in cash and 4.5 to 6.5 quarters of cheap corn, which was barely enough to keep a family alive without income from land or a wife's employment. The rewards of trades such as potting must have been similarly meager. The multiplicity of small-scale food and drink retailers, as in the modern third world, indicates the widespread poverty that drove people into an activity which yielded at least some small profit.[9]

From the broader viewpoint of Western European history, David Levine characterizes this period as one in which "the secular boom ran out of steam. By 1300, the first cycle of early modernization, which had originated with the positive feedback mechanisms that congealed after the year 1000, was over. Rural Europe had become a low-level equilibrium trap in which demographic pressure seemed to forestall economic advance . . . the benefits of commercialization were largely thwarted."[10]

And many historians have raised questions of a much wider scope about the potential for future economic development within the confines of the manorial economy. John Hatcher has argued that demographic and market conditions were harsher than customary restraints in the late thirteenth century, yet also noting that "as in so many areas of medieval life, however, manorial custom and tradition acted as restraints upon innovation and enterprise."[11] Robert Brenner, a dubious source for the overall structure of class relations in thirteenth- and early fourteenth-century England, aptly paraphrases (and concurs with) the viewpoints of M. M. Postan, remarking that "on average something like 50 per cent of the un-free peasant's total product was extracted by the lord. This was entirely unproductive profit, for hardly any of it was ploughed back into production; most of it was squandered in military expenditures and conspicuous consumption." [12] Rodney Hilton put it more directly when he described the economic behavior of thirteenth-century English landlords: "their interest did not seem to go beyond the exaction of the maximum profit. The *idea* of *reinvesting* profit for the purpose of increasing production seems to have been present in the minds of few of the landlords" (emphasis in original).[13]

And as Christopher Dyer has characterized the system:

> The whole purpose of manors and estates was to concentrate wealth in to the hands of a few, who were then expected not to hoard or save, but to redistribute the goods among their followers and supporters in acts of generous giving. We may indeed be exposing one of the great weaknesses of the feudal economy, and one of the sources of its backwardness, because the rest of society was deprived of resources by the constant demand of the lords. It is scarcely surprising to find that such a consumption oriented society lacked investment capital.[14]

David Herlihy has gone as far as to propose that thirteenth-century England (and the rest of Western Europe) was trapped by the manorial system in a Malthusian deadlock that threatened to hold it "in its traditional ways for the indefinite future." [15]

None of these historians mean to suggest that the manorial system did not have capacity for growth. Yet what is striking here for a comparative historian is the notion of a landholding structure that was highly successful and yet had a limit beyond which it could not go. For the Middle East, the precedent is certainly well established. Scholars of medieval Egypt and other areas of the Islamic world can attest to the case of societies that exhibited remarkable growth in agricultural, civil, and proto-industrial technology, only to lapse into stagnation or decline.

So although England had outgrown the economic structure and sociological framework of early Anglo-Norman Britain, there remained a crucial question that was to play a central role in the post-plague outcome. Did landlords still have the ability to deal with labor scarcity, overcome peasant resistance, and once again intensify the mechanism of coercive surplus-extraction?

Some landlords tried to act alone in their dealings with the peasantry. For example, the abbot of Eynsham raised the price of entry fines in the 1350s and attempted to reinstitute labor dues. Money rent increases and the reimposition of labor dues were to be found on many other estates as well. Other examples include attempts at raising merchet payments and forcing tenants either to take up vacant holdings or to pay for not doing so.[16]

Yet the crucial step taken by the landlords was collective. Landlords articulated their economic demands, using Parliament to enforce them. Armed with the seal of Edward III's authority, Parliament approved first the Ordinance of Labourers (1349) and then the Statute of Labourers (1351).[17] Both of these measures were aimed at unifying landlords and imposing restrictions on wage increases and peasant mobility.[18] Violators—both lord and peasant—were to be punished. At first, these restrictions met with some success: the statutes were applied and at least some of the violators were punished.

However, these laws, combined with other factors (such as the experimental 1381 poll tax), galvanized peasant opposition, contributing to the Wat Tyler uprising. The rebels, appealing to the royal authority of Richard II, sought among other things the complete abolition of serfdom as a legal entity. Richard II made public concessions to the angry mob, concessions that were later rescinded as the rebels were hunted down and defeated.[19]

This rebellion was, in a sense, an unprecedented social insurrection in scale and scope, the like of which was not to be seen again until the seventeenth century.[20] Perhaps it sparked fear in the hearts of landlords and made them more reluctant to provoke the peasantry again. However, from the lens of comparative history, this rebellion should be viewed in a very different light, for this was exactly the type of struggle that would have ensured landlord victory. Armed conflict between unified bodies of heavily armed knights and peasant mobs, even if some of the peasants were armed with the deadly longbow of Crécy and Poitiers, was a highly uneven match.[21] As a unified force (or even cohesive forces of rival baronies), landlords were more than a match for peasant mobs with poorly articulated leadership, often vague goals, and few allies among other elements of society.[22] If this had been the battlefield of landlord-peasant strife, and legal measures had kept the English landlords united, they might well have been able to turn back the clock and change the economic outcome of the plagues' impact.[23]

But the struggle between landlord and peasant was not fought on the battlefield in a series of violent confrontations. It was rather to be a slow, steady, and inexorable war of economic attrition.[24] Rather than fight as armed insurrectionists, peasants simply pursued the increasingly available incentives of labor-market supply and demand and voted en masse with their feet. Peasants were willing and able to abandon estates if rent or wage conditions were not to their advantage.[25] As Rodney Hilton succinctly put it, "The English peasants were able to take advantage of economic and demographic circumstances which were themselves beyond their control, as they were beyond the control of the manorial lords and government."[26]

As the fourteenth century drew to a close, the attempts of landlords to act collectively, to "bargain" collectively—represented by labor legislation—slowly broke down. The fundamental dynamic behind this was the nature of landlord ownership. Despite aspects of absenteeism and the use of an intermediary body of reeves and bailiffs, English landlords remained, as owners, attuned to the revenue problems of their individual estates. Thus each landlord, as an individual economic actor, was faced with the stark reality of the direct effect of labor supply and demand on his revenues.[27] The bonds of ownership between landlord and manor led to individual bargaining on the part of the landlords. Yet landlords bargained as individual agents, whereas peasants relentlessly pressed their demands as a random yet economically collective force driven by the market dynamics of labor scarcity. As a result, economic competition between individual landlords in the labor market became increasingly fierce.[28] The brief attempt at collective landlord action broke down, and the peasants' demands were slowly but surely met: rents dropped, rural wages rose, customary fees and fines were reduced or abolished, and the manorial system, already on the wane, slowly fell apart.[29] The outcome of this battle had the most profound consequences for England's economic response to the plagues.

By the early 1400s, a multitude of economic changes began to take place in rural areas. One of these was the transformation of the geographical usage of land and labor along more economically efficient lines. Just as the previous century had witnessed the expansion of grain agriculture onto soils of marginal fertility, the late fourteenth and early fifteenth century witnessed a reversal of this process on a more dramatic scale. As wave after wave of epidemics depopulated the countryside, the nature of rural labor mobility changed.[30] Peasants slowly drifted away from soils less suited to arable farming. Marginal lands were either abandoned or devoted to pasture.[31] As Norman Cantor describes the situation: "Millions of acres [of forests had been] settled with peasant villages. The space preserved for grazing cattle and sheep in each village [had been] cut back. Less attractive land, on hillsides or on more chalky soil up to [the thirteenth century had fallen] to efforts at cultivation."[32] Aerial photographs show the extent to which villages on marginal land were abandoned after the Black Death.[33]

The increasing number of peasant smallholdings that had sprung up over the last century had been exhausted by the pressure of monoculture cropping without sufficient crop rotation, fallow time, manure, or other means of nitrogen replenishment.[34] These were gradually replaced by larger plots of land (usually under leasehold) where, given more fallow time and more animals per capita, fertility rose and convertible husbandry could be practiced more intensively.[35] The relocation of rural labor and the structural changes in the size of peasant holdings had profound consequences for the agrarian economy as a whole.[36] Although total agricultural output declined, the decline was substantially less than the proportional decline of the population because both the marginal and average products of labor rose as marginal lands were abandoned or transformed. This redistribution thus led to a rise in per capita output for rural labor and a rise in per capita income for England as a whole.

The economic "defeat" of landlords was thus no zero-sum game. In and of itself, the prominent rise in the average and marginal products of agrarian labor meant that falling rents and rising wages were not a simple redistribution of income down the socioeconomic pyramid. Landlord incomes did drop, but they were more than offset by the gains of the rest of the population.[37] The agricultural production function shifted outward on a per capita basis. Furthermore, equally important shifts in demand and in factor endowments of supply were to follow.

As Hatcher remarks of the general rise in living standards, "To use the language of the economist, the real wage was a measure of the marginal productivity of labor, and this in turn must have been closely related to the welfare of the population at large." [38] It must be emphasized that from the landlords' point of view this was nothing less than a catastrophic agrarian depression (a drop in income ranging from twenty-five to fifty percent from 1348 to the mid-fifteenth century). They were the relative losers in terms of land and labor, the two major factor endowments for this period. And as Christopher Dyer points out, they were "caught (metaphorically) between the blade of the [price] scissors." [39] They lost income from falling grain prices; they paid out more cash to hired labor; they received less cash from customary and leasehold rents; and they had to pay more for manufactures (a serious problem given that two-thirds of their expenditures went to goods other than food). Their real income expressed in its power to purchase goods thus dropped even further. Some of this loss was eased by the closing of the price scissors in the fifteenth century, when the price of manufactures fell; but the prices of lower-quality, higher-quantity goods fell more than those of luxury manufactures. The consequent trend was for the aristocracy to consume lower quantities of more refined luxury goods, partly because of the cultural pressure from those below their class enjoying relatively higher incomes.[40] Yet the loss in revenue suffered by landlords was far less than the drop in total agricultural output (total kilograms of grain per year), since most of the loss stemmed from the same factors—lower rents, higher wages, and falling grain prices.[41] Nicholas Mayhew's estimates for 1470 show a very marked rise in living standards for most of the population (i.e., those below the top of the social pyramid).[42]

As peasant incomes grew, elastic demand for noncereal products rose in tandem. Demand for meat and dairy products—the output of land redirected to pasture—increased significantly.[43] Demand for more diversified noncereal crops rose, as did demand for proto-industrial goods, including cloth from the expanded output of wool from pasture.[44] On the supply side of the economy, both landlords and peasants responded by increasing the output of noncereal goods. Landlords, facing a new economic terrain, were forced to adapt. Many of them did, and took advantage of differential factor endowments.[45] Not only did this mean the spread of pasture and increased supplies of meat and dairy products, but it also entailed crop diversification, the expansion of proto-industrial crops such as flax, dye plants, and hemp, and cheaper inputs of raw wool for the growing cloth industry.[46] More than ever before, these items found their way to market. For example, a higher percentage of meat was sold at local markets and in urban areas.[47] Peasants, of their own accord or under the direction and financial encouragement of urban merchants, expanded the realm of proto-industry, shifting, to some extent, the center of gravity from urban guilds to rural industry.[48]

The most prominent example of this shift was in the cloth industry, which grew by a factor of five from the fourteenth to the fifteenth century. Although the export of raw wool to Italy and Flanders plummeted, the production of finished cloth for both the domestic and export markets increased dramatically.[49] Some areas specialized in high-grade cloth for export, previously the domain of Flemish and Italian weavers. The customs revenue of England now came primarily from the export of cloth.[50] As Christopher Dyer succinctly put it, "England, once an exporter of raw materials, now supplied the European markets with manufactured goods."[51]

Yet an even more important factor here was the rural production of goods for the domestic market. In the cloth industry, peasant weavers, both independent producers and weavers working for urban merchants, took advantage of the redistribution of income and produced lower-grade cloth on a mass scale for the domestic market.[52] This type of manufacture—cheaper, lower quality, more homogenous, larger in scale, and produced for a wider income range—was the type of production that set important precursors for later developments in early modern proto-industry.[53] No other rural industry demonstrated as much progress as the cloth industry, and much of its success was confined to the southeast of England.[54] But new developments in other areas of rural industry appeared, widening the potential growth of factor markets in land, labor, and capital.[55] These were to have a significant impact in later Tudor and Stuart England.

Economic opportunities for those below the top of the social pyramid thus expanded, and this created a cycle of positive feedback. This positive feedback loop was in many ways the reverse of what was taking place in Egypt at the same time. The lower and middle strata of England's rural population were slowly pulled toward the marketplace, just as the same group was being pushed away in Egypt. The poorest members of agrarian society figured prominently in this process. Holders of tiny subsistence plots were now able to find more productive outlets for their labor.[56] The same applied to the outsiders of England's economic landscape, those who had retreated into complete autarchy.[57] Whether they took up short-term leaseholds from landlords, entered the agrarian milieu as wageworkers for landlords, or worked for other leaseholders, they were generally able to improve their lot and add to productivity on both the demand and supply side of the economy.[58]

For the middle and upper ranks of the peasantry, the change in the balance of agrarian power also created new opportunities. As customary tenure gradually withered away or changed into various forms of lease-hold, the basket of fines and payments (i.e., heriot, legerwite, mortuary, merchet, multure, tallage, etc.) generally became simplified into a single rental payment.[59] This contributed significantly to the effective power of the peasantry in the fifteenth century, as it entailed a far simpler and more comprehensible system of rental choices. And it added further impetus to labor mobility and made the land market more open and volatile. Opportunities to buy and sell land expanded.[60] Some of the more enterprising upper peasantry were able to amalgamate plots of land into substantial holdings, establishing themselves as prominent members of the growing class of yeoman farmers.[61] Further up the social pyramid, the fifteenth century witnessed a significant expansion of the nascent class of gentry farmers.[62] The growing ranks of the gentry played a role in the dynamics of the class struggle by acting as a further check on the power of the greater landlords.[63] Meanwhile, both yeoman and gentry farmers were distinguished by their openness to new opportunities for profit and their greater flexibility toward new methods of production.[64]

All of these factors taken together—increased per capita income, shifts in income distribution, changes in demand- and supply-factor utilization, and growing opportunities for almost all social segments below the top of the socioeconomic pyramid—made for an economy that was more efficient on a per capita basis and more open to economic change.[65] Each of these elements played an important role in the overall economic recovery that was firmly in place by the end of the fifteenth century.[66]

Peasants in the fifteenth century benefited the most from these changes as the movement away from grain monoculture and the rise in incomes improved their standards of nutrition and housing.[67] This was the so-called "golden age of the peasantry." Some historians have rightly asked how golden an age this could have been with plague epidemics episodically sweeping through villages.[68] Certainly, there was a grisly tarnish to this period. Yet even if we include plague deaths, peasant life spans still increased significantly.[69] But all things considered, it seems rather obvious that starving peasants of the early fourteenth century would gladly have chosen to live in the age of their fifteenth-century descendants. For the peasant, the grim side of the fifteenth-century changes appeared later, in the sixteenth century.[70] An inseparable part of this dynamic shift in economic power was the longer-term consequence of the decline of the manorial system. It is well beyond the scope of this study to discuss these long-term changes. Suffice it to make two comments here: as population grew, leaseholding ultimately turned market forces against a peasantry no longer protected by the customary restraints of the manorial courts. Rack-renting, tenant eviction, etc. became the norm.[71] The golden age was relatively short-lived. Yet, from the colder logic of economic efficiency, many economic historians believe that this was essential to the emergence of agrarian capitalism.[72]

Returning to the economic dynamics of the 1350–1500 period, it is worth posing a final question. Some historians contend that this was one of the worst depressions in English history.[73] Yet, we should ask how one could characterize the 1350–1500 period as a true economic depression. Economic depression, properly defined, entails far more than a drop in total agrarian (or commercial) output because of a drop in population. A real economic depression includes across-the-board, not merely sectoral (i.e., grain price), deflation.[74] Depression further includes a significant rise in unemployment, a considerable drop in per capita income, a notable drop in wages, and a substantial drop in investment devoted to invention and innovation. None of these classic symptoms made more than a brief appearance in the 1350–1500 period. In fact, almost all of these indicators pointed in exactly the opposite direction.[75] Wages rose, unemployment dropped, per capita income rose, and investment in the production of finished (rather than raw) goods increased (at least on a per capita, if not an absolute, basis).[76] If one were to sum up this period for rural development, it would be far more accurate to refer to it as one of beneficial long-term economic restructuring induced by the exogenous impact of depopulation.

FIVE

THE DINAR JAYSHI
AND AGRARIAN OUTPUT
IN ENGLAND AND EGYPT

Historians of Egypt have made several attempts to evaluate the overall output of Egypt's agrarian economy before and after the Black Death. Yet there remain many unanswered questions, and some rather dramatic errors that need correction. This chapter will provide new answers to some of the mysteries. The analysis here will also pose new questions and attempt to restructure some of the methodological approaches to the economic history of Egypt.

The 1315 cadastral survey (*rawk*) conducted by Sultan al-Nasir Muhammad provides us with an excellent starting point for the quantitative section of this study. Despite Heinz Halm's outstanding work on the information provided by Ibn al-Ji'an and Ibn Duqmaq, the survey remains a valuable, though relatively neglected source for the macroeconomic history of Egypt at this time.[1] It is no exaggeration to say that without this source the arguments presented here would remain purely speculative. The 1315 survey offers the best opportunity to get an accurate figure for the agrarian output of Egypt before the plagues. Not only does it give a record of the land area and the relative value of each village in Egypt, but we also know from fourteenth-century sources that this particular survey was conducted with special attention given to accuracy and precision. Tsugitaka Sato has studied the planning and execution of this survey in detail and has concluded that it was carried out under the close supervision of amirs and administered by experts in the lower echelons of the landholding bureaucracy.[2] Ibn Mammati's work of the late Ayyubid period provides a glimpse of procedures used for surveying lands and illustrates the sophistication of the techniques that were employed by the specialists in land management.[3]

Accurate values for the 1315 survey can be established using several methods. The first method of approximation used here will employ the dinar jayshi. The land values for the vast majority of the villages are listed in a money of account known as dinar jayshi. The exact value of the dinar jayshi has always been somewhat of a mystery to historians. It is hoped that the analysis here will finally solve this mystery and, in doing so, explain why the definition of the dinar jayshi has remained so elusive. Some historians of Egypt have accepted a value, quoted in the Mamluk chronicles, of 13.3 dirhams for the dinar jayshi. They have generally accepted this figure as a rough approximation and have been unable to verify its accuracy. Other historians have arrived at different approximations without achieving any scholarly consensus.[4] I will argue here that 13.3 is indeed a very reliable value for 1315. However, this value applies only to the period up to 1315 and not to any period following the cadastral survey conducted that year.

A vital piece of information needed to establish the 1315 value of the dinar jayshi lies in the mid-twelfth century, some one hundred and fifty years before the 1315 land survey. Sato, in his study of the Egyptian landholding system, discusses the genesis of the dinar jayshi. It was first used in 564/1169 and was then called the dinar qaraqushi. This is a critical piece of evidence, because this precursor was not only intended to equal $13\frac{1}{3}$ dirhams, but also deliberately calculated to reflect the value of an ardabb (a unit of volume) made up of an average of the value of wheat, barley, and broad beans.[5] These three crops were the most abundant sources of sustenance in Egypt, particularly for urban residents (although this was less true for the peasants). They were beyond doubt the principal focus of the urban-rural bureaucracy that collected rent from the countryside, and their value reflected that of the surplus-extraction most accurately. Seen in this light, $13\frac{1}{3}$ dirhams, which was the original value of the dinar jayshi, can be viewed in context: it was a money of account that reflected the value of the predominant crops in Egypt. As such, it was a highly useful accounting device when the bureaucracy and the sultanate had a clear understanding of conditions in the rural areas of Egypt.

In the political and economic chaos that followed in the wake of severe depopulation, the value of the dinar jayshi ceased to have any meaning. Ibn al-Ji'an's record of the 1315 survey includes a commentary about the confusion and disarray that confronted the urban-rural bureaucracy in the second half of the fifteenth century. Ibn al-Ji'an was a senior member of the urban-rural bureaucracy, and his testimony provides clear evidence of the decay of administrative systems that had functioned smoothly in the early fourteenth century. He reports that the dinar jayshi (once accurately valued at 13.3 dirhams nuqra per dinar mithqal) no longer had any validity as a unit of account.[6] To make matters worse, he tells us, the valuation of land via the dinar jayshi no longer even gave a sense of the relative value of one village (or rural area) in comparison to another. One village that was worth ten times a second village might now be worth less than the second village. As he tells us in his own words:

> Over the course of time [from the fourteenth to the fifteenth century] conditions changed dramatically and most of the rural areas became wasteland. Additionally, some areas that had been wasteland became settled and other areas that had been settled became wasteland. The exchange rate of the dinar increased [in terms of dirhams] and conditions became more oppressive and [rural decay] became more widespread. Hence the means for calculating the value of rural areas became unreliable ... [In the fourteenth century], the value of one village had been 10,000 dinars jayshi and another 1,000 dinars jayshi [and thus the first village could be valued at ten times the value of the second village]. Under the present circumstances, no such comparison can be made [the values of the two villages might now be the same or even reversed]. There is no way to calculate the present values of rural areas except by approximation and guessing.[7]

The dinar jayshi is thus of great use to the historian for the 1315 survey, but becomes a highly unreliable figure thereafter. However, since we are attempting to establish a value for Egypt's output in 1315, this is highly convenient for our purposes. Estimates for agrarian output for later periods will not employ the dinar jayshi.

A second important point to be borne in mind here is that the dinar jayshi used for the 1315 survey did not vary in its exchange rate with other currencies. Some of the chronicles (notably Ibn Mammati's) give us different rates of exchange for the dinar jayshi based upon the rank or caste of the Mamluk or soldier receiving the pay. For example, whereas an amir might receive fifteen dirhams for one dinar jayshi, a freeborn Turkish auxiliary would receive something like eight.[8] It is patently absurd to assume that anything of the sort took place during the 1315 cadastral survey. The iqtaʿ assignments were made after the survey was completed, not before. This fact alone strongly indicates that the values in the survey did not vary according to rank or other criteria.

More importantly, one must ask if a carefully conducted survey carried out by a sultanate bent upon centralizing its power would have used a complicated sliding scale to obtain a measure of land value. Since the estates of the amirs were scattered and reassigned in an attempt to redistribute power, it seems beyond doubt that the central bureaucracy needed the most accurate indication of the relative land values.[9] In addition, the iqta'at were continually reallocated, every few years in some cases, making it highly inconvenient, if not impossible, for the urban-rural bureaucracy to continually change the value of the land based on a sliding scale. Land also changed hands into and out of endowment and ownership, and neither of these transactions would have been amenable to a sliding scale of land values according to rank. If a sliding exchange scale for the dinar jayshi would ever have been useful, it would have been after the survey, when the scale could be used as a filter between the bureaucracy and the military and could be manipulated by the sultan. If a sliding scale had been used during the survey itself, the rawk would have been rendered almost as useless as it was by the late fifteenth century (when Ibn al-Ji'an recorded the figures from 1315).

Thus, we know that the dinar jayshi was not a fictitious accounting device, nor was it always used as a malleable measure of value by the bureaucracy. The picture that emerges is one of a money of account that was subject to dual usage. As a measure of land value, it was employed as a unit of the ardabb. As a means of payment, it was manipulated by the bureaucracy for salary allocations. The first type of usage, for surveys, strove for accuracy and simplicity; the second, for bureaucratic machination and control of payment flows. Viewed from this perspective, the superficially confusing role of the dinar jayshi becomes logically clear.

Another revealing piece of evidence comes from the Ottoman period. It seems that the dual usage of a measurement that functioned like the dinar jayshi persisted into the early modern period. Stanford Shaw's study of Ottoman Egypt demonstrates that there were two different measures of payment used in the landholding system. The first, known as the *jaraye*, 'aliq, or *feddan* was used to estimate the capacity of one ardabb of wheat or barley for the measurement of land values. The second was known by the same names, but was used exclusively for compensation and was manipulated to lessen the amount paid out. When the jaraye and 'aliq were added together, ardabbs of barley were converted to ardabbs of wheat at the rate of 1.5 to 1. We can see here a descendant of the dinar jayshi. Not only does this demonstrate the persistence of a money of account as a dual instrument of measurement, but it also shows how a figure of 13⅓ dirhams could be arrived at by averaging the prices of prominent agricultural crops.[10]

We now have a clear definition of the underlying basis of the dinar jayshi. However, can we accept the figure of 13⅓ dirhams as a measure of land value for 1315? Fortunately, we are not left in the dark here either. We can double-check the validity of 13⅓ by comparing the total agrarian output in 1315 (as given in dinar jayshi by Ibn al-Ji'an), the prices of these crops around 1315, the rent level in kind, and the rent level in cash. But before we explore these ranges of values, we need to take a short detour and discuss the values of the prevailing currencies in use at the time of the 1315 survey, the dirham nuqra and dinar mithqal. We need to be certain of these values before we double-check the value of the dinar jayshi.

As Warren Schultz has convincingly demonstrated in his study, the values of the dirham and the dinar were also based upon monies of account. Schultz has cleared up much of the confusion surrounding coinage and its use in fourteenth-century Egypt, and shown that both the dinars and dirhams in circulation were of irregular weights and alloys. At the time of the 1315 survey, Egyptians relied on a money of account for each of these coins. For the dinar, it was the dinar mithqal, a quantity of gold coins that added up to values of high-alloy gold that weighed just above 4.25 grams. For the dirham, Schultz concludes that the money of account was the dirham nuqra. Schultz argues that the dirham nuqra was a quantity of silver-based coins that added up to a value of sixty-six percent alloy silver weighing approximately three grams.[11] Schultz's logical conclusion that the dirham nuqra was a money of account is corroborated by evidence from endowment deeds (waqfiyyat). These archival sources (most of which remain unedited and unpublished) are located in the Ministry of Religious Endowments in Cairo, Egypt. The waqfiyyat, taken together with the evidence compiled by Schultz, prove beyond a shadow of a doubt that the dirham nuqra (whatever its original usage may have been) was, in the fourteenth century, being used as a money of account.[12]

The accuracy of this numismatic data allows us to convert dinars jayshi to dirhams nuqra. Subsequently, we can convert the value of dirhams nuqra back into a value of dinars mithqal. The value of these dinars mithqal yields a determinate quantity of gold in both weight and alloy (i.e., approximately 4.25 grams of nominally pure gold) for 1315. Thus, based on the listings of land values in dinar jayshi given in the 1315 survey, we can finally arrive at a reliable approximation for the total agricultural product of Egypt in 1315. But we must first return to the issue of double-checking the value of the dinar jayshi.

Ibn al-Ji'an gives a total revenue (surplus-extraction) figure of 9.58 million dinars jayshi for the 1315 rawk. He also lists land area, which (with extrapolation for missing data) comes out to 3.64 million feddans.[13] We do not need to estimate the exact size of the feddan here, since we can simply use the number of feddans without investigating the actual

TABLE 5.1

Agricultural revenue (total and per feddan) in Egypt, 1315

Region	Feddans[a]	Revenue in dinars jayshi (DJ)	Revenue/ feddan (DJ)	Revenue in dirhams nuqra (DN)[b]	Revenue/ feddan (DN)	Revenue in dinars mithqal (DM)[c]	Revenue/ feddan (DM)
Delta	2,001,745	6,228,455	3.11	82,838,452	41.38	4,141,923	2.07
Upper Egypt	1,634,895	3,355,809	2.05	44,632,260	27.30	2,231,613	1.36
Total	3,636,640	9,584,264	2.64	127,470,711	35.05	6,373,536	1.75

[a]1315 feddans
[b]DN = (DJ)(13.3)
[c]DM = (DN)/20

—————— TABLE 5.2 ——————
Average rent per feddan, 1315
(in dinars jayshi and major crops)

Form of payment	Avg. rent / feddan
Dinars jayshi	2.64
Wheat	2.50
Barley	2.50
Broad beans	2.75

Note: Figures for the three crops are in ardabbs.

area in question. If we divide the total revenue in dinars jayshi by the total number of feddans, we arrive at an average revenue per feddan of 2.64 dinars jayshi.

If we convert the figures in dinars jayshi to dirhams nuqra (multiplying dinars jayshi by 13.3), we get an average revenue of 35.05 dirhams nuqra. We can compare this with rents that were levied in cash. The figure of 35.05 dirhams nuqra fits into the range of cash rents of 30–40 dirhams nuqra given by al-Maqrizi and others.[14]

We can also compare the average revenue in dinars jayshi to rent levels in kind, using the assumption here that the dinar jayshi was supposed to be the equivalent of one ardabb of the three main urban crops (wheat, barley, and broad beans). The rent (revenue) levels in ardabbs for these crops are given by Ibn Mammati, al-Maqrizi, and others.[15] We can see that the revenue in dinars jayshi approximated as ardabbs (2.64) equals the approximate amount levied in kind (2.5 to 2.75 ardabbs per feddan).

This by itself is further evidence that the dinar jayshi was indeed intended to equal an approximate number of ardabbs of the predominant crops of Egypt. It also helps to confirm that the conversion rate of 13⅓ dirhams nuqra per dinar jayshi is correct.

Finally, we can cross-check these figures again, starting with the average revenue per feddan in dinars jayshi of 2.64. When we convert this revenue figure into a prevailing currency of account, the average revenue is 1.75 dinars mithqal. Again, we assume that the figure for dinars jayshi is approximately equal to the average number of ardabbs of the three major urban crops (wheat, barley, and broad beans). By dividing the currency revenue per feddan (1.75 dinars mithqal) of the three major crops by the number of ardabbs of these crops per feddan (2.64), we get what

─────────────────── TABLE 5.3 ───────────────────
Average price of major crops in Egypt,
1300–1347 (a comparison of three sources)

Form of payment	Avg. rent per feddan	Information source	Avg. price for wheat, barley, and broad beans
Dinars jayshi	2.64	1315 survey	0.67
Ardabbs	2.64	Pre-plague prices[a]	0.74
Dinars mithqal	1.75	al-ʿUmari	0.62

Note: Prices for the crops are in dinars mithqal per ardabb.
[a] average price with one standard deviation

should be an average price for the three major urban crops. Dividing the average revenue per feddan of 1.75 dinars mithqal by 2.64 ardabbs yields an average price of 0.67 dinars mithqal for wheat, barley, and broad beans. We can then compare this average price from the survey with the pre-plague market-price average of these three crops. Using one standard deviation, the average price for the three crops from 1300 to 1347 equals 0.744 dinars mithqal. This price differs from the above figure (0.67 dinars mithqal) by only eleven percent.

What is significant here is that the average market price is close to the average used for the 1315 survey. We should not expect an exact match here, as the price average is taken over a roughly fifty-year interval and the pricing average used in 1315 would certainly have used a different set of formulas. Another method of checking market prices with the average used in the survey is to compare them with al-ʿUmari's average prices for wheat and barley (extrapolating for broad beans). Al-ʿUmari's average price for wheat is fifteen dirhams nuqra, ten dirhams nuqra for barley, and twelve dirhams nuqra for broad beans (extrapolated based on average price differential). The average price of these three in dinars mithqal is 0.62, which differs from the average used in the survey by only eight percent.[16]

We have now used three different comparative methods to confirm the proposed methodology of the 1315 land survey. We have compared the average revenue from the survey with cash rent and rent in kind. We have also compared the average three-crop price level derived from the survey with the record of pre-plague prices and with the so-called normal prices given by al-ʿUmari, an official in the Mamluk chancellery and observer of contemporary events. All of these comparisons have demonstrated the

—————— TABLE 5.4 ——————
Total land revenue in Egypt, 1315

Unit of value	Revenue
Dinars jayshi (DJ)	9,584,264
Dirhams nuqra (DN)[a]	127,470,711
Silver (kg)[b]	252,392
Dinars mithqal (DM)[c]	6,373,536
Gold (kg)[d]	27,088

[a]DN = (DJ)(13.3)
[b]silver (kg) = [(DN)(2/3)(2.97)]/1,000
[c]DM = (DN)/20
[d]gold (kg) = [(DM)(4.25)]/1,000

accuracy of the assumptions here. Since we also have established a strong historical basis for the use of the dinar jayshi, we can conclude with some certainty that the results obtained here represent an accurate approximation of the total land revenue (surplus-extraction) calculated by the Mamluk sultanate in 1315. Furthermore, since we know the values of the monies of account used here (i.e., the dinar mithqal and the dirham nuqra), we can convert this land-revenue approximation into exact values of gold and silver.

This gives us an estimate of the total agrarian revenue (rent or surplus-extraction). To calculate a value for the agrarian GDP and total GDP for Egypt in 1315, we need to estimate the average level of rent extracted from arable land in Egypt. This can be done two ways. The average rent can be estimated from the output and rent levels provided by medieval observers. Although this will give us an approximate range of values that we can use, we can back this up with available data from the nineteenth century. The nineteenth-century data used here will be that provided by William Willcocks, a British irrigation engineer. Other sources of data from the nineteenth century show similar results; however, Willcocks's figures not only provide an estimate of total output (as opposed to rent levels alone), but also include all three of the major urban crops. Willcocks was able to observe conditions in Upper Egypt before the flood basin system was replaced by perennial irrigation. We can use his numbers both to cross-check rent levels provided by Mamluk historians and to verify once again the accuracy of the data derived from the 1315 land survey.[17]

Ibn Mammati provides a complete schedule and a set of figures for the winter and summer crops. Although his figures are from the twelfth century, we also have Mamluk sources that give similar sets of data.[18]

──────────── TABLE 5.5 ────────────
*Farming schedules, yields, and rents
for three major crops in Egypt, 1315*

Crop	Sown	Harvested	Seed required	Gross yield	Rent
Wheat	27 Oct–10 Dec	9 May–7 June	0.67–1	2–20	2.5
Barley	27 Oct–10 Dec	9 April–8 May	0.67–1	2–20	2.5
Broad beans	11 Nov	9 April–8 May	0.5	2–20	2.5–3

Note: Figures for seed, yield, and rent are in ardabbs per feddan.

──────────── TABLE 5.6 ────────────
Average rent for three major crops in Egypt, 1315

Crop	Avg. yield	Avg. seed deduction	Net yield	Avg. rent	Rent[a]
Wheat	11.00	0.85	10.15	2.50	0.25
Barley	11.00	0.85	10.15	2.50	0.25
Broad beans	11.00	0.50	10.50	2.75	0.26
Average	*11.00*	*0.73*	*10.27*	*2.58*	*0.25*

Note: Figures in all columns except the last are in ardabbs per feddan.
[a] per feddan, as a percentage of net yield

The following table gives the schedule, type of seed, yield, and rent for the three major crops.

We can use the figures above to estimate the approximate average rent for the three major urban crops (wheat, barley, and broad beans). In the early nineteenth century, some eighty percent of the arable land was devoted to these three crops alone.[19] Although the percentage devoted to these crops was probably less in the early fourteenth century, the three crops no doubt represented a substantial majority of the winter crop. Taking 10.27 ardabbs (an average of 2 and 20, minus seed) as a net yield for the three crops and 2.58 ardabbs (an average of 2.5, 2.5, and 2.75) as the rent, the average level of rent for these crops is twenty-five percent. This approximate rent level is a very plausible figure, as surplus-extraction in most pre-modern agrarian societies was limited to a maximum of twenty to thirty percent.

Willcocks's data provides us with a comparative measure of agrarian output and a means of calculating rent for the three main urban crops.[20]

—————— TABLE 5.7 ——————
Average rent for three major crops in Egypt, 1315
(derived from late 19th-century figures)

| Crop | Total yield | | Net yield | | |
	Ardabbs / acre[a]	Liters / feddan[b]	Liters / feddan[b]	Ardabbs / feddan[c]	Rent[d]
Wheat	7.00	2,031	1,893	11.48	0.22
Barley	7.00	2,031	1,893	11.47	0.22
Broad beans	6.00	1,740	1,658	10.05	0.27
Average	*6.67*	*1,934*	*1,815*	*11.00*	*0.24*

[a]19th-century ardabb (198 l.); 1 acre = 4,047 m^2
[b]14th-century feddan (5,929 m^2)
[c]14th-century ardabb (165 l.); 14th-century feddan
[d]per feddan, as a percentage of net yield

—————— TABLE 5.8 ——————
Agrarian GDP in Egypt, 1315

Unit of value	Revenue	Agrarian GDP
Dinars jayshi	9,584,264	38,337,056
Dirhams nuqra	127,470,711	509,882,845
Silver (kg)	252,392	1,009,568
Dinars mithqal	6,373,536	25,494,142
Gold (kg)	27,088	108,350

Note: Rent = 25% of net yield; agrarian GDP = revenue/rent = revenue/ (0.25)

His figures are recalculated here to convert from acres (4,047 square meters) into fourteenth-century feddans (5,929 square meters), and from nineteenth-century ardabbs (198 liters) into fourteenth-century ardabbs (165 liters).[21]

The results indicate that the average level of rent derived from nineteenth-century observations is nearly equal to the averages of those reported by Ibn Mammati and other Mamluk chroniclers. Therefore, for the purposes of deriving total agrarian GDP from the total agrarian revenue, an approximation of twenty-five percent rent (surplus-extraction) will be used here.

We can also use the nineteenth-century figures to double-check our

——————————— TABLE 5.9 ———————————
Agrarian GDP in Egypt, 1315 (derived from late 19th-century figures)

Crop	Total yield[a]	Net yield[b]	Pre-plague price[c]	Unit of value	Total agrarian GDP
Wheat	7.00	11.48	0.90	Dinars mithqal[d]	29,759,432
Barley	7.00	11.47	0.71	Gold (kg)[e]	126,478
Broad beans	6.00	10.05	0.63	Dirhams nuqra[f]	595,188,632
Average	*6.67*	*11.00*	*0.74*	Silver (kg)[g]	1,178,473

Note: There were 3,636,640 14th-century feddans under cultivation.
[a] per acre (4,047m²) in 19th-century ardabbs (198 l.)
[b] in 14th-century ardabbs (165 l.) per 14th-century feddan
[c] market price of 1 ardabb in dinars mithqal (DM)
[d] DM = (net yield)(price)(feddans)
[e] gold (kg) = [(DM)(4.25)]/1,000
[f] DN = (DM)(20)
[g] silver (kg) = [(DN)(2/3)(2.97)]/1,000

estimate of the total agrarian GDP. We can multiply the average number
of ardabbs per feddan from Willcocks's data by the number of feddans
recorded by the 1315 survey.[22] We can then multiply this total by the average market price of the three major urban crops. The total will not give
us an exact figure for agrarian GDP; for that, we would need to calculate
the yields, cropped areas, and prices of each of the winter and summer
crops. Since we do not have this information, or even enough information to make any kind of approximation along these lines, we will have to
resort to an estimate based on the three major crops. These crops almost
certainly took up the majority of the arable land for the winter season. If
we make an estimate that bases agrarian GDP solely on these three crops
alone, we run the risk of calculating a total that is either too high or too
low. However, a couple of factors should be borne in mind here. A rough
tally of the prices and yields listed in the chronicles for the other crops
shows that though a good number of them were less valuable than wheat,
barley, or beans (e.g., clover, cumin, caraway, turnips, and melon), an
equal number of them were more valuable than these three crops (e.g.
flax, onions, garlic, and sugar), and many of them were of the same value.
We run the risk of erring on either side, but the three crops we are using seem to run in the middle of the range of value. This should not be a
surprise. Unless the analysis of the methodology of the 1315 survey was
mistaken, these three crops should reflect an average value upon which
the total agrarian GDP can be based.

TABLE 5.10
Total GDP in Egypt, 1315

GDP	Dinars mithqal	Gold (kg)	Dinars nuqra	Silver (kg)
Agrarian	25,494,142	108,350	509,882,845	1,009,568
Nonagrarian	8,498,047	36,117	169,960,948	336,523
Total	33,992,189	144,467	679,843,793	1,346,091

Note: Agrarian GDP = 75% of total GDP; nonagrarian GDP = 25% of total GDP

The results here, based on an extrapolation from nineteenth-century output, differ by only fifteen percent from the total agrarian GDP based on the 1315 survey. This would seem to confirm that we have an accurate approximation for Egypt's total agrarian GDP in 1315. Since the nineteenth-century output figures were only used to double-check the derivation from the 1315 survey, the calculations from the 1315 survey will be used as our working approximation for agrarian GDP.

The final step of this section will be to calculate the total GDP of Egypt. As a rough approximation, we will assume that twenty-five percent of the total GDP was nonagricultural in origin, a relatively high figure for the large premodern agrarian economy, but one that takes into account the large urban areas as well as domestic and long-distance trade flows.

For a comparison of Egypt and England, GDP approximations from Nicholas Mayhew will be used for England in 1300 and 1500.[23] Although an extensive series of economic studies have looked at late medieval England, scholarly consensus remains elusive. Nevertheless, Mayhew's exceptional talents as an economic historian suggest that his figures are the best possible quantitative assessment available. Mayhew's statistics are based upon a careful analysis of a variety of macroeconomic indicators, including population levels and the primary variables of Fisher's equation ($MV = PT$). Fisher's equation employs the quantity theory of money, in which M = the quantity of money in the economy, V = the velocity of circulation of money, P = the price level, and T = the quantity of output (real GDP; GDP deflated). Mayhew openly admits his own qualifications concerning the precision of his results. However, his approximations seem accurate enough: though they may vary by degree (i.e., containing errors of perhaps twenty to thirty percent), they do not vary by orders of magnitude (i.e., numbers that are off by a margin of one hundred percent or more). Their precision thus matches the relative accuracy of the figures presented here for Egypt, and his figures provide a good basis for

TABLE 5.11
Total and agrarian GDP in England, 1300

Unit of value	Total GDP	Agrarian GDP
Pounds sterling	4,660,000	3,961,000
Pence[a]	1,118,400,000	950,640,000
Silver[b] (kg)	1,487,472	1,264,351
Gold[c] (kg)	114,421	97,258

Note: Agrarian GDP = 85% of total GDP
[a]pence = (pounds)(240)
[b]silver (kg) = [(pence)(1.33 g. silver / penny)]/1,000
[c]bimetallic ratio = 13; gold (kg) = (silver kg)/13

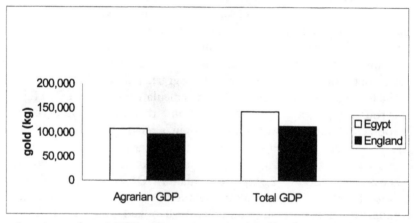

Agrarian and total GDP of Egypt (1315) and England (1300) in kilograms of gold

comparison. Mayhew's numbers presented here show the total and agrarian GDP for England in pounds sterling, gold, and silver.[24]

The pre-plague agrarian and total GDP for England and Egypt can be compared here. It should be noted that the comparison does not serve as a perfectly accurate measure of value, since prices for goods differed in each country. However, a precious-metal comparison will provide a rough indication of the scale of output for both countries. These numbers clearly show that the agrarian and total GDPs for England and Egypt were roughly equivalent before the onset of the plague epidemics.

It is far more difficult to obtain an accurate set of values for Egypt's agrarian output and GDP in the period following plague depopulation. The Mamluk sultanate never again attempted anything approaching the

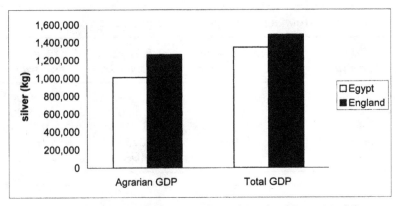

Agrarian and total GDP of Egypt (1315) and England (1300) in kilograms of silver

scale of the 1315 cadastral survey. For the fifteenth century, there are only a few scattered references to the values of individual villages and the revenue collected by specific administrative departments of the sultanate (diwans).[25] The first comprehensive statement we have for revenue after the plagues comes from Ibn Iyas. Writing in the early sixteenth century, immediately following the Ottoman occupation of Egypt, Ibn Iyas informs us that the total annual revenue from agriculture amounted to 1.3 million dinars ashrafi in specie and 600,000 ardabbs in kind (300,000 ardabbs of wheat and 300,000 ardabbs of barley, broad beans, and other crops).[26] The price of wheat in the early sixteenth century, based on a running average from the late fifteenth and early sixteenth centuries (with one standard deviation) was approximately 1.65 dinars ashrafi. The price of barley and broad beans can be calculated from an average of their prices relative to wheat. Barley averaged sixty-two percent the price of wheat and broad beans averaged seventy-six percent the price of wheat over the course of the fifteenth century.[27] Assuming the price of barley to be 1.023 dinars ashrafi per ardabb and broad beans to be 1.254 dinars ashrafi per ardabb, an approximation of the total agrarian revenue based on these numbers yields the following total.

The same numbers can then be converted into gold and silver, using the weights and alloys of the prevailing coinage (dinars ashrafi for gold and *nisf fidda* for silver). At a rent rate of twenty-five percent, the agrarian GDP can then be calculated. These figures, however, do not include land endowed to support mosques, madrasas (higher-level teaching institutions), kuttabs (schools for reading the Qur'an), fountains, other char-

———————————— TABLE 5.12 ————————————
Total agrarian revenue in Egypt, 1517

Unit of payment	Rent assessed (ardabbs)	Price per ardabb (DA)	Rent assessed (DA)
Dinars ashrafi (DA)	—	—	1,300,000
Wheat	300,000	1.650	495,000
Barley	150,000	1.023	153,450
Broad beans	150,000	1.254	188,100
		Total revenue (DA)	2,136,550

———————————— TABLE 5.13 ————————————
Agrarian and total GDP in Egypt, 1517

Unit of value	Total rent revenue	Agrarian GDP[c]	Total agrarian GDP[d]
Dinars ashrafi (DA)	2,136,550	8,546,200	12,208,857
Gold (kg)[a]	7,371	29,484	42,121
Silver (kg)[b]	85,665	342,660	489,514

[a]gold (kg) = [(DA)(3.45)]/1,000
[b]silver (kg) = [(DA)(30)(2.97)(0.5)(0.9)]/1,000
[c]agrarian GDP without endowed lands; rent revenue = 25% of agrarian GDP; agarian GDP = (rent revenue)/(0.25)
[d]endowed lands = 30% of total arable land; total agrarian GDP = (agrarian GDP)/(0.7)

itable institutions, and family endowments. Land in this category was included in the 1315 survey and should be included here. Furthermore, there was a marked increase in endowed lands over the course of the fifteenth century. It is estimated that at least thirty percent of agricultural lands were endowed by the time of the Ottoman conquest of Egypt in 1517.[28] The figures below for total agrarian GDP are adjusted upwards to reflect this trend.

A comparison can be made here between Egypt's agrarian GDP in 1315 and 1517. There are two ways of calculating the change in output over this period. The first method compares the agrarian GDP expressed in kilograms of gold and is shown below.

The second method is an attempt to represent the real agricultural output of goods produced. Averaging the prices of the three major urban

———— TABLE 5.14 ————
Change in agrarian GDP in Egypt,
1315–1517, in kilograms of gold

Year	Agrarian GDP in gold (kg)
1315	108,350
1517	42,121
Percentage change	−61

———— TABLE 5.15 ————
Change in agrarian GDP
in Egypt, 1315–1517, in ardabbs

Year	Total agrarian GDP (ardabbs)
1315	38,337,056
1517	15,993,603
Percentage change	−58

crops (wheat, barley, and broad beans) from Table 5.12 yields 1.31 dinars ashrafi per ardabb. Multiplying this by the figure for total agrarian GDP in ardabbs (12,208,857) yields a figure for total agrarian GDP of 15,993,603 ardabbs. This is the same method that was employed during the 1315 land survey. It has the potential disadvantage of either underestimating or overestimating the prices of other crops. However, as with the 1315 survey, an analysis of the higher- and lower-priced crops shows that the three major urban crops fall roughly in the middle of the price range. Although this method is an approximation, it has the great advantage of canceling out changes from the inflation or deflation of prices, and so gives us an approximation of the total agricultural output in real terms. An estimation of changes based on prices alone runs the risk of obscuring the real output, since changes in the value of monetary stocks and the velocity of money can skew the real picture. The average prices used above for wheat, barley, and broad beans are used here to calculate the total agrarian GDP for 1517 in terms of ardabbs.

For 1315, the number of mixed-crop ardabbs is, as we have shown above, equal to the number of dinars jayshi. Hence, the total agrarian

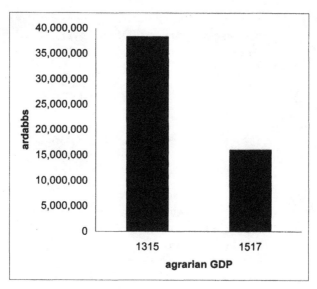

Agrarian GDP of Egypt, 1315 and 1517, in mixed-crop
ardabbs

GDP for 1315—38,337,056 dinars jayshi—is also equal to a total agricultural output of 38,337,056 ardabbs. A comparison of the total agrarian GDP in "real" goods is shown here.

The difference is not great, but the calculation by ardabbs shows a slightly smaller drop (fifty-eight percent) than that based on gold coinage (sixty-one percent). In either case, the drop is precipitous, and it demonstrates the magnitude of devastation that ensued in the wake of the plagues.

It is worthwhile to explore one more means of obtaining an approximation of Egypt's post-plague agrarian GDP. This will take us beyond the temporal bounds of this study, but it has the advantage of providing a cross-check for the numbers reported by Ibn Iyas. After the Ottomans conquered Egypt, they tried several times to survey the value of Egypt's agrarian wealth. The best-documented source is the census of 1596–1597, which has been translated into English.[29] This underutilized source will provide us with another approximation, and an analysis of the figures reported will confirm the accuracy of Ibn Iyas's numbers. However, the numbers from the Ottoman census can only be understood in the context of the early history of Ottoman Egypt. A brief discussion of the early Ottoman occupation and administration of Egypt is called for here.

The Ottomans, in their desire to extract resources from this potentially rich province, went to great lengths to inspect, administer, and invest in Egypt in hopes of reaping rewards from this "cash cow." That they went to such efforts and carefully documented them is hardly surprising, given the fact that their empire was highly centralized during this time. During the late sixteenth and early seventeenth centuries, the Ottoman Empire had greater control of Egypt than at any other period.[30]

After subduing the Mamluks and putting down subsequent revolts, the Ottomans adopted a system of *emanet* for the administration of Egypt's rural economy. This was chosen from among the three major agrarian rent systems that the Ottomans had in place over the vast expanse of their empire: *timar*, *iltizam*, and *emanet*. The two former systems employed a degree of tax farming (in which Ottoman soldiers would pocket a substantial portion of the peasant rent in return for military duties). However, emanet was a system whereby treasury officials (emins) collected the rent in full (via a bureaucracy that was similar to the one employed by the Mamluks), processed it, and then distributed it as salaries to the soldiers of Ottoman Egypt (Janissaries and Mamluks among them).[31]

Emanet was an agrarian system that was supposed to deliver the full proceeds of surplus-extraction to the Cairo treasury, where it would be recorded by Ottoman officials before being disbursed to soldiers. The Ottomans had also confiscated most of the endowments (particularly family endowments) that had proliferated over the course of the fifteenth century.[32] In theory, the Ottoman budget of 1596–1597 should have accounted for close to all of the surplus-extraction levied from the Egyptian peasantry. However, the actual Ottoman control of the landholding system was not so complete and comprehensive as the rules of the emanet system would suggest. Many rural areas remained endowed, despite the Ottoman attempts to confiscate these holdings. More importantly, the salaried emins never had complete control over the landholding system. In addition to the fragmented survivals of the Mamluk iqta' system, another type of landholding arrangement was beginning to emerge by the late sixteenth century. This was the iltizam system, an Ottoman legal structure by which land was sold at auction for tax farming. Using this legal framework, Mamluks were slowly able to reassert their control over Egypt's agrarian economy over the course of the seventeenth and eighteenth centuries. By the time Napoleon's expedition reached Egypt, the Ottoman authorities were only processing twenty-one percent of the total land revenue.[33]

At the end of the sixteenth century, the growth of the iltizam system had only just begun. A conservative approximation is used here, estimating that the Ottoman treasury in Cairo collected roughly half of the total

TABLE 5.16

Agrarian GDP in Egypt, 1596–1597

Income source	Paras	Silver (kg)[a]	Gold (kg)[b]
Land tax	40,789,691	27,737	1,541
Sale of treasury grains	3,045,853	2,071	115
Special arrears	178,476	121	7
Grain tax from mukataas	339,667	231	13
Grain revenue from poll tax	1,597,021	1,086	60
Total land revenue	45,950,708	31,246	1,736
Agrarian GDP, accounting for			
Rent revenue[c]	183,802,832	124,986	6,944
Emins[d]	367,605,664	249,972	13,887
Endowments[e]	432,477,252	294,085	16,338

Note: Figures are rounded to the nearest whole unit.
[a] 1 para = 0.68 g silver; silver (kg) = [(paras)(0.68)]/1,000
[b] bimetallic ratio = 18; gold (kg) = (silver kg)/18
[c] rent rate = 25%; agrarian GDP = revenue/0.25
[d] emins collected 50% of surplus extraction; AGDP (emins) = [AGDP (rent)]/0.5
[e] 15% of land held under endowment; AGDP (endowments) = [AGDP (emins)]/0.85

surplus-extraction from the peasantry. It is also assumes that some ten to twenty percent of the land remained under endowment. With a tax rate of roughly twenty-five percent, the total agrarian GDP can be estimated from the overall budget of 1596–1597.[34]

Taken at face value, these numbers would seem to suggest a dramatic plunge in agrarian output (of at least fifty percent) from 1517 to 1596–1597. However, the figures here are greatly distorted by the influx of gold and silver from the New World. The agricultural output in real terms can once again be evaluated using an ardabb that reflects the price of the major urban crops. This method works particularly well for the Ottoman budget, since the Ottomans used an averaging formula for crops (the jarare, ʿaliq, or feddan referred to above) that was similar in form to the dinar jayshi.[35] We can thus convert the total agrarian GDP into ardabbs and use this as a much more accurate comparison for agricultural output in 1315 and 1517.

Using the Ottoman tax evaluation whereby one ardabb equaled twenty-five paras, the figure for total agrarian GDP in ardabbs (17,299,090) can be converted into paras (432,477,250).

TABLE 5.17

Change in agrarian GDP in Egypt,
1315 to 1517 to 1596–1597

Year	Total agrarian GDP (ardabbs)
1315	38,337,056
1517	15,993,603
% change	−58
1596–1597	17,299,090
% change from 1315	−55
% change from 1517	+8

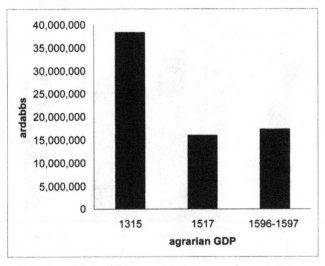

Agrarian GDP of Egypt, 1315, 1517, and 1596–1597,
in ardabbs

A comparison of output in ardabbs then yields the above figures for 1315, 1517, and 1596–1597.

As can be seen from these figures, the total agricultural output (agrarian GDP) in 1596–1597 was still appreciably lower than in 1315. However, agricultural output at the time of the Ottoman budget was above the level of 1517. This was due to the Ottomans' reestablishment of centralized control over the Egyptian economy. The Ottomans were at least partially successful in restoring the irrigation system, as the level of investment in irrigation repairs shown in the budget clearly demonstrates

——————————— TABLE 5.18 ———————————
Change in total GDP in England, 1300 to 1470 to 1526

Year	Population	Total GDP	Total GDP (deflated)	Per capita GDP	Per capita GDP (deflated)
1300	6,000,000	4,660,000	4,660,000	0.77	0.78
1470	2,300,000	3,500,000	3,510,000	1.52	1.52
% change	−62	−25	−25	+97	+95
1526	2,300,000	5,000,000	3,880,000	2.17	1.69
% change from 1300	−62	+7	−17	+182	+117

Note: GDP figures are in pounds sterling.

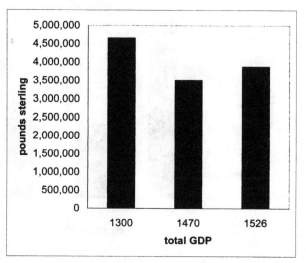

Total GDP of England, 1300, 1470, and 1526,
in pounds sterling

(about 2.5 percent of the budget revenue was set aside for irrigation repairs).[36] Ottoman efforts to encourage agricultural settlement and subjugate Bedouin tribes also help explain the increase in output over the eighty years from 1517 to 1596–1597.[37]

The numbers for the Ottoman budget are clearly an approximation; they are not supposed to reflect an exact measure of agrarian output. However, the approximations used suggest that the final numbers may be in error by margins of twenty percent or so, but certainly not by any

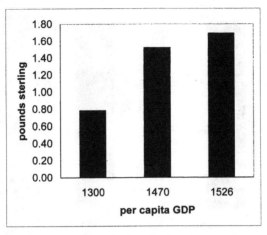

*Per capita GDP in England, 1300, 1470,
and 1526, in pounds sterling*

TABLE 5.19

*Change in agrarian GDP in Egypt
(1315–1517) compared to change in total
GDP in England (1300–1526)*

Country	GDP
Egypt	(total agrarian GDP)[a]
1315	38,337,056
1517	15,993,603
% change	*−58*
England	(total GDP)[b]
1300	4,660,000
1526	3,800,000
% change	*−17*

[a]in ardabbs
[b]in pounds sterling (deflated)

orders of magnitude. The final tally of comparative figures for 1315, 1517, and 1596–1597 clearly reflects the logic of historical circumstances during this period. The overall intention of using the Ottoman budget here was to provide an historical cross-check for the figures provided by Ibn Iyas. It seems clear that they have confirmed the picture of overall trends in Egypt's agrarian economy over this long time span.

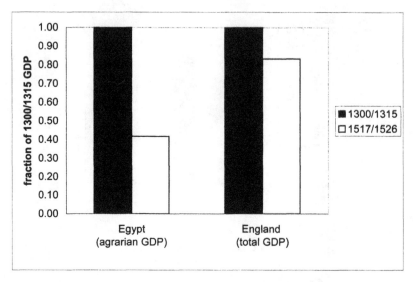

Relative fall in agrarian and total GDP in Egypt and England from 1300/1315 to 1517/1526

A comparison with England's post-plague economy can now be made. The lack of a measure of value comparable to the three-crop ardabb prohibits us from making any direct comparisons of agrarian and total GDP for post-plague Egypt and England. Nevertheless, using Mayhew's figures, we can compare the level of absolute and per capita changes in GDP from before and after the plagues. (Since we do not have exact figures for Egypt's population, per capita changes in agrarian or total income cannot be compared here. However, they will be explored below when we examine prices and wages.) Mayhew's numbers here will be used to show the total drop in England's GDP and the output per capita, both of these figures deflated by Mayhew's use of Fisher's equation ($MV = PT$).[38]

The changes in GDP for England and agrarian GDP for Egypt are compared below. Although the two sets of figures do not form an exact match, the predominance of agriculture in England's GDP makes the contrast valuable for this study.

SIX

PRICES AND WAGES:
A REEVALUATION

Shifting the focus away from agrarian output and GDP to an analysis of prices and wages for Egypt and England will allow us to estimate relative changes in income per capita. The overall picture will also provide crucial information about the relative changes in the two agrarian economies.

The data for prices and wages provided for Egypt and England is abundant in comparison with the other quantitative data assessed in this chapter. The price and wage "scissors" also stand in stark contrast to each other. Briefly put, the overall picture in England after the plagues is that grain prices dropped and wages rose. In Egypt, the opposite occurred: grain prices rose while wages dropped. Although there are some complicating features that will be discussed, the opposing direction of the scissors in the two countries (after the plagues) is unmistakable. A comparison of the purchasing power of wages for grain reveals a dramatic picture.

The section that follows balances a set of prices and wages from 1300 to 1350 with a matching set from 1440 to 1490. The two periods form a good comparison with each other for several reasons. The objective is to demonstrate the long-term effects that demographic decline had on prices and wages in the two economies. For a comparison, two periods of equal length bear the most consistent possible measures. Fifty years serves as the best fit for these two fixed spans of time. The year 1300 is the best starting date, since price data for Egypt is scarcer before the start of the fourteenth century. Moreover, commencing Egypt's price series in 1300 allows us to take account of the expansion in dikes and canals carried out by the early Mamluk sultanate. During the second half of the thirteenth century and the first half of the fourteenth century, the rulers of Egypt were able to increase the amount of arable land by as much as fifty percent.[1] The success of the early Mamluk regime in stimulating agrarian development had a significant impact on prices, and is as crucial to an accurate interpretation of the economic trajectory of Egypt from 1300 to 1500 as the catastrophic failure of the later regime to maintain agricultural productivity after the demographic collapse. The year 1350 (or rather 1347 in Egypt and 1348 in England, when the initial plagues struck) is an obvious end point for the first price series.

The year 1440 is an appropriate starting point for the second fifty-year series. Since it is some ninety years after the initial plague hit both countries, it allows for economic events triggered by demographic collapse to have played themselves out. Both countries were close to reaching the nadir of population by 1440, with the worst plague in Egypt (after the Black Death itself) occurring in 1429–1430. By 1440, enough time had passed for the reactionary efforts of English landlords—as expressed in the Statute of Labourers—to fade into oblivion. In Egypt by 1440, the effects of the landholding system under demographic strain had taken much of their toll on the dike-and-canal system. The year 1440 is an excellent starting point for Egypt if reliable comparative indicators of prices in precious metals are to be used. Before 1440, Egypt had been subject to wild fluctuations in the value of its copper currency. After 1440, the value of copper currency, as expressed in the dirham min al-fulus (its money of account) had become relatively stable. Equally or more importantly, by 1440 silver had once again (as in the period 1300–1350) become a currency of frequent, perhaps comprehensive, usage. Before 1440, silver had been so scarce that in the early fifteenth century it was effectively absent from the Egyptian economy. By starting at 1440, we can use silver as a comparative index. If the starting point for the second data set were placed before 1440, only gold would be available for a precious-metal comparison. Although gold will be used here to back up silver for comparison, it is a more tenuous measure of value for 1300–1350, since it was neither minted nor widespread in England during the early fourteenth century.[2] (The problems associated with using nominal currency, i.e., pence or dirhams, will be discussed below.)

For Egypt, the price data has been subject to one standard deviation. Only the price of wheat is used here, as the other two regularly reported staple crops (barley and broad beans) follow the trend of wheat prices quite closely.[3]

As can be seen here, wheat prices were significantly higher in the post-plague period of 1440–1490. Again, the other two regularly reported crops follow a similar trend. The tables that follow show grain prices in England for the same two periods, in ten-year intervals. Barley and peas

TABLE 6.1

Wheat prices in Egypt, 1300–1350

Year	Season/ month	Dirhams nuqra[a]	Dinars mithqal[a]	Silver (g)[a]	Silver (g) per liter	Gold (g)[a]	Gold (g) per liter
					Price of wheat		
1300	January	17.0	1.00	33.66	0.20	4.25	0.03
1300	February	14.0	0.82	27.72	0.17	3.49	0.02
1300	April	14.5	0.73	28.71	0.17	3.08	0.02
1300	Fall	20.0	1.00	39.60	0.24	4.25	0.03
1300	Spring	27.0	1.35	53.46	0.32	5.74	0.03
1300	Summer	20.0	1.00	39.60	0.24	4.25	0.03
1300	October	20.0	1.00	39.60	0.24	4.25	0.03
1300	Fall	15.0	0.75	29.70	0.18	3.19	0.02
1303	Fall	40.0	2.00	79.20	0.48	8.50	0.05
1303	Fall	25.0	1.25	49.50	0.30	5.31	0.03
1306	Spring	20.0	0.50	39.60	0.24	2.13	0.01
1306	Fall	40.0	0.50	79.20	0.48	2.13	0.01
1307	Fall	50.0	2.50	99.00	0.60	10.63	0.06
1309	Fall	50.0	2.50	99.00	0.60	10.63	0.06
1317	Fall	2.0	0.10	3.96	0.02	0.43	0.00
1324	January	10.0	0.25	19.80	0.12	1.06	0.01
1324	January	17.0	0.43	33.66	0.20	1.81	0.01
1326	February	5.5	0.28	10.89	0.07	1.17	0.01
1328	January	13.0	0.65	25.74	0.16	2.76	0.02
1328	January	17.0	0.85	33.66	0.20	3.61	0.02
1336	February	15.0	0.75	29.70	0.18	3.19	0.02
1336	February	50.0	2.50	99.00	0.60	10.63	0.06
1336	December	40.0	2.00	79.20	0.48	8.50	0.05
1337	Winter	9.0	0.45	17.82	0.11	1.91	0.01
1338	Spring	20.0	1.00	39.60	0.24	4.25	0.03
1341	May–June	15.0	0.75	29.70	0.18	3.19	0.02
1341	May–June	30.0	1.50	59.40	0.36	6.38	0.04
1342	January	6.0	0.55	11.88	0.07	2.32	0.01
1343	Fall	10.0	0.50	19.80	0.12	2.13	0.01
1343	Fall	20.0	1.00	39.60	0.24	4.25	0.03
1346	May	55.0	2.75	108.91	0.66	11.69	0.07
1346	June	30.0	1.50	59.40	0.36	6.38	0.04
1346	September	35.0	1.75	69.30	0.42	7.44	0.05
1346	September	55.0	2.75	108.91	0.66	11.69	0.07
Avg. w/1 std. dev.		19.30	0.90	38.21	0.2316	3.82	0.0231

Note: All data includes one standard deviation.
[a]per ardabb

TABLE 6.2
Wheat prices in Egypt, 1440–1490

Year	Month(s)	Dirhams min al-fulus[a]	Dinars ashrafi[a]	Silver (g)[a]	Silver (g) per liter	Gold (g)[a]	Gold (g) per liter
				Price of wheat			
1440	January	300	1.05	35.17	0.21	3.68	0.022
1440	February	330	1.16	38.69	0.23	4.05	0.024
1440	March	225	0.79	26.38	0.16	2.76	0.017
1444	Apr.–May	200	0.70	23.45	0.14	2.46	0.015
1449	June–July	300	1.05	35.17	0.21	3.68	0.022
1449	July–Aug.	290	1.02	34.00	0.21	3.56	0.021
1449	Aug.–Sep.	400	1.40	46.89	0.28	4.91	0.029
1449	October	600	2.11	70.34	0.43	7.37	0.044
1450	Feb.–Mar.	800	2.81	93.79	0.57	9.82	0.059
1450	June–July	500	1.75	58.62	0.36	6.14	0.037
1450	Aug.–Sep.	650	2.28	76.20	0.46	7.98	0.048
1451	April	900	3.16	105.51	0.64	11.05	0.066
1451	August	900	3.16	105.51	0.64	11.05	0.066
1451	September	900	3.16	105.51	0.64	11.05	0.066
1452	Jan.–Feb.	800	2.50	83.53	0.51	8.75	0.053
1452	Apr.–May	400	1.25	41.77	0.25	4.38	0.026
1452	Nov.–Dec.	320	1.00	33.41	0.20	3.50	0.021
1456	February	270	0.84	28.19	0.17	2.95	0.018
1456	August	260	0.81	27.15	0.16	2.84	0.017
1456	December	470	1.12	37.39	0.23	3.92	0.023
1459	November	300	0.71	23.87	0.14	2.50	0.015
1462	July	270	0.85	28.50	0.17	2.99	0.018
1462	July	450	1.42	47.51	0.29	4.98	0.030
1462	August	350	1.11	36.95	0.22	3.87	0.023
1464	Mar.–Apr.	360	1.14	38.00	0.23	3.98	0.024
1465	June	350	1.00	33.41	0.20	3.50	0.021
1466	January	420	1.20	40.10	0.24	4.20	0.025
1466	February	600	1.71	57.28	0.35	6.00	0.036
1466	March	540	1.54	51.55	0.31	5.40	0.032
1466	April	1,000	2.86	95.46	0.58	10.00	0.060
1466	May	350	1.00	33.41	0.20	3.50	0.021
1468	January	500	1.43	47.73	0.29	5.00	0.030
1468	May	600	1.70	56.80	0.34	5.95	0.036
1468	June–July	700	2.00	66.83	0.41	7.00	0.042
1468	August	750	2.14	71.50	0.43	7.49	0.045
1468	September	900	2.57	85.87	0.52	9.00	0.054
1468	October	400	1.14	38.09	0.23	3.99	0.024

TABLE 6.2
(continued)

Year	Month(s)	Price of wheat					
		Dirhams min al-fulus[a]	Dinars ashrafi[a]	Silver (g)[a]	Silver (g) per liter	Gold (g)[a]	Gold (g) per liter
1468	October	900	2.57	85.87	0.52	9.00	0.054
1468	November	900	2.57	85.87	0.52	9.00	0.054
1468	December	900	2.57	85.87	0.52	9.00	0.054
1469	March	600	1.70	56.80	0.34	5.95	0.036
1469	April	600	1.71	57.28	0.35	6.00	0.036
1469	June–July	1,000	2.86	95.46	0.58	10.00	0.060
1469	Aug.–Sep.	1,350	3.86	128.88	0.78	13.50	0.081
1470	July	850	2.28	76.18	0.46	7.98	0.048
1472	Apr.–May	350	1.00	33.41	0.20	3.50	0.021
1484	Aug.–Sep.	400	1.00	33.41	0.20	3.50	0.021
1486	October	1,000	2.50	83.53	0.51	8.75	0.053
1486	November	1,100	2.75	91.88	0.56	9.63	0.058
1487	Aug.–Sep.	1,200	3.00	100.24	0.61	10.50	0.063
Avg. w/1 std. dev.		596.1	1.78	59.48	**0.3610**	6.23	0.0378

Note: All data includes one standard deviation.
[a]per ardabb

TABLE 6.3
Change in wheat prices in Egypt
from 1300–1350 to 1440–1490

Year	Price of wheat (liter)	
	Silver (g)	Gold (g)
1300–1350	0.2316	0.0231
1440–1490	0.3610	0.0378
% change	+56	+64

(rough equivalents to Egypt's regularly reported barley and broad beans) have been included along with wheat. The price of barley and peas fell more precipitously than did the price of wheat.[4]

The "price resilience" of English wheat in the face of a relative decrease in demand and a rise in the supply of grain crops was probably due

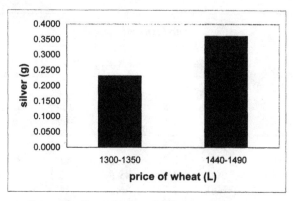

Price of a liter of wheat in Egypt, 1300–1350
and 1440–1490, in grams of silver

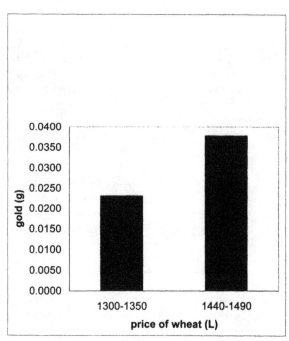

Price of a liter of wheat in Egypt, 1300–1350
and 1440–1490, in grams of gold

TABLE 6.4

Change in wheat prices in England from 1300–1350 to 1440–1490

Year	Price of wheat			
	Shillings[a]	Pence[b]	Silver (g)[b]	Gold (g)[b]
1300–1310	5.37	0.22	0.30	0.02
1310–1320	7.94	0.33	0.44	0.03
1320–1330	6.90	0.29	0.38	0.03
1330–1340	5.24	0.22	0.29	0.02
1340–1347	4.88	0.20	0.27	0.02
Average	*6.07*	*0.252*	*0.336*	*0.024*
1440–1450	4.93	0.20	0.15	0.01
1450–1460	5.63	0.23	0.17	0.02
1460–1470	5.60	0.23	0.17	0.02
1470–1480	5.76	0.24	0.17	0.02
1480–1490	6.85	0.28	0.20	0.02
Average	*5.75*	*0.236*	*0.172*	*0.018*
% change	*−5*	*−6*	*−49*	*−25*

[a]per quarter
[b]per liter

TABLE 6.5

Change in barley prices in England from 1300–1350 to 1440–1490

Year	Price of barley			
	Shillings[a]	Pence[b]	Silver (g)[b]	Gold (g)[b]
1300–1310	4.18	0.17	0.23	0.02
1310–1320	6.23	0.26	0.34	0.03
1320–1330	5.02	0.21	0.28	0.02
1330–1340	4.22	0.17	0.23	0.02
1340–1347	3.81	0.16	0.21	0.02
Average	*4.69*	*0.194*	*0.258*	*0.022*
1440–1450	3.36	0.14	0.10	0.01
1450–1460	4.04	0.17	0.12	0.01
1460–1470	4.10	0.17	0.12	0.01
1470–1480	4.30	0.18	0.13	0.01
1480–1490	4.22	0.17	0.13	0.01
Average	*4.00*	*0.166*	*0.120*	*0.01*
% change	*−15*	*−14*	*−53*	*−45*

[a]per quarter
[b]per liter

TABLE 6.6

Change in pea prices in England from 1300–1350 to 1440–1490

Year	Price of peas			
	Shillings[a]	Pence[b]	Silver (g)[b]	Gold (g)[b]
1300–1310	3.68	0.15	0.20	0.02
1310–1320	5.22	0.22	0.29	0.02
1320–1330	4.35	0.18	0.24	0.02
1330–1340	3.79	0.16	0.21	0.02
1340–1347	3.24	0.13	0.18	0.01
Average	*4.06*	*0.168*	*0.224*	*0.018*
1440–1450	2.74	0.11	0.08	0.01
1450–1460	2.67	0.11	0.08	0.01
1460–1470	3.00	0.12	0.09	0.01
1470–1480	3.18	0.13	0.09	0.01
1480–1490	4.61	0.19	0.14	0.01
Average	*3.24*	*0.132*	*0.096*	*0.01*
% change	*−20*	*−21*	*−57*	*−44*

[a]per quarter
[b]per liter

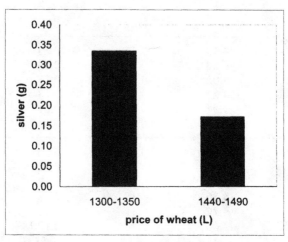

*Price of a liter of wheat in England, 1300–1350
and 1440–1490, in grams of silver*

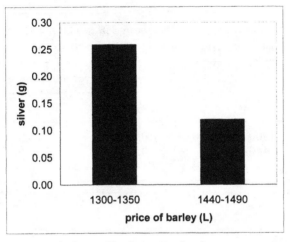

Price of a liter of barley in England, 1300–1350
and 1440–1490, in grams of silver

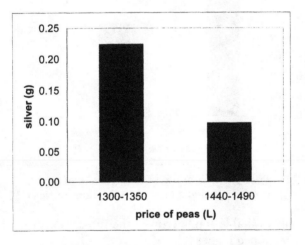

Price of a liter of peas in England, 1300–1350
and 1440–1490, in grams of silver

to the greater elasticity of its demand curve. When living standards for
the majority of the population improved in the fifteenth century, wheat—
which had been a luxury in the early fourteenth century (e.g., during the
great famine of 1315–1317)—was more highly prized than other crops
that had served as substitutes during difficult times. When wheat became

TABLE 6.7
Comparison of the change in wheat prices in England and Egypt, 1300–1350 to 1440–1490

Year	Price of wheat in silver (g)[a]	
	England	Egypt
1300–1350	0.336	0.2316
1440–1490	0.172	0.3610
% change	−49	+56

[a]price for 1 liter

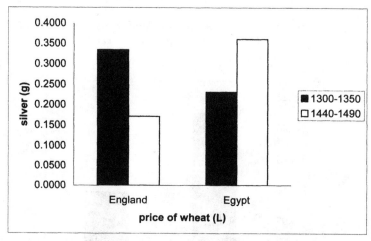

Price of a liter of wheat in England and Egypt,
1300–1350 and 1440–1490, in grams of silver

a more readily available staple crop in the fifteenth century, relative demand for it remained higher.[5]

As can be seen from these figures, grain prices fell in England while they rose in Egypt. The fall in grain prices for England is much more dramatic when the prices are expressed in constant weights of silver rather than nominal currency (the English penny). Choosing between nominal and precious-metal prices brings us into the realm of the great debate over the scale, scope, and impact of monetary flows in fourteenth- and fifteenth-century Europe. A full analysis of this debate would be very protracted, and could easily be the subject of a separate study (as it has been for many English medievalists).[6]

One could argue that a discussion of this subject is superfluous. A reader familiar with the monetary situation can choose among the various indices of prices shown here (e.g., nominal, constant weights of silver, and constant weights of gold). A comparison of purchasing power in terms of grain will be given below, and the use of nominal versus precious-metal prices will make no difference in this case, as the two nominal currencies (or two precious metals) will cancel each other out. The comparison of Egyptian and English agrarian living standards is, in the end, more important than any absolute comparison of prices and wages.

Nevertheless, since this study will attempt to provide a wider scope for comparative indices, some equal measure of value is called for. Egypt had no standard currency with which one could compare the pre-plague and post-plague periods. Egypt's coinage before the plague was different in so many respects from its coinage after the plague that a comparison of nominal currency would be deceptive. (The closest match would be the dinar, which will be used sporadically below. However, the dinar's weight and usage changed significantly from the fourteenth to the fifteenth century.)[7] A brief discussion of the nominal and fixed-weight monetary standards is needed here.

David Farmer does not give prices and wages in constant weights of precious metal (silver in this case), saying that "such exercises ignore the value of silver relative to the stock in the economy in which it circulates."[8] The problem with this logic is that it is just as loaded with unstated assumptions as the reverse proposition would be. That is, if one were to use constant weights of silver (or another precious metal) without making an attempt to calculate the money supply or monetary stocks, one would be just as prone to error. By contending that currency should not be converted into precious metals, Farmer is tacitly asserting that the monetary stock is fluctuating in a manner that is exactly proportional to the change in the precious-metal content of the currency. (The English penny declined in silver content from 1.44 grams sterling silver, i.e., 1.332 grams of silver, in 1300 to 0.78 grams sterling silver, i.e., 0.7215 grams of silver, in 1500.) Farmer is positing an exact monetary ratio where he never establishes one, which is arguably just as bad as positing the reverse. (One might support Farmer's contention by arguing that the silver penny had a familiarity of usage, a tradition of expectations that overcame its extrinsic value. However, this assumption smacks of modern perceptions of money usage; certainly, medieval merchants, and perhaps peasants, were acutely aware of and attentive to the vital changes in the extrinsic value of currency.)

Fortunately, quite a few studies of the late-medieval English economy

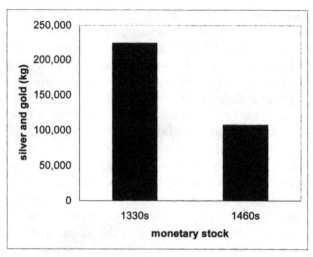

*Monetary stock of England, 1330s and 1460s,
in kilograms of silver and gold*

can shed light on this question. Peter Spufford, drawing on earlier work by monetary historians such as John Day, has analyzed the bullion famine in Europe, evaluating both the silver famine of the late fourteenth century and the more generalized bullion famine of the mid-fifteenth century.[9] Spufford observes that the royal mint of England was one of the few European mints to stay open during the worst of the latter famine (even increasing its mint output, albeit slightly, in the 1450s).[10] The resilience of the English mint may have been linked to the increased production of cloth for export (and a favorable balance of trade), particularly when Italy, which had ready access to the early fifteenth-century Bosnian and Serbian silver mines, assumed a dominant role in the cloth trade with England in the 1400s.[11] For the purposes of this study, Spufford's data tables for the monetary stock in England are particularly useful. Looking at averages of England's monetary stock that fall into the middle of the 1300–1350 and 1440–1490 periods, we can see that the total stock of bullion fell by approximately one-half from the first period to the second.[12]

Given that the silver content of the English penny dropped by roughly one-half over the same period (from 1.332 grams of silver in 1300–1350 to 0.7215 grams of silver in 1440–1490), one might be tempted to conclude that Farmer's use of nominal currency alone is the correct method to use. A cursory glance at Fisher's identity ($MV = PT$) would suggest that a fifty percent drop in real prices balanced the fifty percent drop in the monetary stock.

However, this argument neglects the drop in population. By the late fifteenth century, England's population had reached its nadir, and was roughly half that of the 1300–1350 period. Once population is factored in, the argument is reversed: although there may have been only half as much precious metal available in England, there were only half as many people left to make use of it.[13] With population factored in, constant weights of silver would seem to be a more accurate index of prices; nominal prices distort the picture by underestimating the fall in real prices.

Nicholas Mayhew's examination of Fisher's equation lends further credence to the notion that constant weights of silver should be employed for this analysis.[14] Mayhew estimates that the nominal level of the money supply was equal in 1300 and 1470 (in both cases the total figure is 900,000 pounds sterling). With the drop in population and the reduced silver content of the English penny factored in, this would again argue for the use of constant weights of silver as a method of comparing prices over the two periods.[15] However, as Mayhew aptly puts it, "we are groping towards general orders of magnitude, rather than advancing hard figures."[16] In the end, we cannot arrive at an exact figure to balance the equation. Although I prefer to use constant weights of silver, both nominal and "real" prices are presented here, and, as stated above, the most important index (purchasing power for agrarian goods) does not rely upon either method, since the two cancel each other out.

It is more difficult to harmonize two data sets of wages for the same periods (1300–1350 and 1440–1490). Nevertheless, a few roughly equivalent categories have been chosen, and will serve to provide a general picture. The contrast is striking: wages in England rose significantly while wages in Egypt declined precipitously.

Egypt's wages have never been carefully analyzed. Eliyahu Ashtor's data, assembled over fifty years ago, has been supplemented with new material here. The wages presented here are, for the most part, taken from unpublished endowment deeds. This new data, coupled with previously published material, will provide a more accurate picture.[17] The wages for England have been taken from David Farmer and Christopher Dyer, both very reliable sources for the nominal wages over the pre- and post-plague periods.[18]

Table 6.12, on page 107, summarizes the wage trends in pence and silver for England and dinars and silver for Egypt. The nominal wages

TABLE 6.8

Change in tradesmen's wages in England, 1300–1350 to 1440–1490 (carpenter and slater/tiler)

Year	Carpenter's wages				Slater/tiler and helper's wages			
	Pence[a]	Pence[b]	Silver (g)[b]	Gold (g)[b]	Pence[a]	Pence[b]	Silver (g)[b]	Gold (g)[b]
1300–1310	2.89	772.5	962.37	74.03	5.17	1,292.5	1,721.61	132.43
1310–1320	3.10	775.0	1,032.30	79.41	5.82	1,455.0	1,938.06	149.08
1320–1330	3.12	780.0	1,038.96	79.92	5.04	1,260.0	1,678.32	129.10
1330–1340	3.20	800.0	1,065.60	81.97	5.38	1,345.0	1,791.54	137.81
1340–1347	3.03	757.5	1,008.99	77.61	5.22	1,305.0	1,738.26	133.71
Average	3.068	767.0	1,021.64	78.59	5.33	1,331.5	1,773.56	136.43
1440–1450	5.17	1,292.5	932.54	84.78	8.23	2,057.5	1,484.49	134.95
1450–1460	5.45	1,362.5	983.04	89.37	9.63	2,407.5	1,737.01	157.91
1460–1470	5.42	1,355.0	977.63	88.88	9.75	2,437.5	1,758.66	159.88
1470–1480	5.83	1,457.5	1,051.59	95.60	9.82	2,455.0	1,771.28	161.03
1480–1490	5.71	1,427.5	1,029.94	93.63	9.17	2,292.5	1,654.04	150.37
Average	5.516	1,379.0	994.95	90.45	9.32	2,330.0	1,681.10	152.83
% change	+80	+80	−3	+15	+75	+75	−5	+12

[a] per day
[b] per year

TABLE 6.9

Change in tradesmen's wages in England, 1300–1350 to 1440–1490 (thatcher and thatcher's helper)

Year	Thatcher's wages				Thatcher's helper's wages			
	Pence[a]	Pence[b]	Silver (g)[b]	Gold (g)[b]	Pence[a]	Pence[b]	Silver (g)[b]	Gold (g)[b]
1300–1310	2.5	625.0	832.5	64.04	1.00	250.0	333.00	25.62
1310–1320	3.0	750.0	999.0	76.85	1.25	312.5	416.25	32.02
1320–1330	3.0	750.0	999.0	76.85	1.00	250.0	333.00	25.62
1330–1340	3.0	750.0	999.0	76.85	1.25	312.5	416.25	32.02
1340–1347	3.0	750.0	999.0	76.85	1.25	312.5	416.25	32.02
Average	2.9	725.0	965.7	74.28	1.15	287.5	382.95	29.46
1440–1450	5.25	1,312.5	946.97	86.09	4.00	1,000.0	721.50	65.59
1450–1460	5.50	1,375.0	992.06	90.19	3.25	812.5	586.22	53.29
1460–1470	4.75	1,187.5	856.78	77.89	3.75	937.5	676.41	61.49
1470–1480	5.25	1,312.5	946.97	86.09	3.75	937.5	676.41	61.49
1480–1490	6.00	1,500.0	1,082.25	98.39	3.75	937.5	676.41	61.49
Average	5.35	1,337.5	965.01	87.73	3.70	925.0	667.39	60.67
% change	+84	+80	0	+18	+222	+222	+74	+106

[a] per day
[b] per year

TABLE 6.10

Change in tradesmen's wages in Egypt, 1300–1350 to 1440–1490 (custodian and doorkeeper)

Year	Custodian's annual wages			Doorkeeper's annual wages		
	Dinars	Silver (g)	Gold (g)	Dinars	Silver (g)	Gold (g)
1303	17.4	692.49	73.95	12.0	477.58	51.00
1303	15.0	596.97	63.75	18.0	716.36	76.50
1325[a]	15.0	596.97	63.75	36.0	1,432.73	153.00
1325	—	—	—	18.0	716.36	76.50
Average	*15.8*	*628.81*	*67.15*	*21.0*	*835.76*	*89.25*
1461	1.43	47.73	4.93	—	—	—
1464	3.79	126.68	13.08	3.79	126.68	13.08
1466	10.29	343.67	35.49	10.29	343.67	35.49
1474	8.57	286.39	29.57	10.29	343.67	35.49
Average	*6.02*	*201.12*	*20.77*	*8.12*	*271.34*	*28.02*
% change	*−62*	*−68*	*−69*	*−61*	*−68*	*−69*

[a]custodian's wages are for 1331

TABLE 6.11

Change in tradesmen's wages in Egypt, 1300–1350 to 1440–1490 (water carrier and reader)

Year	Water carrier's annual wages			Reader's annual wages		
	Dinars	Silver (g)	Gold (g)	Dinars	Silver (g)	Gold (g)
1303	18.0	716.36	76.5	12.0	477.58	51.00
1331	—	—	—	15.0	596.97	63.75
Average	*18.0*	*716.36*	*76.5*	*13.5*	*537.27*	*57.38*
1444	—	—	—	4.21	140.68	14.53
1461	—	—	—	1.43	47.73	4.93
1464	7.58	253.36	26.16	1.90	63.34	6.54
1464	3.79	126.68	13.08	0.95	31.67	3.27
1466	—	—	—	10.29	343.67	35.49
1474	14.57	486.87	50.27	9.43	315.03	32.53
Average	*8.65*	*201.12*	*29.84*	*4.70*	*157.02*	*16.21*
% change	*−52*	*−60*	*−61*	*−65*	*−71*	*−72*

TABLE 6.12

Comparison of the change in tradesmen's wages
in England and Egypt, 1300–1350 to 1440–1490

Annual wages of English tradesmen

Year	Carpenter		Slater/tiler & helper		Thatcher		Thatcher's helper	
	Pence	Silver (g)	Pence	Silver (g)	Pence	Silver (g)	Pence	Silver (g)
1300–1350	767	1,021.64	1,331.5	1,773.56	725.0	965.70	287.5	382.95
1440–1490	1,379	994.95	2,330.0	1,681.10	1,337.5	965.01	925.0	667.39
% change	+80	−3	+75	−5	+84	0	+222	+74

Annual wages of Egyptian tradesmen

Year	Custodian		Doorkeeper		Water carrier		Reader	
	Dinars	Silver (g)	Dinars	Silver (g)	Dinars	Silver (g)	Dinars	Silver (g)
1300–1350	15.80	628.81	21.00	835.76	18.00	716.36	13.5	537.27
1440–1490	6.02	201.12	8.12	271.34	8.65	288.97	4.7	157.02
% change	−62	−68	−61	−68	−52	−60	−65	−71

TABLE 6.13

Change in tradesmen's purchasing power in England, 1300–1350 to 1440–1490, in liters of wheat

	Annual purchasing power in liters of wheat			
Year	Carpenter	Slater/tiler & helper	Thatcher	Thatcher's helper
1300–1350	3,054.70	5,302.94	2,887.44	1,142.87
1440–1490	5,790.61	9,784.00	5,616.36	3,884.21

TABLE 6.14

Change in tradesmen's purchasing power in Egypt, 1300–1350 to 1440–1490, in liters of wheat

	Annual purchasing power in liters of wheat			
Year	Custodian	Doorkeeper	Water carrier	Reader
1300–1350	2,906.92	3,863.63	3,311.69	2,483.98
1440–1490	549.37	741.13	789.27	428.75

TABLE 6.15

Comparison of the change in tradesmen's purchasing power in England and Egypt, 1300–1350 to 1440–1490

	Average annual purchasing power[a]	
Year	English tradesmen[b]	Egyptian tradesmen[c]
1300–1350	3,096.99	3,141.56
1440–1490	6,268.80	627.13
% change	+102	−80

[a] in liters of wheat
[b] carpenter, slater/tiler and helper, thatcher, thatcher's helper
[c] custodian, doorkeeper, water carrier, reader

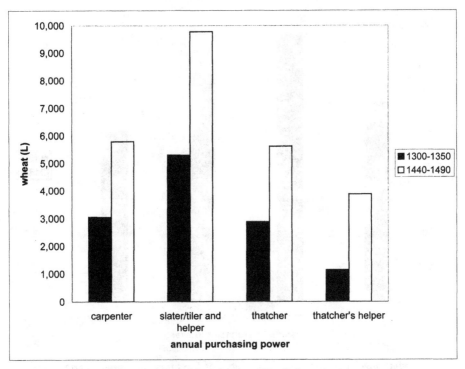

*Annual purchasing power of four types of English tradesmen, 1300–1350
and 1440–1490, in liters of wheat*

for Egypt do not have the same continuity of those in England, as the currency changed over the two periods evaluated.

A far more telling index for the purposes of comparison is the purchasing power of wages for an agrarian commodity. Wheat is used here, but any other staple food crop would yield virtually the same results.

The striking contrast between the average purchasing power for agrarian goods in England and Egypt substantiates the arguments presented in earlier chapters about the changes in the marginal, average, and total products of labor. For England, the increase in purchasing power and per capita income would be inexplicable unless one accepts at least some of the historical arguments concerning land usage before and after the plagues. It was argued above that England's overpopulation (a relative overpopulation given the available level of technology) caused expansion onto lands of marginal soil fertility, which had diminishing yields because of the scarcity of animal manure. Overpopulation also led to diminishing yields because of reduced fallow time and crop rotation, an increased

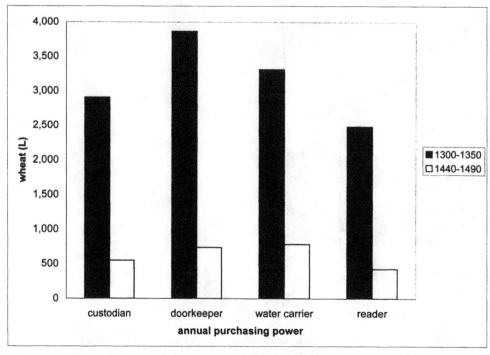

Annual purchasing power of four types of Egyptian tradesmen, 1300–1350 and 1440–1490, in liters of wheat

number of inefficient smallholdings, and limitations on agricultural reinvestment because of smallholding and the nature of the manorial system. All of these factors, it was argued, were reversed after the plagues swept through England. Each one of these elements has also been the subject of historical debate. It is possible that some of these measures did not play a major role, and it is certain that they did not apply to every area of England. However, it is impossible to account for the dramatic change in agrarian purchasing power (and per capita income) unless several of these elements played a significant role in most areas of England. The data compiled above essentially proves that the marginal and average products of labor in England increased dramatically after the plagues. The increase in purchasing power and per capita income also allows for a quantified estimate of the changes in the marginal, average, and total products of labor, which will be explored below, as they were in earlier chapters.

The contrast between purchasing power in England and Egypt also shows that the outcome in England need not have proceeded in this fashion. The typical picture of rising wages, falling rents, and falling grain

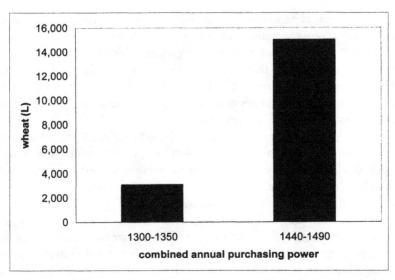

Combined average annual purchasing power of four types of English tradesmen, 1330–1350 and 1440–1490, in liters of wheat

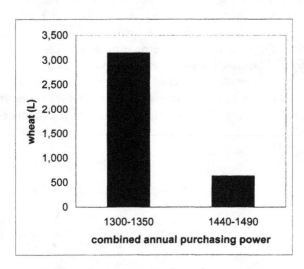

Combined average annual purchasing power of four types of Egyptian tradesmen, 1330–1350 and 1440–1490, in liters of wheat

prices that is associated with the plagues in Western Europe applied given only certain socioeconomic parameters. The structure of landholding in England fell within these parameters. Egypt provides a stunning example here of reversed effects from depopulation. Wages fell, rents remained stable, and grain prices rose. The landholding system in Egypt gave rise to an outcome that challenges traditional assumptions about the plagues' typical impact on agrarian economies.

The data presented here provides quantified confirmation of the arguments presented concerning developments in Egypt's agrarian economy. Egypt's landholders, it was argued, were well equipped to combat the demands of scarce labor. At the same time, the landholding system as a whole was all too vulnerable to the challenge of depopulation on a macroeconomic level. Dikes and canals (particularly the large sultanic dykes and canals that interlinked the smaller village systems) decayed and fell into ruin. Peasants did not relocate to the most suitable areas, where the irrigation system may have remained more intact. Peasants either remained in their villages, resorting to autarchic modes of subsistence (e.g., millet, sorghum, waterfowl, fish, etc.) or fled to urban areas. Bedouins moved in to inhabit decayed areas of the irrigation system, where their relatively autarchic lifestyle flourished. Again, as with England, not all of the explanations offered above necessarily applied. However, the dramatic evidence supplied here by the quantitative data, combined with the testimony of Mamluk-era observers, demonstrates that most of these factors must have played a significant role. As in the case of England, the quantitative data, barring some other study not observed in the chronicles of Mamluk Egypt, proves that events played out in the manner outlined above.

SEVEN

CONCLUSION

The great historical plague is usually associated with falling rents, falling grain prices, rising wages, and changes in landholding systems. Egypt did not follow this course of development. Egypt's landholding structure, a substantial success before the attack of *Yersinia pestis*, determined a dramatically different outcome from the one depicted in most historical studies. Egypt's rents increased, its grain prices rose, wages dropped precipitously, per capita incomes fell, and the landholding system stayed more or less intact. The outcome in Egypt stands out in dramatic relief when compared with that in England.

No one has ever clearly answered the question of why the plagues had such a particularly disastrous economic impact on Egypt. This study has proposed an answer to that question through the lens of comparative history. As Robert Brenner pointed out in his contentious (and, see below, at times erroneous) examination of European economies and their relation to demography, "The obvious difficulty with this whole massive structure [i.e., a fixation on demography] is that it simply breaks down in the face of comparative analysis. Different outcomes proceeded from similar demographic trends at different times and in different areas of Europe."[1] Or, as he further contends, reactions to changing demography resulted in "opposite outcomes—depending on the social-property relationships and balances of class forces."[2] Where English landholders failed in their efforts to collectively confront a scarce rural labor market, Egyptian landholders triumphed brilliantly. The consequences were a disaster for Egypt's rural economy, the backbone of its economic power. Egypt was left in ruins by the time the Ottomans turned it into a province in 1517. It is important here to critique a central part of Brenner's thesis in his famous debate. The comparison between Egypt and England demonstrates that it was not, as Brenner has maintained in his comparison of western and eastern Elbian Germany, the strength of peasant communal power that engendered contrasting outcomes, but rather it was the structure of the landholding system itself that determined the character of the denouement of the drastic depopulation wrought by the waves of plague.[3]

The results shown in this study should prompt European and Middle Eastern historians alike to probe more deeply into the trajectories that drove the East and the West in different developmental patterns in the late Middle Ages and the early modern period. This close comparison of England and Egypt shows that, contrary to some world historians' beliefs, not all Old World economies were at parity before the dramatic developments that followed the discovery of the New World. It also challenges the conclusions of other historians who maintain that the blocking of economic progress in Egypt and other non-Western economies was a foregone conclusion. Without the dramatic exogenous shock of the plague, the story of Egypt's development would probably have been very different. However, as demonstrated above, the reaction of England, Egypt, and other parts of world civilization to demographic loss in the wake of the plagues was dependent on the overall structure of the ruling classes' relationship to the agrarian economy.

The decline of Egypt's economy after the Black Death put an end to power in the heartland of the Arab world. Newcomers (Ottomans and Safavids) soon took the place of the Mamluk Empire. Did they, however, retain the achievements of their Mamluk forebearers? Certainly there is much to be said for the grandeur of Ottoman mosques, Safavid paintings, and a host of other achievements, but what might have been lost?

It might be better to ask what could have been gained. Egypt and other areas in the heartland of the Arab world were bastions of impressive achievements in science and technology before the Black Death. After the Black Death, they slipped into relative quiescence. A dramatic illustration of the dichotomy of before and after can be seen in two Egyptian monuments to higher learning (as well as worship). The Sultan Hasan mosque, built before the economic consequences of the Black Death were felt in Egypt, was an endowed institution devoted to the training of doctors and astronomers and containing an impressive body of literature outside the scope of traditional Islamic religious studies. By contrast, the edifice of the ruling potentate (Muhammad Bey Abu al-Dhahab) in eighteenth-century Egypt contained almost nothing related to secular studies, its library and endowment devoted solely to traditional and conservative religious training.[4]

Imagine, counterfactually, the impressive achievements and power of the Ottoman Empire harnessed to a robust and flourishing realm of science and technology in the Arab heartland that it ruled. One can wonder how different might have been their conquests in Europe and the sieges of Vienna had not the Arab heartland been stripped of its former dynamic character. How different would the astronomical observatories and mosque-madrasa complexes of the Ottomans have been if they had been coupled with an efflorescent contribution from Egypt and other areas of the Arab world? How different might the Ottomans' achievements in technology have been if Egypt's proto-industries had not fallen into oblivion? It would be worth exploring the scale and scope of decline for the Ottoman period that is suggested by Cairo's export stagnation in the following areas: metallurgy, military equipment, pottery, ceramics, tanned leather, leather items, parchment, paper, bookbinding, construction, cut stone, furniture, prepared and processed food, and textiles.[5]

To call the plagues the singular cause of Egypt's failure to progress to some form of industrialization, like that eventually realized in England, lies far beyond the bounds of this study. However, similar cross-regional microcomparisons may yield more answers to this great historical mystery and pose further challenging questions for scholars. The ground covered by smaller-scale comparisons can feed into the larger framework of grand comparisons taken up by macrohistorians.

Egypt should be compared with Syria, where a similar landholding system was applied to a different geographical base. Egypt should be compared with Iran, where localized *qanats* (underground water aqueducts) may have engendered a rural-centered, localized response, a response that may have been somewhat similar to that in England and may have accounted for the majestic rise of Safavid Persia. Egypt should be compared with Ottoman Anatolia and the Balkans as well as the dying Byzantine domain. Egypt should be compared with regions of Eastern Europe, the arena in which Brenner maintains that the peasants were defeated by the landlords and pressed into serfdom by the lack of cohesion in their communal village structures.[6] Egypt should be compared with the Italian city-states, where the power of urban landlords over the *contado* may have resembled the power of Egypt's urban elite; such a study may foster a better understanding of the different impacts of urban- and rural-based landholding social structures. Of particular importance, Egypt should be compared with China, where irrigation geography seems to have been somewhat similar, and may have engendered similar outcomes. Equally fascinating would be a comparison with Angkor and the dramatic collapse of the Khmer irrigation economy that occurred at the time of this pandemic. England also offers a focal point of comparison for these areas. All of these cross-regional comparisons are worth doing because they open up new doors for comparative historians to engage in cross-cultural studies and eliminate some of the vast generalizations inherent in larger world-historical comparisons.

In today's world, where Western capitalism reigns triumphant over a globalized and interconnected world economy, these questions are not simply a matter of debate for scholars intent on establishing the causes and contingencies of comparative development in the distant past. They are, rather, of signal importance for our ability to confront the future with the insight, wisdom, and humility that will be needed to understand changes in the global economic climate. A world bound together by transnational corporate capitalism seems to be the answer to many economists' dreams. (It may, indeed, be the answer for the near-term future.) Nevertheless, we must continue to pose broader questions about our mode of economic progress.

History teaches us that stubborn pride in a socioeconomic system that seems to be working (the English manorial system, the Mamluk caste system) can be mistaken and indeed very dangerous. In their studies of global economies and culture, economists, sociologists, and political scientists should constantly question economic postulates that seem to be firmly grounded. History also teaches us that developmental patterns change dramatically over time. New structures and new thinkers emerge and defy traditional economic and cultural norms. We would be indeed arrogant if we were to assume we have reached the "end of history" with our current model of liberal global capitalism.

We are also being dangerously parochial if we assume that our future economic decisions should be guided simply by gauging a proper mix of recent experiments in free-market capitalism and socialist welfare economics. The distant past lives on to inform us that an entirely new economic system could well emerge. In the twenty-first century, we should not face this with unexamined dismay, as Egypt's and England's leaders did. If we were to hold fast to our economic system during a time of acute crisis and economic change, we might well be courting disaster. In the age of new diseases such as AIDS and SARS and of climate changes such as global warming, we should learn from the cases of England and Egypt that we must be open to new modes of economic adaptation. If we put stubborn faith in our established paradigms, as Egypt's and England's leaders did, we wander blindly down the path of historical contingency. We could be lucky, as England turned out to be. But chance could lead us the other way, to the road of Egypt's decline. The lesson of Egypt and England teaches us that an abiding belief in a system that has worked in the past can be a very dangerous thing indeed.

THE MARGINAL PRODUCT
OF LABOR RECONSIDERED

The data in this study allows for a quantified estimate of the changes in the marginal, average, and total products of labor in a graphical format. The graphical models presented here propose to illustrate the basic features of England and Egypt's economies in the wake of the Black Death. They clarify the changes that took place in both economies and create a more easily conjured relationship with the quantitative data presented thus far. As with all economic models, the structure of the economies as depicted in the graphs has been simplified so that certain basic features can be analyzed and understood. (To state one of the most obvious principles of economics, any model that seeks to depict all aspects of a real economy is no longer a model and is of no value for functional analysis.)

A brief review of the economic concepts that underlie the graphs will be provided first. Not all historians are intimately familiar with the way in which the marginal, average, and total products of labor operate in an economy, and the graphs for Egypt are not typical of those presented in basic macroeconomic texts.

The graphs employ the basic economic concepts of the factors of production (fixed factors and variable factors), the total product, the average product, and the marginal product. A fixed factor is something, such as land or capital, which does not vary in quantity. The variable factor is something, such as labor, which does vary in quantity. The total product (TP) is the total amount of something that is produced in a given period of time. The average product (AP) is the total product divided by the number of units of a variable factor used to produce it. The marginal product (MP) is the change in the total product resulting from the addition of one more unit of the variable product.

One can make a simple analogy here to help explain the relationship between the three (*TPN*, *APN*, and *MPN*, where N stands for labor). Imagine that we are observing a car in motion. Labor, on the *x*-axis (abscissa) represents the amount of time that transpires. For the total product of labor (total output), the *y*-axis (ordinate) represents the distance traveled by the car in a given period of time (*x*-axis). For the marginal product of labor (the change in the total output per additional unit of labor), the *y*-axis represents the velocity at a given moment in time (e.g., 1 second, 2 seconds, etc.). For the average product of labor, the *y*-axis represents the average velocity travelled from time zero. Finally, for changes in the slope of the *MPN* curve as labor is added, the *y*-axis would represent the acceleration or deceleration of the car

Thus, if the *MPN* graph is a flat horizontal line, one would have a car at zero acceleration travelling at a constant velocity. The corresponding *TPN* graph would be a straight diagonal line moving upward along the *x*-axis. This would be the distance travelled by the car at a constant velocity over time. If the *MPN* graph were a straight diagonal line, moving upward or downward along the *x*-axis, one would have a car accelerating or decelerating at a constant rate (i.e., acceleration would be represented as a straight line at some level on the *y*-axis moving along the *x*-axis). If the *MPN* graph were curved rather than straight, one would have a car changing its rate of acceleration or deceleration. The *TPN* and *MPN* graphs are products of differential calculus. The *APN* graph is not (as it is simply the *TPN* divided by the total amount of labor in use, or, in this example, the average velocity of the car from when the car was started to the present time). If we imagine a car traveling at a constant rate of acceleration, *A*, we can represent the relationship between the *TPN* and the *MPN* (as labor is added) in terms of three differential equations:

^ = Exponent (raised to the power of)
* = Multiplied by
/ = Divided by

1. Acceleration $= d^2(x)/dt^2 = Ai$
Where *Ai* represents the constant number for the acceleration.

If we integrate this differential equation, we obtain the equation for velocity:

2. Velocity $= dx/dt = \int A = Ai^*(t) + Vi$
Where *Vi* represents the initial velocity and *t* represents time.

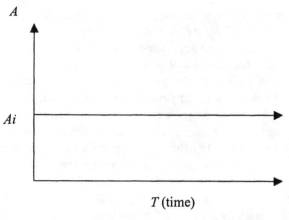

Constant acceleration

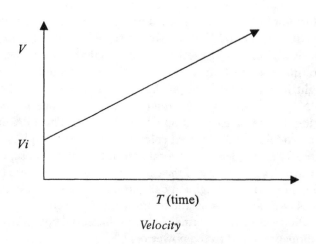

Velocity

If we integrate this differential equation again, we obtain the equation for the distance travelled:

3. Distance $= \int A^*(t) + Vi = \frac{1}{2} Ai^*(t^2) + Vi^*(t) + Di$
Where Di represents the initial distance along the x-axis.

For our purposes we have the following variables:
$MP =$ (the change in total product resulting from the addition of a variable factor) divided by (the change in the variable factor due to the addition of one more unit)

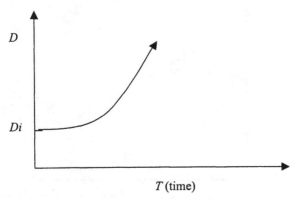

Distance traveled

The total product and factors of production can be represented by any one of the following equations:

$Y = A^*F^*(L, N)$
$Y = A^*F^*(K, N)$
$Y = A^*F^*(L, K, N)$

Where:
Y = total product
A = total factor productivity (a number representing the overall productivity)
L = quantity of land employed
N = quantity of labor employed
K = quantity of capital employed
F = a function relating Y to land (L), labor (N), and capital (K)

The variable factors used here will be labor and, later, capital. The fixed products will be land and capital. The law of diminishing returns states that if increasing amounts of a variable factor (e.g., labor) are applied to a fixed factor (e.g., capital or land), eventually a situation will be reached in which each addition of the variable factor adds less to total product than did the previous unit; that is, the marginal product (*MP*) of the variable factor (labor) will decline. If, for example, the fixed factor is capital and the variable factor is labor, each unit of labor gets a declining amount of capital to assist it as the total output grows. Increases in labor eventually begin to add diminishing amounts to the total output (total product).

In many basic economic graphs the marginal product of labor (*MPN*) is shown dropping from the outset, with the *TPN* increasing at a decreasing rate (see Figures A.4 and A.5 below). What must be remembered is

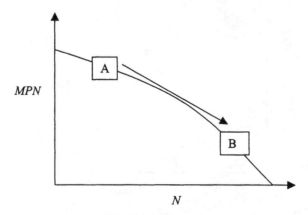

*Effect of overpopulation on the marginal
product of labor*

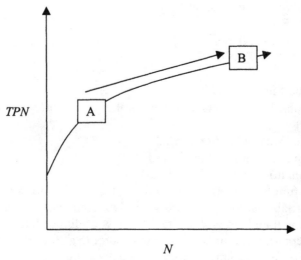

Effect of overpopulation on the total product of labor

that the x-axis of the graph usually does not start from the point where you only have one unit of labor (e.g., 1 person). The typical *MPN* graph begins at the point of diminishing marginal returns to labor (i.e., declining *MPN* sloping downward). This scenario leads to decreasing returns to labor when population increases, and increasing returns to labor when the population drops.

A particularly famous historical example of diminishing returns is the case of England, as analyzed in Chapter 4, before and after the Black Death depopulation. At the end of the thirteenth century, England's population was quite high relative to land, and land scarcity had brought living standards to a precariously low level. The marginal and total products of labor would have moved from A to B in Figures A.4 and A.5. The disastrous weather that followed in the years 1315–1317 ushered in a horrific famine in which as much as ten percent of the population is estimated to have died from starvation and malnutrition. By contrast, following mass depopulation from the Black Death and repeated outbreaks of *Yersinia pestis*, England entered the so-called "golden age of the peasantry," when fifteenth-century survivors enjoyed a period of lower rents, higher wages, and a generally improved standard of living. The marginal and total products of labor would have moved from C to D in Figures A.6 and A.7.

Now I would like to draw the reader's attention away from the right-hand side of this graph to the less-familiar other half and to demonstrate the concept of eventually diminishing returns to labor. That is, when the equilibrium point is pushed back far enough (toward a very low level of labor), the economy will find itself with positive marginal returns. At this low threshold of manpower, labor is so scarce that even with premodern agricultural capital, each additional unit will yield more output than the previous unit (from E to F in Figure A.8).

Not surprisingly, it is hard to visualize this situation in preindustrial history, except perhaps through reference to increasing commercialization and growing markets. The simplest way to conceptualize this scenario for a medieval dry-farming regime is to view it on a microeconomic level and imagine one peasant trying to utilize 1,000 acres of newly assarted land. In addition to the land, he has in his possession some primitive capital in the form of domestic animals and agricultural implements: a herd of pigs; an abundance of cows, oxen, horses, and sheep; plows, carts, scythes, winnowing forks, and other miscellaneous goods needed for mixed husbandry. One peasant (one unit of agricultural labor) might be able to put much of the land to good use, especially if he left most it for pasture. But imagine if a second unit of labor (a second peasant) were added to the existing land and capital. This additional peasant would, by employing the underutilized capital (agricultural implements), be able to devote more of the land to effective mixed-husbandry and to increase the total output of the 1,000 acres by more than one hundred percent (the increase shown here is two hundred percent, from 1 unit to 3 units of produce, grain and pastoral), thus adding more to the total product than did the previous unit of labor (on Figure A.9).

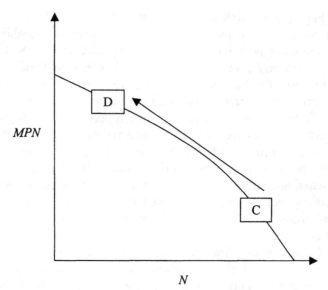

Effect of depopulation on the marginal product of labor

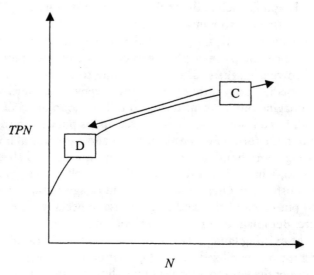

Effect of depopulation on the total product of labor

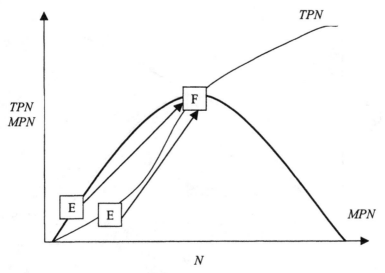

Effect of depopulation on the total and marginal products of labor

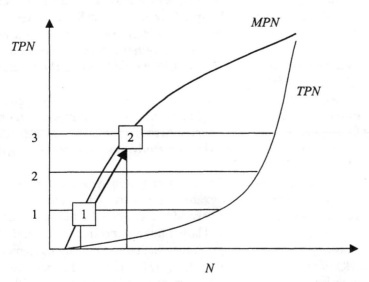

Effect on the total and marginal products of labor of moving from one peasant to two

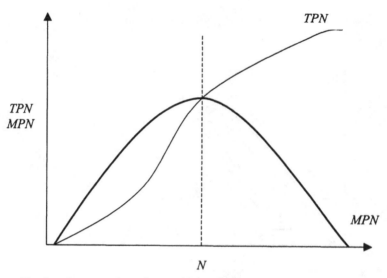

Total and marginal products of labor before and after equilibrium

This synergy would thus lead to positive marginal returns to labor, holding land and agricultural capital fixed. Eventually, as three, then four, and then five units of labor were added, we would reach a point where the more-familiar diminishing marginal returns began to set in, and, as shown again in Figure A.10, *MPN* would begin to show negative marginal returns to labor.

The synergy for a dry-farming regime is thus most easily visualized if we picture it on a very local level. How it applies to the macroeconomies of dry farming is not the main concern here. The concept becomes one of cardinal importance, however, when we study the dynamics of irrigation economies.

Above a certain threshold of size, an irrigation system can potentially serve as an ideal archetype for examining positive returns to scale. If an irrigation network is extended beyond the boundaries of local channels directly fed by a natural river, and larger interconnecting canals and dikes are used, the agrarian economy will then include an enormous element of capital (K) in addition to the usual labor (N) and land (L) that one finds in a premodern economy. The modern production function can then be applied: $Y = A*F*(KLN)$, where Y equals total output, A is a coefficient of labor efficiency, F is a constant, K is capital, L is land, and N is labor.

Let us reexamine the example from Chapter 2 of a basin irrigation system in which transverse and longitudinal dikes trap floodwater from a natural river that feeds a man-made canal (Figure A.11).

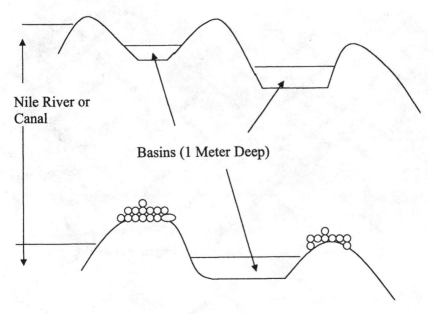

Nile River or
Canal

Basins (1 Meter Deep)

Basin schematics of the Nile (after Willcocks)

Seen from above, one can visualize a village irrigation system in which one large man-made canal feeds most of the village basins, and a few are fed by a natural river (Figure A.12).

If, in this microeconomic scenario, labor (N) is reduced by a significant margin, more than fifty percent (for example), the villagers will no longer have enough manpower to keep the main canal and dike in working order, and it will slowly decay, as shown in Figures A.13, A.14, and A.15.

This is how Egypt's basin irrigation system functioned during the Mamluk period (1250–1500). As detailed in Chapter 2, every June the Indian Ocean monsoon brings a torrent of rain to the Ethiopian highlands. This enormous (and relatively uniform) deposit of water then cascades down the Blue Nile and the Atbara River, bringing with it an abundant supply of nutrient-rich topsoil from Ethiopia. Prior to the construction of the Aswan Dam, this cascade of floodwater, joined with the perennial supply of equatorial water from the White Nile, would inundate the Nile Valley and Delta, reaching a peak in September (in Cairo) before subsiding from October to November.

Man-made canals of various sizes were then employed to draw this water away from the Nile and into flood basins. Dikes were used to trap the water and to allow the moisture to sink into the basins before the sowing of seeds. The alluvium washed down from the Ethiopian high-

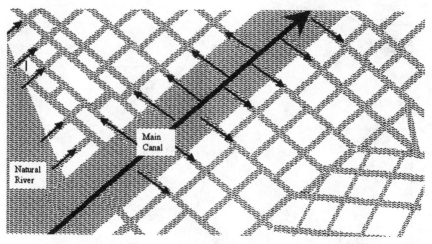

Basin schematic for a functional irrigation system

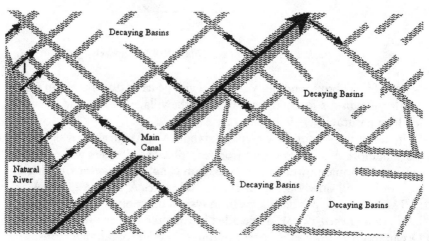

Basin schematic for a damaged irrigation system at decay stage 1

lands provided an annual supply of fertilizer that in conjunction with the sophisticated crop rotation employed by the Egyptians of the Islamic era guaranteed an annual seed-to-yield ratio of up to 1:10 for the winter crop. We have seen how Egypt's irrigation system was divided into two levels of control, *sultani* and *baladi*. The baladi system functioned as the local network of dikes and canals for a single village; the sultani system was a regional network of dikes and canals, divided by nomes ("provinces," Arabic *'iqlim*), that linked the baladi systems together.

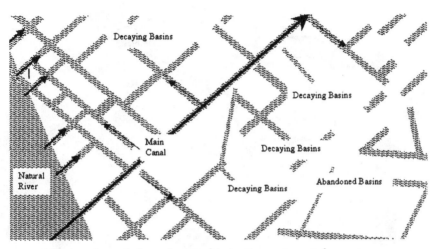

Basin schematic for a damaged irrigation system at decay stage 2

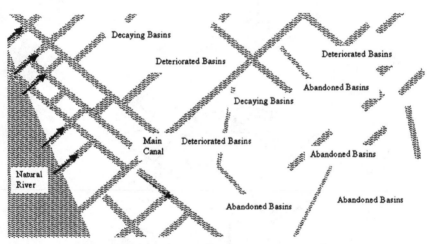

Basin schematic for a damaged irrigation system at decay stage 3

1 = Buhayra
2 = Fuwwa
3 = Nastrawiyya
4 = Dumyat
5 = Sharqiyya
6 = Qalyubiya
7 = Minufiyya
8 = Gharbiyya
9 = Daqhaliyya

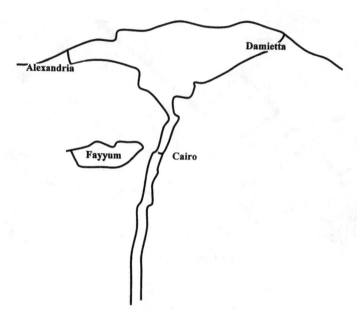

Nile Delta and river valley

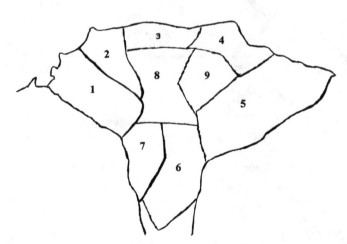

Nomes in the Nile Delta in the 14th and 15th centuries

If the system were struck with depopulation, baladi systems might continue to function smoothly for awhile, but if labor were not used to maintain the interconnecting sultani systems, then all of the baladi systems not directly connected to a natural river or natural canals would begin to decay in precisely the fashion shown in Figures A.13, A.14, and A.15. If population were not redirected and redistributed on the level of the sultani nome, the entire nome's irrigation network would begin to decay in the manner shown in Figures A.8 and A.9 (where the equilibrium point moves from F to E on Figure A.8 and from 2 to 1 on Figure A.9).

This would entail the point of equilibrium moving from F to E on Figure A.18, that is, the total agrarian output would decrease faster than population. The drop in Y (TPN) would be more than the proportionate drop in N in the equation $Y = A^*F^*(K, L, N)$ because the capital was no longer being utilized (as in our example of the one man in a thousand-acre plot). Of course, in this example the capital would also be decaying, and the road back from E to F (in Figure A.18) would require an extensive investment of resources in manpower over a fairly lengthy period of time.

This is the macroeconomic scenario that Egypt encountered in the wake of the Black Death. As detailed in Chapters 5 and 6, not only did Egypt's agrarian output drop by about fifty-eight percent, but Egypt's price and wage scissors were also exactly the opposite of what we should expect for a region hit with massive depopulation. We have seen that the standard picture of falling grain prices and increasing wages was reversed in Egypt. In Egypt, wages fell while grain prices rose. The graphical analysis in this chapter shows exactly how and why this occurred. Yes, Egypt's population was decimated by *Yersinia pestis*, as were the populations of England and many other countries. However, Egypt's agrarian economy lay on the other (left-hand) side of the marginal product curve. Rather than seeing increasing marginal returns to labor with depopulation, Egypt witnessed decreasing marginal returns.

When we consider that we are dealing with underutilized and ruined capital (i.e., the sultani irrigation networks), we can see that we are moving from F to E on Figure A.18. The decrease in output was greater, significantly greater, than the decrease in population. The drop in output was so much greater than that of population that grain, not people, became the scarce commodity in the wake of a horrifying plague. This, combined with rural-to-urban flight, also helps explain why people were the relatively abundant factor, whereas grain, the largest commodity in Egypt's premodern economy, was the relatively scarce factor. Or, to be more precise, capital (K), in the form of large canals that needed to be

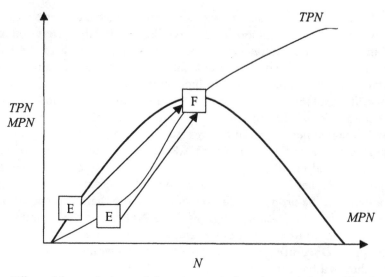

Effect of depopulation and decaying capital on the total and marginal products of labor

dredged with animal power, manpower, and simple equipment, and dikes that needed to be shored up with mud, straw, and a minimum amount of foundation stone, was now the scarce factor in the equation $Y = A*F*(K, L, N)$ and land (L) was the abundant factor.

The economic dilemma here can also be illustrated by another graphical production function. The one shown below includes the decay of capital (K) as well as manpower (N). A reduction in the amount of capital (canals, dikes, etc.) can be represented by a production function that is shifted downward, with an altered slope, at the same time that depopulation is producing decreasing marginal returns to labor.

The data presented in this appendix has demonstrated the basic quantitative economic changes that occurred in England and Egypt. Agrarian output fell precipitously in Egypt, but far less dramatically in England (nearly recovering its previous level of agrarian production by the early sixteenth century). Grain prices dropped in England but rose in Egypt. Wages and per capita income rose in England and fell in Egypt. A comparison of the agrarian purchasing power in both countries illustrates an even more dramatic picture, showing that the bulk of the population in England enjoyed a very substantial increase, while Egypt's population (with the exception of the landholders) suffered an enormous decrease.

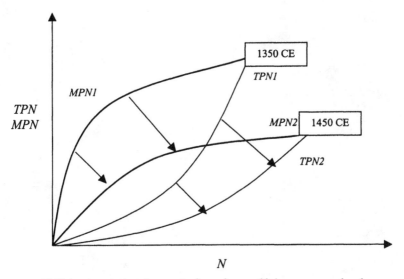

Shift in the total and marginal products of labor as a result of depopulation and decaying capital

The graphical illustrations, coupled with the analyses presented in Chapters 1, 2, and 3, have demonstrated why these changes occurred. The effects of the landholding structures on both economies, as evaluated in the graphs, have clarified, through a simplified economic model, the manner in which the divergent changes took place. Through the lens of comparative history, a new picture has emerged of exactly how the plagues devastated Egypt. This chapter has offered a clearer analysis that solves much of the mystery of Egypt's demise and corrects some of the previous erroneous assumptions about the economic history of Egypt in this period.

NOTES

CHAPTER 1

1. Taqi al-Din al-Maqrizi, *Kitab al-suluk li-ma'rifat duwal al-muluk* (cited hereafter as *Suluk*), ed. Sa'id 'Abd al-Fattah 'Ashur (Cairo: 1957–1973), 2:776.

2. K. N. Chaudhuri, *Asia before Europe: Economy and Civilization of the Indian Ocean from the Rise of Islam to 1750* (Cambridge: Cambridge Univ. Press, 1990), 100. For general studies of the plague in historical perspective, see John Norris, "East or West? The Geographic Origin of the Black Death," *Bulletin of the History of Medicine* 51 (1977): 1–24; Daniel Williman, ed., *The Black Death: The Impact of the Fourteenth-Century Plague* (Binghamton, N.Y.: State Univ. of New York Press, 1982); Philip Ziegler, *The Black Death* (New York: John Day, 1969); Colin Platt, *King Death: The Black Death and Its Aftermath in Late Medieval England* (Toronto: Univ. of Toronto Press, 1996); Mark Ormand and Phillip Lindley, eds., *The Black Death in England* (Stamford, UK: Paul Watkins, 1995); Rosemary Hor rox, ed. and trans., *The Black Death* (Manchester and New York: Manchester Univ. Press, 1994); Norman Cantor, *In the Wake of the Plague: The Black Death and the World It Made* (New York: Free Press, 2001).

3. Cantor, *Wake of the Plague*, 25.

4. Ibid.

5. For the medical aspects of the plague, see Chester David Rail, *Plague Ecotoxicology: Including Historical Aspects of the Disease in the Americas and the Eastern Hemisphere* (Springfield, Ill.: Charles C. Thomas, 1985); Thomas Butler, *Plague and Other* Yersinia *Infections* (New York: Plenum, 1983); Graham Twigg, *The Black Death: A Biological Reappraisal* (London: Batsford Academic and Educational, 1984); Lawrence Conrad, "The Plague in the Early Medieval Near East" (PhD diss., Princeton University, 1981); K. L. Gage, "Plague," in *Topley and Wilson's Microbiology and Microbiological Infections*, ed. L. Colliers, A. Balows, M. Sussman, and W. J. Hausles, 3:885–903 (London: Edward Arnold Press, 1998); G. L. Campbell and D. T. Dennis, "Plague and Other *Yersinia* Infec-

tions," in *Harrison's Principles of Internal Medicine* 14th ed., ed. D. L. Kasper et al. (New York: McGraw-Hill, 1998), 975–983.

6. M. Bahmanyar and D. C. Cavanaugh, *Plague Manual* (Geneva: World Health Organization, 1976), 46.

7. See Butler, *Plague and Other Infections*, 31.

8. Robert Perry and Jacqueline Fetherston, "*Yersinia pestis*: Etiologic Agent of Plague," *Clinical Microbiology Reviews* 10, no. 1 (January 1997): 51.

9. Ibid., 53.

10. Conrad, "Plague in the Near East," 31–35.

11. If the bubo bursts within a week, the victim will usually survive.

12. Ziegler, *The Black Death*, 27.

13. Butler, *Plague and Other Infections*, 82.

14. See Dols's well-informed discussion of outbreaks between the plague of Justinian and the Black Death, *The Black Death in the Middle East* (Princeton, N.J.: Princeton Univ. Press, 1977), 27–35, 305–314. William Tucker has kindly provided me with an unpublished list of recurrent plague epidemics that haunted the Mediterranean and Arab world between the plague of Justinian and the Black Death.

15. Michael Dols, "Ibn al-Wardi's Risalah al-Naba' 'An al-Waba'," as quoted in Don Nardo, ed., *The Black Death* (San Diego, Calif.: Greenhaven Press, 1999), 42–44.

16. al-Maqrizi, *Suluk* 2:772.

17. See Dols, "Ibn al-Wardi," 49.

18. Nardo, *The Black Death*, 15.

19. J. Stewart, *The Nestorian Missionary Enterprise: The Story of a Church on Fire* (Edinburgh: T&T Clark, 1928), 209. See also Ziegler, *The Black Death*, 15.

20. Ziegler, *The Black Death*, 15.

21. See, for example, Cantor, *Wake of the Plague*, 11–16. His discussion of this hypothesis is based on the research of zoologist Graham Twigg and archeologist Edward Thompson.

22. That some historians still believe that overpopulation in Europe was an important factor in plague mortality, via a malnourished population, is a testament to the neglect of the plague's widespread impact outside of Europe. Ziegler quotes previous historians who have held this view. He accepts a moderate view that balances an ecologically vulnerable population in Europe with the lethality of the Black Death (*The Black Death*, 19–23).

23. Al-Maqrizi states, "It killed enormous numbers of people in China, few people were left alive there, but it killed less people in India" (*Suluk*, 2:774).

24. Both David Herlihy and Rosemary Horrox suggest that the Black Death resulted from the appearance of a new, mutant strain of *Y. pestis*. See David Herlihy, *The Black Death and the Transformation of the West*, ed. Samuel Cohn, Jr. (Cambridge, Mass.: Harvard Univ. Press, 1997), 30–31; Horrox, *The Black Death*, 7.

25. Conrad, "Plague in the Near East," 90.

26. Ibid., 96.

27. Ibid., 314.

28. Ibid., 310–325.

29. McNeill, *Plagues and Peoples*, 46

30. Ibid., 50–51.

31. Perry and Fetherston, "Agent of Plague," 49.

32. Rail, *Plague Ecotoxicology*, 12–13.

33. McNeill, *Plagues and Peoples*, 15.

34. Conrad, "Plague in the Near East," 438.

35. Horrox, *The Black Death*, 7.

36. Medical researchers concur with this theory. McNeill is one of many historians who have postulated that the plague was spread by Mongol trade routes (*Plagues and Peoples*, 140–147). The record of the earliest disease sites and the contemporary (1330s) and calamitous outbreak in China, where the plague may have killed perhaps sixty-five percent of the population, certainly suggests a focal point in the Central Asian steppe. See William Naphy and Andrew Spicer, *The Black Death: A History of the Plagues, 1345–1730* (Stroud, UK: Tempus Publishing, 2001), 27–35.

37. Conrad has suggested that *Pulex irritans* may have played a role in epidemic outbreaks of *Y. pestis* ("Plague in the Near East," 18).

38. Ziegler, *The Black Death*, 15–16.

39. Bahmanyar and Cavanaugh, *Plague Manual*, 46–47; Butler, *Plague and Other Infections*, 50–52.

40. Butler, *Plague and Other Infections*, 17–22.

41. Conrad, "Plague in the Near East," 8.

42. See Dols's extended discussion of transmission (*Black Death in the Middle East*, 42–67).

43. For a general description of *waqf* in medieval Egypt, see Muhammad Muhammad Amin, *Al-Awqaf wa'l-Hayat al-Ijtima'iyya fi Misr* (Cairo: Dar al-Nahda al-'Arabiyya, 1980). See also, Muhammad 'Afifi, *Al-Awqaf wa'l-Hayat al-Iqtisadiyya fi Misr fi'l-Asr al-'Uthmani* (Cairo: al-Hay'a al-Misriyya al-'Amma lil-Kitab, 1991).

44. See Chapter 5 for a full discussion of the previous estimates and sources for the value of the *dinar jayshi*.

45. Stanford J. Shaw, *The Budget of Ottoman Egypt, 1005–1006/1596–1597* (The Hague: Mouton, 1968).

46. See Chapter 5.

47. Karl Wittfogel, *Oriental Despotism: A Comparative Study of Total Power* (New Haven, Conn.: Yale Univ. Press, 1957).

48. T. H. Aston and C. H. E. Philpin, eds., *The Brenner Debate: Agrarian Class Structure and Economic Development in Pre-Industrial Europe* (Cambridge: Cambridge Univ. Press, 1985).

49. There are numerous studies by both specialists and generalists that lay out this basic pattern. For a recent summary, see, for example, Naphy and Spicer, *History of the Plagues*, 41. For a more detailed summary, see Christopher Dyer, "Rural Europe," in *The New Cambridge Medieval History: Vol. VII, c. 1415–c. 1500*, ed. Christopher Allmand, 106–120 (Cambridge: Cambridge Univ. Press, 1998).

50. Robert Brenner's work on Western and Eastern Europe after the plagues is probably the most well-known and contentious example of a comparison that extends beyond Western Europe.

51. Although clover was used in England in the sixteenth century, its use did not become widespread until the nineteenth. See Bruce Campbell and Mark Overton, "A New Perspective on Medieval and Early Modern Agriculture: Six Centuries of Norfolk Farming, c. 1250–c. 1850," *Past and Present* 141 (November 1993), 59.

52. For the quantitative information that lies behind these graphs, see Chapter 5.

53. See Wittfogel, *Oriental Despotism*. For recent defenses of this theory, see David Landes's short discussion in *The Wealth and Poverty of Nations: Why Some Are So Rich and Some So Poor* (New York: Norton, 1999). The hydraulic study is certainly more applicable to other irrigation systems where centralized control was a necessity.

54. Karl W. Butzer, *Early Hydraulic Civilization in Egypt: A Study in Cultural Ecology* (Chicago: Univ. of Chicago Press, 1976).

55. Roger Bagnall, *Egypt in Late Antiquity* (Princeton, N.J.: Princeton Univ. Press, 1993).

56. R. P. Duncan-Jones, "The Impact of the Antonine Plague," *Journal of Roman Archaeology* 9 (1996), 108–136.

57. Ibid., 121.

58. Ibid., 123–124.

59. Ibid., 124.

60. See Chapter 5 for a calculation of Egypt's total GDP in gold (144,467 kg). This is compared here with Ashtor's estimate for the total value of exports to the northern Mediterranean as being 2,343 kg of gold. See Eliyahu Ashtor, *Les métaux précieux et la balance des payements du Proche-Orient à la basse époque* (Paris, 1971), 65–96.

61. Nicholas Mayhew estimates that the total value of England's exports amounted to about four percent of its GDP at this time; see Mayhew, "Modelling Medieval Monetisation," in *A Commercialising Economy: England, 1086 to c. 1300*, ed. Richard Britnell and Bruce Campbell, 55–77 (Manchester: Manchester Univ. Press, 1995).

62. Herlihy, *Black Death and Transformation*, 40–46.

63. Ibid., 51. In his list of technological innovations, Herlihy has included the fifteenth-century modification of earlier forms of the printing press by Johannes Gutenberg (as scribes became more expensive and less skilled), the rapid development of shipbuilding technology (where the objective was to build bigger ships manned by smaller crews), and advances in firearms technology.

64. The pioneering Middle East historian Eliyahu Ashtor, often cited by European historians, has been the most prominent advocate of this theory. See, for example, Ashtor, "The Economic Decline of the Middle East in the Later Middle Ages: An Outline," *Asian and African Studies: Journal of the Israel Oriental Society* 15 (1981): 253–286; "Levantine Sugar Industry in the Later Middle Ages: An Example of Technological Decline," *Israel Oriental Studies* 7 (1977): 226–280.

65. See, for example, Immanuel Wallerstein, *The Modern World System* (New York: Academic Press, 1976); Samir Amin, *Eurocentrism* (New York: Monthly Review Press, 1989); Andre Gunder Frank, *World Accumulation, 1492–1789* (New York: Monthly Review Press, 1978); J. M. Blaut, *Eight Eurocentric Historians* (New York: Guilford Press, 2000).

66. Samuel Cohn, Jr., introduction to Herlihy, *Black Death and Transformation*, 10–12 (emphasis added).

67. Blaut, *Eight Eurocentric Historians*, 66–67.

68. Ibid., 67.

69. Michael Cook, "Islam: A Comment," in *Europe and the Rise of Capitalism*, ed. Jean Baechler, John A. Hall, and Michael Mann (Oxford: Basil Blackwell, 1988), 131–135.

70. It is a testament to the pressure faced by historians and sociologists trying to tackle the East and West that a scholar of such preeminence as Janet Abu-Lughod can, in an otherwise exceptional masterpiece, briefly contend that Egyptian peasants were, in contrast to their European counterparts, unable to resist landlords' surplus extraction pressure in the wake of the plague because "the 'serfs' had no forests to which they could flee" (*Before European Hegemony: The World System, AD 1250–1350* [Oxford: Oxford Univ. Press, 1989], 238). Ecologically, nothing could be further from the truth: forests provide only the most marginal possibilities for subsistence (one could potentially herd truffle-eating pigs), whereas desert scrublands provide an excellent refuge for peasants who might be forced or willing to adopt the lifestyle of the Bedouin.

CHAPTER 2

1. For a discussion of the changes in historians' estimates of mortality, see Horrox, *The Black Death*, 229–236.

2. Dols, *Black Death in the Middle East*, 172–200.

3. Michael Dols, "The General Mortality of the Black Death in the Mamluk Empire," in *The Islamic Middle East, 700–1900: Studies in Social and Economic History*, ed. Abraham Udovitch, 404–411 (Princeton, N.J.: Darwin Press, 1981).

4. Dols points out that "unlike the European experience of plague, the recurrences in the Middle East had a far more damaging impact on population—a cumulative effect far greater than that of the Black Death itself" (*Black Death in the Middle East*, 4).

5. For example, al-Maqrizi's estimates for the pre-plague population of one category of peasant farmers in Assyut (6,000) are in accord with my own estimates derived from the 1315 land survey. See al-Maqrizi, *Suluk*, 2:786, and Chapter 5 of this study.

6. The population estimate for pre-plague Egypt is based on an analysis of the 1315 land survey. A figure of 6 million is a conservative approximation based on the output of grain and other crops analyzed in Chapter 5 of this study. Estimates of population densities on irrigated land dovetail well with this figure. Evidence

presented for the cadastral survey and quantitative references in the chronicles point to a flourishing pre-plague irrigation system. Estimates for a population density of some 280 people per square kilometer yield an approximate figure of slightly less than 6 million inhabitants in a cultivated area of 20,000–22,000 square kilometers. For an estimate of population density on irrigated and non-irrigated land, see Karl A. Wittfogel, "The Hydraulic Civilizations," in *Man's Role in Changing the Face of the Earth* (2 vols.), ed. William L. Thomas, Jr., 152–164 (Chicago: Univ. of Chicago Press, 1956).

7. *Mamluk* translates as "owned" in Modern Standard Arabic. In medieval Egypt, it was used to mean "slave-soldier."

8. Before the late fourteenth century, the majority of the slave children were brought from Central Asia.

9. Khalil bin Shahin al-Zahiri, *Kitab zubdat kashf al-mamalik wa bayyan al-turuq wa'l-masalik*, ed. Paul Ravaisse (Paris: Imprimerie Nationale, 1894), 106; Ahmad ibn 'Ali al-Qalqashandi, *Subh al-a'sha' fi-sina'at al-insha'* (14 vols.) Cairo, 1913–1919, 4:19; Mahmud Ibn Ahmad al-'Ayni, *'Iqd al-juman fi ta'rikh ahl al-zaman*, ed. Muhammad Muhammad Amin (Cairo: Al-Hay'at al-Masriyya al-'Amma l'il-Kitab, 1987–1992), 72–76.

10. The amir "had a coat of arms (rank, runuk), with a special design serving as an emblem, such as a cup (hanab), an inkwell (dawat), a napkin (bugja), a fleur-de-lis (faransisa), and the like. This coat of arms, which bore a colour of the amir's choice, was painted on the gates of his house and other possessions, such as the grain storehouses, the sugar refineries, the ships, as well as on his sword, his bow, and the caparisons (barkustuwanat) of his horses and camels" (David Ayalon, "Studies on the Structure of the Mamluk Army," Part II, *Bulletin of the School of Oriental and African Studies* 15 [1953], 461–462).

11. Ibn Taghri-Birdi, *al-Nujum al-zahira fi muluk Misr wa'l-Qahira*, 16 vols., ed. and trans. William Popper as *History of Egypt, 1382–1469*, 3 vols. (Berkeley and Los Angeles: Univ. of California Press, 1954–1957), 2–8, 48–52; al-Zahiri, *Kitab zubda*, 113ff.; Amin, *al-Awqaf*, 72; al-Qalqashandi, *Subh*, 4:61–64.

12. There were some exceptions. An auxiliary body of soldiers known as the "Ajnad al-Halqa" formed a separate landholding group, but their status had already dwindled and declined more rapidly after the plagues. See al-Qalqashandi, *Subh*, 4:15–16; Taqi al-Din al-Maqrizi, *Kitab al-mawa'iz wa'l-i' tibar bi-dhikr al-khitat wa'l-athar* (cited hereafter as *Khitat*), 2 vols. (Cairo, 1853–1854), 1:87–91.

13. As with all historical precedents, there were some deviations from this sociological paradigm, yet this standard was generally adhered to. See Carl Petry, "A Paradox of Patronage during the Later Mamluk Period," *Muslim World* 73 (1983), 192.

14. al-Qalqashandi, *Subh*, 13:118–123; Petry, "Paradox of Patronage," 188.

15. al-Maqrizi, *Suluk*, 3:563; Amin, *al-Awqaf*, 72.

16. Amin, *al-Awqaf*, 93.

17. Ibn Hajar al-'Asqalani, *'Inba' al-ghumr bi-'anba' al-'umr*, ed. Hassan Habashi (Cairo: al-Majlis al-'Ali, 1969–1972), 6:134.

18. al-Maqrizi, *Khitat*, 1:90; al-Qalqashandi, *Subh*, 3:52; Tsugitaka Sato, "The Evolution of the Iqta' System under the Mamluks: An Analysis of al-Rawk al-Husami and al-Rawk al-Nasiri," *Memoirs of the Research Department of the Toyo Bunko (the Oriental Library)* 37 (1979), 99–131; Tsugitaka Sato, *State and Rural Society in Medieval Islam* (Leiden, Neth.: E. J. Brill, 1997); Hassanein Rabie, *The Financial System of Egypt, AH 564–741/AD 1169–1341* (Oxford: Oxford Univ. Press, 1972), 56; Jennifer M. Thayer, "Land Politics and Power Networks in Mamluk Egypt" (PhD diss., New York Univ., 1993), 45–46. The scattering of estates took place during the famous 1315 cadastral survey (*rawk*) conducted under the auspices of the Sultan al-Nasir Muhammad. There were many changes that the sultan attempted to effect in the wake of the 1315 rawk. There has been much confusion among scholars about the nature of these changes and their impact on landholding in Mamluk Egypt. For example, most scholars contend that bureaucrats working for the sultan were withdrawn from many of the villages in Egypt and that the changes allowed the amirs more direct control over their estates. However, it seems clear that it was in fact just the opposite. It represented a bungled attempt on the part of al-Nasir Muhammad to rob the amirs of many of their estates and to reduce their control over those that were left to them. The ultimate (and unintended) victims of this rawk were the Ajnad al-Halqa.

19. Petry, "Paradox of Patronage," 184.

20. *Waqfiyya Raqam 1019* (Cairo: Wizarat al-Awqaf [Ministry of Religious Endowments, hereafter WA]); *Waqfiyya Raqam 901*, WA; *Waqfiyya Raqam 92*, WA; *Waqfiyya Raqam 3195*, WA; *Waqfiyya Raqam 883*, WA; *Waqfiyya Raqam 140*, WA; *Waqfiyya Raqam 809*, WA; *Waqfiyya Raqam 720*, WA; al-As'ad Ibn Mammati, *Kitab al-qawanin al-dawanin*, ed. A. S. Atiya (Cairo, 1943), 297–306; al-Maqrizi, *Suluk*, 1:61; al-Zahiri, *Kitab zubda*, 78, 129–130; al-Qalqashandi, *Subh*, 3:522–526, 4:18; 'Abd al-Rahman Ibn Abi Bakr al-Suyuti, *Husn al-muhadara fi akhbar Misr wa'l-Qahira* (Beirut: Dar al-Kutub al-'Ilmiyya, 1997), 2:131; Carl Petry, *The Civilian Elite of Cairo in the Later Middle Ages* (Princeton, N.J.: Princeton Univ. Press, 1981), 15–36, 203–220.

21. The word *diwan* in this context means the body of civil servants who were attached to a particular leader; in this case, either the sultan or one of the amirs.

22. al-Maqrizi, *Suluk*, 3:558; Ibn Hajar al-'Asqalani, *al-Durar al-kamina*, 6 vols. (Cairo, 1929–1932), 5:178, 348; Petry, "Paradox of Patronage," 185–186.

23. al-'Asqalani, *al-Durar al-kamina*, 5:77, 246, 343; 6:130; Petry, *Civilian Elite*, 15–36, 313.

24. Petry, *Civilian Elite*, 273, 313. It seems that most of the bureaucrats were Coptic Christians at the start of the Mamluk era, a factor that may have contributed to their lower status in society. During the 1350–1500 period, the vast majority of them converted to Islam. However, their devotion to Islam remained suspect. They were called *Musalima*, a term conveying that they were recent converts. This epithet also conveyed the impression that their motives for conversion were questionable and may have been driven by their desire to hold higher offices

in the civilian hierarchy. See al-ʿAsqalani, *al-Durar al-kamina*, 5:355, 6:172; al-Qalqashandi, *Subh*, 5:459–460, 13:159–160; Huda Lutfi, "Coptic Festivals of the Nile: Aberrations of the Past?" in *The Mamluks in Egyptian Politics and Society*, ed. Thomas Philipp and Ulrich Haarmann, 254–282 (Cambridge: Cambridge Univ. Press, 1998), 268.

25. Ibrahim ʿAli Tarkhan, *al-Nizam al-Iqtaʿi fiʾl-Sharq al-Awsat fiʾl-ʿUsur al-Wusta* (Cairo: Dar al-Katib al-ʿArabi at-Tabaʾa waʾl-Nashra, 1968), 223, 234.

26. al-Qalqashandi, *Subh*, 3:256; 4:18, 31; 6:192–193; 11:92–93, 314, 319; 13:118, 160, 201; al-Maqrizi, *Suluk*, 3:594–595; al-Maqrizi, *Khitat*, 2:215–216; Robert Irwin, *The Middle East in the Middle Ages: The Early Mamluk Sultanate, 1250–1382* (London and Sydney: Croon Helm, 1986), 92–94. See also Hammud ibn Muhammad ibn ʿAli al-Najidi, *al-Nizam al-Naqdi al-Mamluki* (Alexandria: Muʾassasat al-Thaqafa al-Jamiʾiya, 1993), 180–181. Najidi points out that the prevailing money of account was used to pay muqtis for the value (ʿibra) of their iqtaʿ revenue. If the assignment or collection of rent were an individual versus a collective matter, then why would this mechanism be used at all? If landholding for military service, for a Mamluk soldier in the ranks, was individual rather than collective, then the soldiers would simply collect their wheat or grain from their iqtaʿs and convert it into cash in the most favorable way possible. This intermediate role strongly implies that rents were not set on an individual basis.

27. al-Qalqashandi, *Subh*, 3:51–53, 4:61–64, 6:192–193; Tarkhan, *al-Nizam*, 96–97; al-Maqrizi, *Khitat*, 2:229; al-Zahiri, *Kitab zubda*, 113ff., 130; *Waqfiyya Raqam 1019*, WA; *Waqfiyya Raqam 901*, WA; *Waqfiyya Raqam 3195*, WA; Petry, "Paradox of Patronage," 188–189; Petry, *Civilian Elite*, 133, 145.

28. Given the short financial time horizon of the landholders and the apparent problems that this could cause, it would be reasonable to ask why this system worked so well before the depopulation set in. As we will see below, the bureaucracy, coupled with a strong ruling sultan, not only kept the system under control, but also enabled Egypt's agrarian economy to flourish before the plagues. As will be shown, systemic weaknesses, which existed in both Egypt and England's landholding systems, became debilitating for Egypt only with the onset of the plagues and the vicious circle created by the initial drop in resources, rural depopulation, and the way in which Egypt's landholding system responded to these twin blows to its economy.

29. Irwin, *Middle East*, 152.

30. For example, see Bagnall, *Egypt in Late Antiquity*, 116–157.

31. William Popper, *The Cairo Nilometer* (Berkeley: Univ. of California Press, 1951), 87, 248, 250, 256; William Willcocks, *Egyptian Irrigation*, 2nd ed. (London: Spon, 1899), 230. The date of the maxima, the highest level reached by the Nile in a given year, differed from the date of plenitude, when the level on the Nilometer measured 16 cubits (*dhiraʿ*), an important distinction that will be discussed below.

32. For the following, see al-Maqrizi, *Khitat*, 1:60ff; Ibn Mammati, *Kitab al-qawanin*, 205–233; D. S. Richards, "A Mamluk Petition and a Report from the Diwan al-Jaysh," *Bulletin of the School of Oriental and African Studies* 40

(1977): 14-15; Helen Rivlin, *The Agricultural Policy of Muhammad 'Ali in Egypt* (Cambridge, Mass.: Harvard Univ. Press, 1961); P. S. Girard, "Memoire sur l'agriculture, l'industrie, et le commerce de l'Égypte," in *Description de l'Égypte, État Moderne*, Vol. 2, Part 1 (Paris: 1813), 497, 557, 564.

33. For a discussion of some these maintenance works, see Tsugitaka Sato, "Irrigation in Rural Egypt from the Twelfth to the Fourteenth Centuries," *Orient: Report of the Society for Near Eastern Studies in Japan* 8 (1972), 81-92; *State and Rural Society*, 220-233. See also Carl Petry, *Protectors or Praetorians?: The Last Mamluk Sultans and Egypt's Waning as a Great Power* (Albany: State Univ. of New York Press, 1994), 106, 114-115, 124-125nn, 128nn.

34. This instrument was a large triangular box, measuring roughly a meter to a side, known as *garraafa* or *garaariif*. See al-Zahiri, *Kitab zubda*, 128; Stanford Shaw, *The Financial and Administrative Organization and Development of Ottoman Egypt, 1517-1798* (Princeton, N.J.: Princeton Univ. Press, 1962), 227-228.

35. See al-Zahiri, *Kitab zubda*, 128; Shaw, *Financial Organization*, 227-228. This mud was also used as fertilizer in areas that had not received a heavy coating of alluvium from the flood.

36. For the Ayyubid period, see Ibn Mammati, *Kitab al-qawanin*, 205-233. The basic division is reiterated in al-Maqrizi's *Khitat* and other sources from the fourteenth and fifteenth centuries.

37. In the Ottoman period, the term "jusur al-sultani" is clearly spelled out as entailing canals in addition to the dikes; see Shaw, *Financial Organization*, 226-229. Fifteenth-century sources, such as al-Zahiri, *Kitab zubda*, 129-130, also make this apparent. The usage of the term *jisr* when it was applied to administrative categories and not to a specific dike (which is the literal meaning of the word) strongly suggests that this meaning was intended throughout the Ayyubid, Mamluk, and Ottoman periods.

38. This conception of the division differs, in some of its details, from that suggested by Sato; see below.

39. Although Sato's discussion correlates with this in general, he argues that the sultanic network was intended only for the provinces of al-Gharbiyya and ash-Sharqiyya ("Irrigation in Rural Egypt," 85-86; *State and Rural Society*, 225-227). Whereas this might still embrace one-third to one-half of the agrarian revenue (depending on the administrative division and economic circumstances in different periods), it seems clear that this is not the intended meaning of Ibn Mammati and al-Maqrizi, whose texts Sato relies upon for this geographic specification, nor other chroniclers of the Ayyubid and Mamluk periods. See Ibn Mammati, *Kitab al-qawanin*, 232, and al-Maqrizi, *Khitat*, 101, where the sultanic network is explicitly designated as serving the public welfare and where the terms "al-sharqiyya" and "al-gharbiyya" are used in a grammatical context that means "the eastern areas" and "the western areas," not the provinces of these names (whose divisions, in any case, changed over time).

40. Sato also provides some valuable details on the management of baladi networks in the Fayyum; see "Irrigation in Rural Egypt," 81-84; *State and Rural Society*, 221-225.

41. al-Maqrizi, *Khitat*, 1:101. Here I am assuming his use of *mustakhdimun min al-diwan* is intended to refer to the central bureaucracy. It is possible that this system was also coordinated by the provincial walis. Al-Maqrizi also mentions that there had also been another management and taxation system before this one. It involved tax farmers, and seems to refer to the early Ayyubid or Fatimid period.

42. al-Zahiri, *Kitab zubda*, 129.

43. For the following, I am indebted to Sato's detailed studies of irrigation works in the Ayyubid and early Mamluk periods ("Irrigation in Rural Egypt," 81–92; *State and Rural Society*, 220–233).

44. This was not always the case in the early Mamluk period. However, the ability of central government to combat the practice of corvée is significant in contrast to actions in the later period.

45. Sato, *State and Rural Society*, 229.

46. Ibid.; al-Maqrizi, *Khitat*, 1:171; al-Maqrizi, *Suluk*, 2:111–113.

47. The canal of Abu'l-Manajja, crucial to the irrigation of al-Sharqiyya province, was excavated in the late Fatimid period, 511/1117. See Sato's chart of irrigation reconstruction (*State and Rural Society*, 228).

48. Tarkhan, *al-Nizam*, 75–76. In Chapter 5, I will discuss the issue of land area, the quantitative history of the cadastral surveys, and other evidence that supports this view.

CHAPTER 3

1. al-'Asqalani, *'Inba' al-ghumr*, 5:137, 6:16, 18; al-Suyuti, *Husn*, 2:259, gives a list of plague outbreaks that follow the same seven-year recurrence cycle that has been documented for England.

2. al-Qalqashandi, *Subh*, 3:516.

3. In many villages, the rents actually increased, or at least appeared to increase, as we will see below.

4. Andre Raymond discusses elite infighting over scarce resources at some length. See Raymond, *Cairo*, trans. Willard Wood (Cambridge, Mass.: Harvard Univ. Press, 2000) 141, 160, 168–169.

5. Rodney Hilton, "A Crisis of Feudalism," in *The Brenner Debate*, ed. Aston and Philpin, 132–133; Dols, *Black Death in the Middle East*, 277.

6. al-Qalqashandi, *Subh*, 2:811, 3:515–516; Petry, *Civilian Elite*, 220. In the case of Royal Mamluks, this was usually accomplished via the auspices of the *Diwan al-Jaysh*. For higher amirs and their Mamluk entourages, their own bureaucratic resources monitored repairs.

7. al-Zahiri, *Kitab zubda*, 129; al-Qalqashandi, *Subh*, 3:515–516.

8. al-Maqrizi, *Suluk*, 4:564 in 824/1421, 4:618 in 825/1422, 4:646 in 826/1423, 4:678 in 828/1425, 4:709–710 in 829/1426, 4:750–753 in 830/1427, 4:806–809 in 832/1429, 4:834 in 833/1430, 4:863 and 4:874 in 835/1432, 4:903–904 in 837/1434, 4:831 and 4:950 in 838/1435; al-Maqrizi, *Khitat*, 1:101; Muhammad ibn Khalil al-'Asadi, *Kitab al-taysir wa'l-i'tibar*, ed.

Ahmad Tulaymat (Cairo, 1968), 92–93; Ibn Taghri-Birdi, *Hawadith al-duhur fi mada al-ayyam wa'l-shuhur*, 8 vols., ed. William Popper (Berkeley and Los Angeles: Univ. of California Press, 1930–1931), 4:673; Ibn Iyas, *Nuzhat al-umam fi'l- 'aja' ib wa' l-hukm*, ed. Muhammad Zaynham Muhammad 'Azab (Cairo: Maktab Madbuli, 1995), 182; Ibn Iyas, *Bada'i' al-zuhur fi-waqa'i' al-duhur*, 5 vols., ed. Mustafa Muhammad (Cairo: al-Hayat al-misriyya al-'amma li'l-kutub, 1982), 5:114–115, 124–125; al-Suyuti, *Husn*, 2:302.

9. Which included, among other things, a low Nile flood.

10. al-Maqrizi, *Khitat*, 1:101. Once again, the use of corvée labor and the economic problems associated with it were hardly new to Egypt. But they seem to have taken on a much larger dimension in the 1350–1450 period.

11. For the number of villages in Fatimid times (i.e., 10,000), contrasted with a realistic number for 838/1435 (i.e., 2,170), see al-Maqrizi, *Suluk*, 3:912–913. For the height of the Striped Palace, which al-Maqrizi gives as 500 cubits (*dhira'*; anywhere from 230 to 340 meters, depending on the cubit used), see al-Maqrizi, *Khitat*, 2:210. For land area under cultivation, see his extensive discussion of the history of the land tax, where he reports the area to be 1 million feddans in the fifteenth century and 100 million feddans in former times.

12. al-Maqrizi, *Suluk*, 4:481.

13. As represented mainly by the religious endowment deeds and other fragmentary data, the Geniza, Ibn al-Ji'an's compilation of army registers, etc.

14. See Shoshan's treatment of 24 million feddans as reported for the ninth century (and recorded in al-Nuwayri, *Nihayat al-arab fi funun al-adab*, 1:266) in Shoshan, "Money, Price, and Population in Mamluk Egypt" (PhD diss., Princeton Univ., 1978), 19–20.

15. See al-Maqrizi's reports of dike and canal decay and the neglect of their maintenance by the amirs (and see below for a further discussion of these observations): *Suluk*, 4:564 in 824/1421, 4:618 in 825/1422, 4:646 in 826/1423, 4:678 in 828/1425, 4:709–710 in 829/1426, 4:750–753 in 830/1427, 4:806–809 in 832/1429, 4:834 in 833/1430, 4:863 and 4:874 in 835/1432, 4:903–904 in 837/1434, 4:831 and 4:950 in 838/1435.

16. al-'Asadi, *Kitab al-taysir*, 92–93; Hassanein Rabie, "Some Technical Aspects of Egyptian Agriculture in Medieval Egypt," 62.

17. al-Qalqashandi, *Subh*, 3:300.

18. As cited in Ibn Iyas, *Bada'i al-zuhur*, 4:159.

19. Ibn Iyas, *Nuzhat*, 182.

20. Ibn Iyas, *Bada'i al-zuhur*, 4:104.

21. Petry, *Protectors or Praetorians*.

22. Ibid., 106, 114–115, 124–125n2.

23. Ibid., 114–115.

24. Muhammad Muhammad 'Ali Abu Zayd, *al-Nil wa Misr* (Cairo: Dar al-Hidayat, 1987), 28–34.

25. al-Maqrizi, *Suluk*, 4:863, 874.

26. Ibid., 4:931, 950.

27. See the references above for the thirteenth, fourteenth, and fifteenth centuries: al-Maqrizi, *Khitat*; Ibn Iyas, *Nuzhat*; the range that they give for the pre-

1350 period seems to be about 4 cubits (each being 0.46m) but certainly no less than 3 cubits.

28. See the table in Popper, *Cairo Nilometer*, 180.

29. al-Maqrizi, *Suluk*, 4:646 in 826/1423, 4:678 in 828/1425, 4:709-710 in 829/1426, 4:750-752 in 830/1427, 4:806 in 832/1429, 4:834 in 833/1430, 4:903-904 in 837/1434, 4:931 and 4:950 in 838/1435.

30. Petry, *Protectors or Praetorians*, 105; Stuart Borsch, "Nile Floods and the Irrigation System in Fifteenth-Century Egypt," *Mamluk Studies Review* 4 (2000), 131-145.

31. Willcocks, *Egyptian Irrigation*, 90, 229, 235, 291.

32. This particular description is for the pre-plague period, but it illustrates the general process. Significantly, for the contrast with the fifteenth century, the damage in this case was corrected by a project organized by the central government. See al-Maqrizi, *Suluk*, 2:130, 166, and Sato, *State and Rural Society*, 230.

33. For the two years which followed the disastrously low Nile of twelve cubits and twenty-one fingers (596/1200), 'Abd al-Latif al-Baghdadi reports that the flood waters "receded without the country having been sufficiently watered, and before the convenient time, because there was no one to arrest the waters and keep them on the land" (*Kitab al-'ifada*, 253-254).

34. The Egyptians were well aware of the European silver famine; see al-Maqrizi, *Suluk*, 3:515. Although it was also an exogenous factor in this area, its role in the economic outcome was part of Egypt's reaction to the crisis.

35. *Waqfiyya Raqam* 140, WA; al-Maqrizi, *Suluk*, 4:3, 131, 165, 205, 226, 306, 942-943; al-Qalqashandi, *Subh*, 3:510-512, 515.

36. Ibn Taghri-Birdi, *Hawadith*, 2:237, 3:503-510; al-Maqrizi, *Suluk*, 4:436, 441, 549, 630, 794, 943, 1090-1092.

37. Tarkhan, *al-Nizam*, 240-241.

38. al-Qalqashandi, *Subh*, 3:519-522; Tarkhan, *al-Nizam*, 100. The destabilization of rural exchange also had a dramatic impact on the ability of even the most well-informed peasants to adapt to changed economic circumstances. Overall, it led to a demonetization and decommercialization of rural areas, especially the highly commercialized delta. This was to have serious ramifications for the decline of proto-industrial crops such as flax. It also inhibited crop diversification. Both of these broader outcomes, the crisis of currency and the movement to a barter system, were polar opposites of contemporary developments in England. Relative to that of Egypt, England's currency remained stable during this period, despite the bullion famine. And the overall trend of commercialism in England at this time led to an increased use of currency rather than a rise in the barter system.

39. Petry, "Paradox of Patronage," 204.

40. Tarkhan, *al-Nizam*, 482; al-Zahiri, *Kitab zubda*, 107, 130.

41. al-Maqrizi, *Suluk*, 4:345; Thayer "Land Politics," 134.

42. al-Maqrizi, *Suluk*, 2:843, 861, 899-900, 908, 909-910.

43. Ibid., 2:899, 909-914.

44. This was made worse by the fact that villages were, to a great extent,

tightly closed communities organized along family lines. Outsiders could hardly be certain of a warm welcome, even if the village were more prosperous and functional.

45. Dols, *Black Death in the Middle East*, 163–165.

46. William Tucker, "Natural Disasters and the Peasantry in Mamluk Egypt," *Journal of the Economic and Social History of the Orient* 24 (1981): 215–224.

47. It is possible that this form of social uprooting and alienation, from a familiar rural setting to a new urban one, was a prime factor in stimulating conversion from Coptic Christianity to Islam.

48. Boaz Shoshan, "Grain Riots and the 'Moral Economy' in Cairo, 1350–1517," *Journal of Interdisciplinary History* 10 (1980), 462–467; Ira Lapidus, "The Grain Economy of Mamluk Egypt," *Journal of the Economic and Social History of the Orient* 12 (1969), 11–14; Sa'id 'Abd al-Fattah 'Ashur, *al-Mujtama' al-Misri fi 'Asr Salatin al-Mamalik* (Cairo: Dar al-Nahda al-'Arabiyya, 1993), 45–46.

49. In 818/1415, during a time of civil disorder and drought, peasants fled from the delta to Cairo seeking grain; see al-Maqrizi, *Suluk*, 4:332.

50. Lapidus, "Grain Economy," 8.

51. Amalia Levanoni, *A Turning Point in Mamluk History: The Third Reign of al-Nasir Muhammad ibn Qalawun, 1310–1341* (Leiden, Neth.: E. J. Brill, 1995), 173.

52. For example, in 825/1422, as the grain economy in parts of Upper Egypt collapsed, peasants were reported to be living on sorghum alone; see al-Maqrizi, *Suluk*, 4:603. In his famine treatise, *Ighathat al-'Ummah bi-Kashf al-Ghummah*, al-Maqrizi refers to peasants withdrawing from the agricultural economy; see Adel Allouche, *Mamluk Economics: A Study and Translation of Al-Maqrizi's Ighathah*, (Salt Lake City: Univ. of Utah Press, 1994), 54. For the subdivision of basins and the growing of dhurra and sorghum during the Ottoman period, see Kenneth M. Cuno, *The Pasha's Peasants: Land, Society, and Economy in Lower Egypt, 1740–1858* (Cambridge: Cambridge Univ. Press, 1992), 18. Willcocks observed this in great detail while Upper Egypt was still under a system of basin irrigation (*Egyptian Irrigation*, 59–66).

53. Among the many studies which highlight this problem, see Jean-Claude Garcin, *Un centre musulman de la Haute-Égypte médiévale: Qus* (Cairo: Institut français d'archéologie orientale, 1976), 468–507. See also al-Maqrizi, *Suluk*, 7:710; al-Zahiri, *Kitab zubda*, 34–41; 'Ashur, *al-Mujtama'*, 59–63; 'Ashur, *al-'Asr al-Mamalik fi Misr wa'l-Sham*, 3rd. ed. (Cairo, 1994).

54. It was often the practice of the Bedouins to deliberately break the dikes as a means of taking over and adapting the land for their use. See, for example, al-Maqrizi, *Suluk*, 2:832–833; Petry, *Protectors or Praetorians*, 124–125; Richard Cooper, "Land Classification Terminology and the Assessment of the Kharaj Tax in Medieval Egypt," *Journal of the Economic and Social History of the Orient* 17 (1974), 96, 100.

55. 'Ashur, *al-Mujtama'*, 59–63; al-Zahiri, *Kitab zubda*, 34–41; Cooper "Land Classification," 91–102; al-Maqrizi, *Khitat*, 1:100–101; Ibn Mammati, *Kitab al-qawanin*, 201–204.

56. Ibn Mammati, *Kitab al-qawanin*, 258–260; Willcocks, *Egyptian Irrigation*, 379–382.

57. al-ʿAsqalani, *ʿInbaʾ al-ghumr*, 5:21; Garcin, *Qus*, 468–507. Shaw notes that it took the Ottomans over a century to subdue Bedouin tribes in Upper Egypt, a task that was never fully completed (*Financial Organization*, 12–13, 19).

58. For example, see Bagnall, *Egypt in Late Antiquity*, 116–157.

CHAPTER 4

1. Rodney Hilton gives some examples of multiple landlords with holdings in one village. See Hilton, *Class Conflict and the Crisis of Feudalism: Essays in Medieval Social History* (London: Hambledon Press, 1985), 3.

2. Graeme Snooks, "The Dynamic Role of the Market in the Anglo-Norman Economy and Beyond, 1086–1300," in *A Commercialising Economy*, ed. Britnell and Campbell, 29, 43.

3. The existence of a labor market was well established in Egypt and had been intensified during the early Mamluk period. This can be clearly seen if one studies the prevailing rent payments reported in the late Fatimid and early Ayyubid periods for basic urban food crops such as wheat, barley, and broad beans. Compare, for example, the payments in kind for pre–Mamluk Egypt (as recorded by Ibn Mammati and al-Makhzumi) with the payments in cash for the Mamluk period (as recorded by Ibn Zahir, al-Maqrizi, al-Qalqashandi, and others). Peasants, especially in Lower Egypt, were expected to pay their rent in cash (in silver or copper coin in the fourteenth century and in copper coin in the fifteenth century). They were able to do so largely because of the existence of a substantial network of rural markets that ensured a two-way flow of goods between urban and rural areas. In cases where the peasant did not have ready cash in hand, there were numerous private merchants who bought grain in the countryside and sold it in the city for a higher price. This relatively neglected subject needs further treatment, but was given considerable attention in Thayer, "Land Politics."

Before the Black Death, peasant mobility was relatively widespread. Different forms of land tenure were available to the peasant in addition to itinerant work during the harvest season. Many of these alternatives dropped out of use in the fifteenth century under pressure from resource-hungry landholders, only to reappear, in an altered form, under the Ottoman landholding system; see Cuno, *Pasha's Peasants*. A full discussion of this subject lies outside the boundaries of this study, but will be the subject of a later work.

The existence of a factor market for land is a more complicated matter. There was a long established precedent for the effective buying and selling (on the peasant level) of the usufruct of the land (where the landholder would not change hands). In addition to this, *iqtaʿat* were bought and sold at intervals during the Mamluk period (especially that of the Ajnad al-Halqa). Finally, there was a land market that hinged upon the use of religious endowments known as *ahli waqf* (as opposed to *khayri waqf*). The former, or family, waqf could be passed along from generation to generation until all descendants of the family had died. Only then would the full proceeds be donated to a charitable foundation. (The strictly charitable use of khayri [altruistic] waqf was more firmly though not exclusively enforced). Although the administrative features of these *awqaf* mirrored the iqtaʿat in almost all respects, their quasi-legal use as an instrument to buy, sell, and effectively own land allowed room for a private economy in land to operate in parallel with the iqtaʿat system. This system lacked the efficiency of an outright ownership system, and was in many ways a reaction to the desire to elude the iqtaʿat system via the well-established and tolerated legal legerdemain known as *hiyal* (literally, "trick" in Arabic). The brilliant and comprehensive study of the awqaf system by the late Muhammad Muhammad Amin (*Al-Awqaf*) needs to be supplemented with further work on the dynamics of this system in fifteenth-century Egypt. Once again, this lies outside the scope of this study, but may soon be the subject of a work by ʿImad Abu Ghazi of Cairo University.

4. Edmund B. Fryde, *Peasants and Landlords in Later Medieval England, c. 1380–1525* (New York: St. Martin's, 1996), 3–6; Rodney Hilton, *The English Peasantry in the Later Middle Ages* (Oxford: Oxford Univ. Press, 1975), 58–59; Horrox, *The Black Death*, 240, 242.

5. John Hatcher argues that under the harsh demographic conditions of the late thirteenth century, many villeins clung to the customary restraints of servile tenure (as opposed to the more precarious terms of leasehold tenancy); see Hatcher, "English Serfdom and Villeinage: Towards a Reassessment," in *Landlords, Peasants, and Politics in Medieval England*, ed. T. H. Aston, 255–261 (Cambridge: Cambridge Univ. Press, 1987). Landlord preference for hired labor might be seen as another reflection of this trend; see David Stone, "Productivity of Hired and Customary Labor: Evidence from Wisbech Barton in the Fourteenth Century," *Economic History Review*, 2nd ser., 50, no. 4 (1997), 641. Christopher Dyer stresses the more traditional view of thirteenth-century manorialism: the rent conditions and restrictions faced by villeins were worse than for those of "free" status; see Dyer, *Standards of Living in the Later Middle Ages: Social Change in England, c. 1200–1520* (Cambridge: Cambridge Univ. Press, 1989), 137–138. See also Rodney Hilton's introduction to Aston, *Landlords, Peasants, and Politics*; Tim North, "Legerwite in the Thirteenth and Fourteenth Centuries," *Past and Present* 111 (May 1986): 3–16.

6. Hilton, *English Peasantry*, 60–61; Larry R. Poos, *A Rural Society after the Black Death: Essex, 1350–1525* (Cambridge: Cambridge Univ. Press, 1991), 246; Hatcher "English Serfdom," 249–250, 270, 281–282.

7. Richard H. Britnell, *The Commercialisation of English Society, 1000–1500* (Cambridge: Cambridge Univ. Press, 1993), 23; Hilton, *English Peasantry*, 43; Dyer, *Standards of Living*, 25, 35–37; North, "Legerwite," 16.

8. Robert Brenner lambastes the focus on markets and commercialization in the timeline of European progress to capitalism. He sees it as two steps removed (the second step being a focus on demography) from his own focus on the structure of class relations and the dynamics of surplus-extraction. As he observes, "both Postan and Le Roy Ladurie have chosen to construct new models largely by substituting a different objective variable, population, for the old, discredited

one, commerce" ("Agrarian Class Structure and Economic Development in Pre-Industrial Development," 30).

9. Dyer, *Living Standards*, 133–134. In the monetary system used in England at this time twelve pence (pence being symbolized here by *d*) equaled one shilling (symbolized here by *s*), and twenty shillings equaled one pound.

10. David Levine, *At the Dawn of Modernity* (Berkeley and Los Angeles: Univ. of California Press, 2001), 161, 287.

11. Hatcher, "English Serfdom," 262.

12. Brenner, "Agrarian Class Structure," 31.

13. Hilton, *Class Conflict*, 213.

14. Dyer, *Living Standards*, 7.

15. Herlihy, *Black Death and Transformation*, 51.

16. Rodney Hilton, *The Decline of Serfdom in Medieval England*, 2nd ed. (London: Macmillan, 1983), 42; Hilton, *English Peasantry*, 60–62; Pamela Nightingale, "Capitalists, Crafts, and Constitutional Change in Late Fourteenth-Century London," *Past and Present* 124 (August 1989), 33. See her reference to D. Moss and L. Murray, "Land and Labour in Fourteenth-Century Tottenham," *London and Middlesex Archaeological Society* 24 (1973), 213–214; Stone, "Hired and Customary Labor," 653–655.

17. A. Luders et al., ed., *Statutes of the Realm, 1101–1713*, 11 vols. (London, 1810–1828), 1:307–308, 311–313, as quoted in Horrox, *The Black Death*, 287–289, 312–316.

18. Fryde, *Peasants and Landlords*, 5–6; Dyer, *Living Standards*, 148; Poos, *Rural Society*, 233, 240–241; Britnell, *Commercialisation*, 218.

19. Fryde, *Peasants and Landlords*, 5–6.

20. Other uprisings provide similar examples of the failure of violent collective action on the part of the peasantry. In addition to the rebellion led by Jack Cade in the mid-fifteenth century, see Hilton, *English Peasantry*, 70–71, on the anti-Yorkist peasant uprising suppressed by Edward IV in 1464. It should be noted that the 1388 additions to the statute of laborers mandated the confiscation of baselards, daggers, and swords from the peasantry. However, instead of having their longbows confiscated, peasants were ordered to engage in regular archery practice rather than other holiday pastimes. The more limited disarmament of peasants in England provides an interesting contrast with the contemporaneous disarmament of villages in Egypt (where only local enforcement agents of the landholding apparatus were allowed to retain weapons of any kind). There are obvious military and social distinctions between a society that employed rural, lower-middle-strata elements in effective combination with armored horsemen and other soldiers, and one that did not. The overall relative strength and cohesiveness of peasant communities on a broader sociological level—including aspects of the legal system—remains an important arena for future comparative research. For England, see Mavis E. Mate, "The East Sussex Land Market and Agrarian Class Structure in the Late Middle Ages," *Past and Present* 139 (1995), 65; Luders, *Statutes*, 2:56–58, as quoted in Horrox, *The Black Death*, 325.

21. Approaching this episode from a completely different, seemingly ahistorical viewpoint, Norman Cantor describes the potential outcome of this revolt as

one that could have led to "a working-class takeover of the government and a socialist state." The peasants "had that possibility within their grasp" and "came close to bringing down the government and establishing a Christian socialist regime" (*Wake of the Plague*, 23, 98–99).

22. Rodney Hilton stresses the importance of the failure of juridical measures to foster unity among the landlords: "If it was true, as we have suggested, that well-paid work for wages offered an alternative to the servile peasant lot, the enforcement of labor legislation, if successful, would have blocked that alternative. This would have strengthened the position of the landlords as against the villeins." Further along Hilton argues, "It was not inevitable that the economic difficulties of the later Middle Ages should result in the loosening of the bonds of serfdom . . . it is therefore difficult to avoid the conclusion that in England, in addition to the mobility and scarcity of labor, surplus of land and shortages of tenants, such non-economic factors as the refusal of tenants to accept the implications of serfdom and the inability of landholders to force them to do so were responsible also for the favorable situation for tenants in the fifteenth century" (*Decline of Serfdom*, 38, 57).

23. Hatcher, "English Serfdom," 281–283; Britnell, *Commercialisation*, 200.

24. Horrox, *The Black Death*, 238; Dyer, *Living Standards*, 147.

25. There were also legal actions aimed at imposing agricultural labor dues on artisans and their apprentices to attempt to force them to work on rural estates during harvest time; see Luders, *Statutes*, 2:56–58, as quoted in Horrox, *The Black Death*, 324.

26. Hilton, *Decline of Serfdom*, 56–57.

27. Fryde, *Peasants and Landlords*, 3; Britnell, *Commercialisation*, 219–221.

28. Dyer, *Living Standards*, 42; Hilton, *Decline of Serfdom*, 39; Britnell, *Commercialisation*, 219.

29. Dyer, *Living Standards*, 42, 97, 146–147, 221; Fryde, *Peasants and Landlords*, 147, 160; Hilton, *English Peasantry*, 24, 35–38, 64–67; Hilton, *Class Conflict*, 13. Phillipp Schofield illustrates the slow pace of this "defeat," emphasizing that the socioeconomic advantages which improved peasant economic conditions (in terms of mobility, rents, wages, etc.) did not fully develop until the fifteenth century. He adds that the plagues have once again assumed the center place as the cause of the collapse of the manorial economy; see Phillipp Schofield, "Tenurial Developments and the Availability of Customary Land in a Later Medieval Community," *Economic History Review*, 2nd ser., 49, no. 2 (1996), 250–251. Along the same lines see Britnell, "Economic Development," in *A Commercialising Economy*, ed. Britnell and Campbell, 25, where he comments, "An argument for the decisive importance of the fourteenth and fifteenth centuries can today only be justified by reference to the decline of serfdom." Compare with Britnell, *Commercialisation*, 217–221.

30. Rural labor was arguably just as mobile prior to the onset of the plagues. But the former pattern was characterized largely by landless labor in desperate search of employment of any kind, whereas the latter pattern took the form of peasants of all strata searching for new and improved economic opportunities. The

latter form was sharply opposed by the landlords. See, for example, Hilton, *Decline of Serfdom*, 33–35; Poos, *Rural Society*, 160–164; Dyer, *Living Standards*, 223; James Ambrose Raftis, *The Estates of Ramsey Abbey: A Study of Economic Growth and Organisation* (Toronto: Pontifical Institute, 1957), 251–252, 258; Raftis, *Tenure and Mobility: Studies in the Social History of the Medieval English Village* (Toronto: Pontifical Institute, 1964), 153; Britnell, *Commercialisation*, 220; Nora Ritchie, "Labour Conditions in Essex during the Reign of Richard II," in *Essays in Economic History*, vol. 2, ed. E. M. Carus-Wilson (London: Edward Arnold, 1962).

31. M. Bailey, *A Marginal Economy?: East Anglian Breckland in the Later Middle Ages* (Cambridge: Cambridge Univ. Press, 1989); Wilhelm Abel, *Agricultural Fluctuations in Europe from the Thirteenth to the Twentieth Centuries*, trans. Olive Ordish (New York: St. Martin's, 1980), 89; Christopher Dyer, "'The Retreat from Marginal Lands': The Growth and Decline of Medieval Rural Settlements," in *The Rural Settlements of Medieval England*, ed. M. Aston, D. Austin, and C. Dyer (Oxford: Blackwell, 1989), 45–57; B. H. Slicher van Bath, *The Agrarian History of Western Europe* (London: Edward Arnold, 1963), 19–20.

32. Cantor, *Wake of the Plague*, 68.

33. Ibid., 68.

34. Dyer, *Living Standards*, 41, 91, 119–120, 125–128; see his reference to Marie Stinson's study, "Assarting and Poverty in Early Fourteenth-Century West Yorkshire," *Landscape History* 5 (1983): 53–67; Nicholas Mayhew, "Population, Money Supply, and the Velocity of Circulation in England, 1300–1700," *Economic History Review*, 2nd ser., 48 (1995), 249; Slicher van Bath, *Agrarian History*, 22.

35. Mate, "East Sussex Land Market," 58, 60; Slicher van Bath, *Agrarian History*, 10, 44; Dyer, *Living Standards*, 127–128, 144, 148–149 (and see his references to numerous studies of rising fertility on 128); Bruce Campbell and Mark Overton have contested this point in the case of Norfolk. See Campbell and Overton, "New Perspective," 38–105. However, they qualify their data on one point (which may have significant implications for the 1350–1500 period) by noting that yield sown per acre is not the same as overall agricultural productivity (output divided by area); see 67, 97–99.

36. Mate, "East Sussex Land Market," 47; and see Bruce Campbell, "Population Pressure, Inheritance, and the Land Market in a Fourteenth-Century Peasant Community," in *Land, Kinship, and Life-Cycle*, ed. Richard Smith (Cambridge: Cambridge Univ. Press, 2002), 87–134.

37. See, for example, Mayhew, "Money Supply," 248–251, and Dyer, *Living Standards*, 151–187.

38. John Hatcher, *Plague, Population, and the English Economy, 1348–1530* (London: Macmillan, 1977), 55.

39. Dyer, *Living Standards*, 103.

40. Ibid., 103–108.

41. For a few examples of estimated losses in landlord revenue, falling rents, rising rural wages, falling grain prices, and the rise in the marginal and total

product of labor, see Dyer, *Living Standards*, 141 (rise in per capita income), 146–147, 171.

42. Mayhew, "Money Supply," 249–250. Note also his Table 1 (244) where he shows a rise in per capita income of modest proportions from 1300 to 1470, and a near doubling of per capita income between 1300 and the early sixteenth century. These figures should also be viewed, as Mayhew does, from the standpoint of "income expressed in terms of its power to purchase . . . goods" (249–250) rather than as monetary indices alone (adjusting for early fourteenth-century stagflation, the late fourteenth- and fifteenth-century excess of grain supply over demand, which caused falling grain prices, etc.; see Dyer, *Living Standards*, 41, 58, 66, 101–102, 113–114, 210, 220, 226, 227, 262–273). Adjusting for the supply of goods and services increases both the 1300–1470 and the 1300–1526 expansions in real per capita income by a considerable degree. Compare this with Mayhew's broader estimates for 1086, 1300, and 1688, and see his analysis of other recent estimates and extrapolations in "Medieval Monetisation," 57–68, 74–75, 195–196. See also Hilton, *Decline of Serfdom*, 44; Richard Lomas, "A Priory and Its Tenants," in *Daily Life in the Late Middle Ages*, ed. Richard Britnell (Stroud, UK: Sutton, 1998); Britnell, *Commercialisation*, 160–164, 168, 184–185, 192; Harry Miskimin, *The Economy of Early Renaissance Europe, 1300–1460* (Cambridge: Cambridge Univ. Press, 1975), 29; Abel, *Agricultural Fluctuations*, 50–67; Evengii Alekseevich Kosminskii, "The Plague De-emphasized," in *The Black Death: A Turning Point in History?*, ed. William Bowsky (Melbourne, Fla: Krieger, 1978), 38–46.

43. Dyer, *Living Standards*, 156.

44. Grenville Astill and Annie Grant, "The Medieval Countryside: Efficiency, Progress, and Change," in *The Countryside of Medieval England*, ed. Astill and Grant (Oxford: Blackwell, 1988), 213–234; Hilton, *English Peasantry*, 38; Mayhew, "Money Supply," 249; Richard Britnell, *Growth and Decline in Colchester, 1300–1525* (Cambridge: Cambridge Univ. Press, 1986), 131–132, 146; Peter Kriedte, *Peasants, Landlords, and Merchant Capitalists: Europe and the World Economy, 1500–1800* (Cambridge: Cambridge Univ. Press, 1983), 31; Miskimin, *Early Renaissance Europe*, 89; Abel, *Agricultural Fluctuations*, 70–72; N. J. G. Pounds, *An Historical Geography of Europe* (Cambridge: Cambridge Univ. Press, 1990), 194; Christopher Dyer, "Changes in Diet in the Late Middle Ages: The Case of Harvest Workers," *Agricultural History Review* 36 (1988), 28–32. Dyer also emphasizes the contrast between demand in the fifteenth century and the thirteenth century, when the quantity of employment was limited by the low demand for goods. Again, this was driven not only by the rise in the per capita level of income—but just as importantly—by the downward redistribution of income; see Dyer, *Living Standards*, 133.

45. Britnell, *Commercialisation*, 177; Kriedte, *Merchant Capitalists*, 14, 18; Poos, *Rural Society*, 16–18, 56–57; Leonard Cantor, *The Changing English Countryside, 1400–1700* (London: Routledge & Kegan Paul, 1987), 18. Factor endowments were utilized in seemingly paradoxical ways. For example, whereas rural part-time weavers in Essex were employed in the midst of relatively high population density and smaller peasant plots of land, parts of southwestern Eng-

land utilized part-time weavers in underpopulated areas where pastoralism left free time for rural labor to engage in weaving.

46. Slicher van Bath, *Agrarian History*, 14; Miskimin, *Early Renaissance Europe*, 35, 55; Mate, "East Sussex Land Market," 57–60. Mate notes that some lords reversed their practice of trying to increase surplus extraction and instead tried to increase and, where possible, diversify production. Mate particularly singles out the knightly families as being especially active in this process; see also Hilton, *English Peasantry*, 45. Hilton also notes that more landlord income was reinvested in agricultural buildings (ibid., 213–214), and Dyer estimates that the percentage of revenue reinvested by landlord aristocracy in buildings for agricultural use more than doubled (from five percent to more than ten percent) between the early fourteenth century and the early fifteenth century (*Living Standards*, 80). That landlords began keeping their own accounts and concentrating on fewer estates, rather than relying exclusively on reeves and bailiffs, is also indicative of increased concentration on flexible and rationalized production (ibid., 94, 100). On cheaper imports of raw wool, see ibid., 143–145.

47. This was true of meat, dairy products, leguminous plants, and grain. Dyer argues that the leasing of demesnes pushed the landlords into the marketplace more often than the sale of demesne product had in the thirteenth century, when hired labor rather than services were generally in use (*Living Standards*, 68, 156, 202).

48. Although there was no direct link between the two, the rise of rural industry in the fifteenth century was accompanied by deurbanization in many areas; see Hilton, *Class Conflict*, 47, 255–257, 265, 277; Nightingale, "Capitalists and Change," 4, 9, 35; Dyer, *Living Standards*, 210: Kriedte, *Merchant Capitalists*, 6–7, 13, 29, 100; Miskimin, *Early Renaissance Europe*, 98. Hilton remarks, "However we interpret urban developments during this period, not even the strictest stagnationist denies the growth of the craft industry in the countryside" (*English Peasantry*, 37–38).

49. Edward Miller, introduction to *The Agrarian History of England and Wales, Vol. 3: 1348–1500*, ed. Miller (Cambridge: Cambridge Univ. Press, 1991), 28–29; Miskimin, *Early Renaissance Europe*, 94–97; Kosminskii, "Plague Deemphasized," 38–46; Nightingale, "Capitalists and Change," 35.

50. Peter Spufford, *Money and Its Use in Medieval Europe* (Cambridge: Cambridge Univ. Press, 1988), 376–377.

51. Dyer, "The Economy and Society," in *The Oxford Illustrated History of Medieval England*, ed. Nigel Saul (Oxford: Oxford Univ. Press, 1997), 169.

52. Michael Zell, "Credit in the Pre-industrial English Woollen Industry," *Economic History Review*, 2nd ser., 49, no. 4 (1996), 686; B. A. Holderness, *Pre-Industrial England: Economy and Society, 1500–1750* (London: Dent, 1976), 154, emphasizes the importance of yeomanry in the process; Kriedte, *Merchant Capitalists*, 34, 125; Fryde, *Peasants and Landlords*, 162. Stephan Epstein argues that the fifteenth-century growth of markets for "mass" commodities within certain regions (i.e., the domestic market within England in this case) was governed by factors that were not necessarily a direct function of the specific type of

landholding system in force ("Cities, Regions, and the late Medieval Crisis: Sicily and Tuscany Compared," *Past and Present* 130 [1991]: 3–50). According to Epstein, these factors were ignored both by Brenner and by Postan and Miskimin in their opposing views of Western Europe's economic development during this period. He points specifically to the "institutional structures which shape peasants' access to markets . . . at the point of distribution" rather than at the point of production (10). According to Epstein, lower scale and more regularized local tolls and tariffs were one of the primary features that could inhibit or enhance the utilization of differential factor endowments, which could in turn determine the development of regional markets for "mass" goods (22). Although this issue is beyond the scope of this article, it is suggestive that England's local tolls seemed to have dropped significantly during the period in question—whereas the opposite seems to have happened in Egypt.

53. The rural cloth industry expanded for a broader income market (Dyer, *Living Standards*, 145, 175–177), but the production of lead (used mainly for roofs, gutters, and water pipes in larger buildings of the aristocracy) and tin (used mainly for pewter, and largely a product for the aristocracy) dropped proportionately with population as landlord incomes declined (103–105).

54. John Fudge, *Cargoes, Embargoes, and Emissaries: The Commercial and Political Interaction of England and the German Hanse, 1450–1510* (Toronto: Univ. of Toronto Press, 1995).

55. Iron mining and bloomeries took second place to the development of the cloth industry, but grew in output and employment on an absolute level (not just per capita); see Dyer, *Living Standards*, 145, 276, and Wendy R. Childs, "England's Iron Trade in the Fifteenth Century," *Economic History Review*, 2nd ser., 36 (1981): 25–47. Important technological innovations in the iron industry were introduced at the end of the fifteenth century, and it is significant that these cut the cost of labor, the scarcest of factor endowments. Both the forge hammer and the blast furnace were introduced and powered by waterwheels. By the early sixteenth century, coal, which was already in use in other industries, began to be processed for the iron-industry blast furnaces because it was needed as a supplement for charcoal. This was the start of coal carbonization techniques that led to the first use of coke 200 years later. These innovations (or expansions in scale) of labor-saving innovations also took place in the cloth industry, where water-powered fulling mills were used more intensively. Hilton also points to relative expansion in other areas of rural industry such as brewing, tanning, and the making of iron implements (*English Peasantry*, 38, 86–89).

56. Hilton, *English Peasantry*, 40, 52, 82.

57. I am using the term "autarchy" here to refer to self-subsistent economies that were not only disconnected from regional market structures (i.e., as self-sufficient as peasant smallholders could be), but were also "outside the boundaries of super-imposed classes and institutions" that relied on surplus extraction for their survival (Hilton, *English Peasantry*, 13). Good examples of autarchy in England would be the fishers and fowlers in the fens and marshes of East Anglia; see Dyer, *Living Standards*, 185. The most obvious example for Egypt would be

the economy of the Bedouin, which was mainly based on subsistence and outside of the political and economic superstructure of Egypt's agrarian and commercial society. Some of the Egyptian peasantry also began to fall into this category, albeit in a very different fashion.

58. Mate, "East Sussex Land Market," 48, 60, 65; Dyer, *Living Standards*, 149–150; Mayhew, "Money Supply," 249; Stone, "Hired and Customary Labor," 652–653; Britnell, *Commercialisation*, 202, 220. Stephan Epstein argues that the importance of peasants as a driving force for innovation has been minimized by economic historians. His view of the peasant as a rational and dynamic actor involved in innovation on the supply side of the economy contrasts sharply with other models of peasant economies that assume both peasant irrationality and a general orientation toward subsistence rather than production for the market (an approach generally favored by both Brenner and Postan—on opposite sides of the Brenner debate); see Epstein, "Cities and Crisis," 5–8. In the context of production in the milling industry, John Langdon makes the same basic argument ("Lordship and Peasant Consumerism in the Milling Industry of Early Fourteenth-Century England," *Past and Present* 145 [1994], 3, 4, 7, 41). As mentioned above, in the wake of depopulation the use of the waterwheel as a labor-saving device was of particular importance as an inducement to further technological innovation. Although the water mill was well developed and in use long before the plagues, it was only after depopulation that it was used on a relatively large scale for activities other than grinding grain.

59. On the transformation of customary tenure, see Hilton, *Decline of Serfdom*, 47–51; Fryde, *Peasants and Landlords*, 161; Hatcher, "English Serfdom," 282. On the simplification of payments, see, for example, Lomas, "Priory and Tenants," 117; North, "Legerwite," 7, 8, 15; Hilton, *Class Conflict*, 122–138. As Dyer points out, this was one of the prominent objectives of villeins seeking free status. The lumping of payments into one basket (by cancellation or amalgamation) was largely achieved by the end of the fifteenth century (*Living Standards*, 69, 138).

60. Hilton, *Class Conflict*, 13–14; Mate, "East Sussex Land Market," 65; Lomas, "Priory and Tenants," 112–113; Dyer, *Living Standards*, 142–143.

61. Peter Gatrell, "Historians and Peasants: Studies of Medieval English Society in a Russian Context," in *Landlords, Peasants, and Politics*, ed. Aston, 413–414; Hilton, *Class Conflict*, 13, 263; Fryde, *Peasants and Landlords*, 165; Lomas, "Priory and Tenants," 111–113; Mayhew, "Money Supply," 149; Mate, "East Sussex Land Market," 55–56. Additionally, during this period, some of the most resourceful yeoman had an exceptionally good chance of entering the ranks of the gentry. Mate provides an interesting example of changing titles for the same person coming before the court of the Star Chamber ("East Sussex Land Market," 63).

62. Britnell, *Commercialisation*, 211ff.

63. See, for example, Hilton, *English Peasantry*, 68–69; Lomas, "Priory and Tenants," 116; Mate "East Sussex Land Market," 62.

64. Kriedte, *Merchant Capitalists*, 29; Mate, "East Sussex Land Market,"

58. Yet it should be noted that not all gentry were so flexible or open to new opportunities; some clung to old methods and often slipped down the social ladder as a consequence; see Dyer, *Living Standards*, 43.

65. Hilton, *English Peasantry*, 42–44; Britnell, *Commercialisation*, 228.

66. At this point, not only had the marginal and average product of labor increased significantly, but the total agrarian product and even landlord revenues were reaching and exceeding their pre-plague levels; see Mayhew, "Money Supply," 244 (Table I for a comparison of 1300 and 1526 output in monetary terms), 248 (for his comment on living standards in the early sixteenth century), and 250–251 (for more analysis of the full recovery in absolute terms in the early sixteenth century). To mention one local case, Durham priory provides an interesting example of an area that had suffered heavy losses in the fifteenth century (not only from the plague but also from Scottish raids) and was now in full recovery; see R. Barrie Dobson, *Church and Society in the Medieval North of England* (London: Hambledon Press, 1996). At this point the output of tin and lead were back up to their pre-plague levels as well and were soon to expand much further in scale; see Dyer, *Living Standards*, 103–104; Cantor, *English Countryside*, 134–135.

67. Dyer, *Living Standards*, 158–159.

68. Hatcher, "English Serfdom," 282; Fryde, *Peasants and Landlords*, 3; Horrox, *The Black Death*, 282.

69. Dyer, *Living Standards*, 182.

70. Hatcher, "English Serfdom," 283.

71. Ibid.

72. Brenner, "Agrarian Class Structure," 48–53; Kriedte, *Merchant Capitalists*, 118–125.

73. Yves Renouard, "The Black Death as a Major Event in World History," in *The Black Death*, ed. Bowsky, 25–34; Fryde, *Peasants and Landlords*, 145.

74. Dyer, *Living Standards*, 103. I am referring here specifically to the price scissors of the late fourteenth century.

75. As David Herlihy remarked of this period, "A more diversified economy, a more intensive use of capital, a more powerful technology, and a higher standard of living for the people—these seem the salient characteristics of the late medieval economy" (*Black Death and Transformation*, 51). Rosemary Horrox has summed up current literature on the economic consequences by remarking that "it is possible to see the fifteenth century as a period of economic decline or stagnation; but there can be very little doubt that most individuals saw their standard of living rise. It was also a period in which many people enjoyed a greater degree of self-determination . . . opportunities in manufacturing and what would now be called the service industries widened" (*The Black Death*, 243).

76. On an absolute level, capital investment did indeed drop. Yet it seems probable from the sources above that it not only increased on a per capita basis, but just as importantly, that the relative composition of capital investment spending changed rather dramatically. True, the pure Marxist critique of feudalism and manorialism is not corroborated by the clear evidence of growth and agrarian re-

investment in the 1086–1348 period, yet it remains true that a high percentage of seigniorial profits was devoted to luxury spending. And one should ask which type of investment was more important to long-term economic growth. Once again, it is true that before 1348 substantial amounts of resources were devoted to bridges, grain waterwheels, and other "utilitarian" developments. Yet, a very substantial portion of capital investment went into building large manor houses for absentee landlords, castles, and enormous cathedrals. All of these investments slowed or came to a halt with the onset of the plagues. Yet, can one possibly argue that these structures were anywhere near as important for long-term economic development as the fifteenth century's smaller residential manor houses, agricultural buildings, fulling mills for cloth manufacture, water-powered hammer forges, and blast furnaces? I think the answer is clearly no, and I would not characterize post-plague England as depressed in the arena of innovative technologies.

CHAPTER 5

1. Heinz Halm, *Ägypten nach den mamlukischen Lehensregistern*, 2 vols. (Wiesbaden: Reichert, 1979; 1982).

2. Tsugitaka Sato, "The Proposers and Supervisors of *al-Rawk al-Nasiri* in Mamluk Egypt," *Mamluk Studies Review* 2 (1998), 73–92.

3. Ibn Mammati, *Kitab al-qawanin*, 279–296.

4. See, for example, Sato, "Evolution of the Iqta' System," 120; Richard Cooper, "A Note on the Dinar Jayshi," *Journal of the Economic and Social History of the Orient* 16 (1973), 317–318.

5. Sato, *State and Rural Society*, 62. It was introduced by Qaraqush Ibn 'Abd Allah al-Asadi after 564/1169, and it was also called *al-dinar al-qaraqushi* and "equaled 13 and ⅓ dirhams or the price of one ardabb of wheat, barley, or broad beans."

6. Ibn al-Ji'an, *Kitab al-tuhfa al-saniyya*, ed. Mortiz (Cairo, 1898), 2–3.

7. Ibid., 3.

8. Ibn Mammati, *Kitab al-qawanin*, 369.

9. Sato, "Evolution of the Iqta' System," 118; al-Maqrizi, *Khitat*, 1:90; *Suluk*, 2:154.

10. Shaw, *Financial Organization*, 220–224.

11. Warren Schultz, "Mamluk Money from Baybars to Barquq: A Study Based on the Literary Evidence and the Numismatic Evidence" (PhD diss., Univ. of Chicago, 1995), 147–149, 163, 234–235.

12. References to the dirham nuqra in the waqfiyyat lack any supporting clauses that one would expect for an existing coin in circulation. The dirham nuqra is simply mentioned without any specification of weight, alloy, or source of issue. The lack of any such formula in these records is highly unusual for an Islamic legal document from this period. As Jeanette Wakin has argued, "Formalism is common to most archaic legal systems, but the Arabic formulary does seem to have become excessively overburdened in this respect." This is particularly true when it comes to the means of payment stipulated in the deed. Wakin adds that

"the most important formulas, if we are to judge by the elaborateness of some of the shurut formulas and the actual practice of the papyri, are those expressing the price. In Tahawi's text, the price is described, and the quality of the coin is also established with the formula 'of standard weight [i.e., seven mithqals] in gold, in minted coin of full weight and good alloy'"; see Jeanette Wakin, *The Function of Documents in Islamic Law: The Chapters on Sales from Tahawi's* Kitab al-Shurut al-Kabir (Albany, N.Y.: State Univ. of New York Press, 1972), 38, 53.

A few examples from the waqfiyyat vividly illustrate this point. In a fourteenth-century waqfiyya for a graveyard, all of the salaries and prices are listed simply by the number of dirhams nuqra, without any further comment. If the dirham nuqra were a real coin in circulation, the lack of precise references to the weight, alloy, quality, and issuing authority of the coin would have opened up a tinderbox for future litigation; see *Waqfiyya Raqam 732*, WA. There are numerous examples from the waqfiyyat that illustrate the same point: see *Waqfiyya Raqam 532*, WA; *Waqfiyya Raqam 713*, WA; *Waqfiyya Raqam 720*, WA; *Waqfiyya Raqam 732*, WA; *Waqfiyya Raqam 759*, WA; *Waqfiyya Raqam 786*, WA.

We also have clear evidence of the opposite case: a tangible, circulating coinage backed by the Mamluk sultanate. The waqfiyyat stipulate that these coins be of good weight and alloy purity. One example is to be found in a fifteenth-century Mamluk document of exchange (*Istibdal*). In this document, payment is made in 500 ashrafi dinars. The documents specify that these coins must be "of good weight" and "free from defects." This clause is the crucial difference that confirms the clear distinction between these coins and the earlier dirham nuqra; see *Waqfiyya Raqam 75*, WA.

There are similar references in the waqfiyyat that prove the same point for coinage backed by the sultanate and circulating at a fixed weight and alloy; see, for example, *Waqfiyya Raqam 532*, WA; *Waqfiyya Raqam 749*, WA; *Waqfiyya Raqam 1019*, WA. Other examples (for both monies of account and circulating currency) can be found in the waqfiyyat in the Egyptian National Archives. See Muhammad Muhammad Amin, ed., *Tadhkirat al-Nabih fi Ayyam al-Mansur wa Banihi* (Cairo, 1982), 2:401–448; Muhammad Muhammad Amin, *Catalogue des documents d'archives du Caire de 239/853 à 922/1516* (Cairo: Institut d'archéologie orientale, 1981).

13. Ibn al-Ji'an, *Kitab al-tuhfa*, 3–4.

14. Al-Qalqashandi, *Subh*, 3:519–522; Sato, "Evolution of the Iqta' System," 115.

15. See, for example, al-Qalqashandi, *Subh*, 3:519–522; Ibn Mammati, *Kitab al-qawanin*, 258–264.

16. Ibn Fadl Allah al-'Umari, *Masalik al-Absar fi Mamalik al-Amsar*, 20:154.

17. Willcocks, *Egyptian Irrigation*.

18. Ibn Mammati, *Kitan al-qawanin*, 258–264.

19. Rivlin, *Agricultural Policy*, 258. The figure of eighty percent discounts "dhurra" (sorghum and millet in the Mamluk period, later Indian corn), which was not collected from peasants during the Mamluk era.

20. Willcocks, *Egyptian Irrigation*, 379–382.

21. The feddan of 5,929 square meters can be verified using the measures of length in use at the time of the 1315 survey. The 165-liter ardabb is larger than that employed by most historians of the Mamluk period. The majority of historians have employed an ardabb of 70 kilograms, or some 92 liters, for wheat. After investigation, I have determined that the smaller ardabb (which is cited in the sources as the "ardabb Masri" and is based on the "small qadah") yields an impossibly small amount of wheat when market prices are evaluated. For example, if the smaller ardabb of 70 kilograms of wheat is compared with market prices for flour, the resulting calculation yields the absurd result that flour is cheaper than wheat. It is conceivable that there could have been an ardabb of wheat equaling approximately 90 kilograms (119 liters of wheat). This would mean that the ardabb of wheat and the ardabb of flour were equal in weight. However, an examination of price ratios reveals that with minimal weight losses upon conversion from wheat to flour added in, flour would still be (in many specific cases cited) more expensive than wheat by weight. Based upon an examination of the price ratios, the charges for cleaning and milling wheat, and the weight loss incurred in cleaning and milling wheat, the most accurate measure seems to be that calculated by William Popper. Popper's ardabb of 275 pounds (125 kilograms and 165 liters for wheat) fits within all of these parameters. For the source of these calculations, see Popper, *Systematic Notes*, 2:100–104. For grain price ratios, see al-Maqrizi, *Suluk*, 3:818, 1133–1134; *Suluk*, 4:712, 718, 780, 794, 799, 964. See also Allouche's comparative prices, *Mamluk Economics*, 99–103, 110–111, and Popper's price ratios in *Systematic Notes*, 2:103. For the varying weight and volume of the ardabb, see al-Qalqashandi's discussion in *Subh*, 3:511–512. For the prices charged for cleaning wheat, milling wheat, and the weight loss involved, see al-Maqrizi, *Ighathat al-Ummah bi-Kashf al-Ghummah*, ed. Sa'id 'Abd al-Fattah 'Ashur (Cairo, 1990), 126–127. Note also that the customary rents in use in 1844 (listed in ardabbs) are close to the ardabb rent listed by Mamluk chroniclers. The similarity of these rents in ardabbs would seem highly suspicious if the ardabb had grown from 92 liters to 198 liters. A smaller change in volume (e.g., from 165 liters to 198 liters) seems much more likely. For the 1844 rents, see Rivlin, *Agricultural Policy*, 262.

22. See Willcocks, *Egyptian Irrigation*, 379–382.

23. Mayhew, "Money Supply," 238–257.

24. Ibid., 244. The value of England's agrarian GDP is based on a rough approximation of urban and rural populations; see Dyer, *Standard of Living*, 23. The value of England's GDP in kilograms of silver is derived from Mayhew's total multiplied by the silver weight of the penny in 1300 (1.44 grams of sterling silver = 1.33 grams pure silver); see Peter Spufford, *Handbook of Medieval Exchange* (London: Offices of the Royal Historical Society, 1986), lix. England's GDP in gold is presented here, but is very imprecise, as it is computed from the bimetallic ratio in Florence at a time when gold currency had not yet been introduced in England; see Spufford, *Handbook of Exchange*, lxi.

25. For example, al-Zahiri, writing in the mid-fifteenth century, gives an estimate of the land values of two large villages (Fariskur and al-Manzala) in the

north of the delta. He also reports that the Diwan al-Mufrad (an administrative department responsible for paying royal Mamluks) had a revenue of some 400,000 dinars and 300,000 ardabbs of wheat, barley, and broad beans. His information on the income of the Diwan al-Mufrad seems to be out of date, since he informs the reader that at the present time "no one knows anything about the condition [of the rural estates of the Diwan al-Mufrad]"; see al-Zahiri, *Kitab zubda*, 34, 107.

26. Omar Toussoun, "Memoirs sur les finances de l'Égypte depuis les pharaons jusqu'à nos jours," *Memoirs de l'Institut d'Égypte* 6 (1924), 153, citing Ibn Iyas, *Bada'i al-zuhur*, 3:266.

27. Popper, *Systematic Notes*, 2:93.

28. Amin, *Al-Awqaf*, 98.

29. Stanford Shaw, *The Budget of Ottoman Egypt 1005–1006/1596–1597* (The Hague: Mouton, 1968).

30. Shaw, *Financial Organization*, 21–22, 63, 95; Shaw, *Ottoman Budget*, 4; Nelly Hanna, *Making Big Money in 1600: The Life and Times of Isma'il Abu Taqiyya, Egyptian Merchant* (Syracuse, N.Y.: Syracuse Univ. Press, 1998), 114–115; Michael Winter, "Ottoman Egypt, 1525–1609," in *The Cambridge History of Egypt, Volume 2: Modern Egypt from 1517 to the End of the Twentieth Century*, ed. M. W. Daly (Cambridge: Cambridge Univ. Press, 1998), 1–5; Daniel Crecelius, "Egypt in the Eighteenth Century," in *Cambridge History of Egypt, Volume 2*, ed. Daly, 59–63.

31. Stanford Shaw, "The Land Law of Ottoman Egypt (960/1553): A Contribution to the Study of Landholding in the Early Years of Ottoman rule in Egypt," *Der Islam* 38 (1962), 109–110; Shaw, *Financial Organization*, 21; Jane Hathaway, "Egypt in the Seventeenth Century," in *Cambridge History of Egypt, Volume 2*, ed. Daly, 38.

32. Shaw, *Financial Organization*, 43, 47.

33. Ibid., 95.

34. For the table of figures, see Shaw, *Ottoman Budget*, 21, 84. For the rate of taxation or rent, see Shaw, *Financial Organization*, 65. This estimate is taken as a rough average from Shaw's reported tax rates (in kind) of ten to fifty percent. It also reflects the rent or tax rate that prevailed under the Mamluk sultanate. Shaw also gives a tax rate in coin (per feddan) of 4–5 paras for 1596–1597, as well as a tax rate in coin of 7–8 paras for the time of Napoleon's expedition (*Financial Organization*, 65). Both of these tax rates in specie are clearly in error. Both of them yield an impossible figure of some 11 million ardabbs (of 4,200 square meters) under cultivation—a ridiculously high figure for any period in Egypt's history. A close examination of Shaw's work leads to the conclusion that the tax rate in kind, coupled with an official valuation of 25 paras per ardabb, is the only possible figure for the Ottoman budget.

35. Shaw, *Financial Organization*, 220–221.

36. Shaw, *Ottoman Budget*, 124; Shaw, *Financial Organization*, 227–228.

37. Shaw, *Financial Organization*, 12–13, 21.

38. Mayhew, "Population," 243–245.

CHAPTER 6

1. Sato, *State and Rural Society*, 229; al-Maqrizi, *Khitat*, 1:171; al-Maqrizi, *Suluk*, 2:111–113; Tarkhan, *al-Nizam*, 75–76; Taghri-Birdi, *Nujum*, 1:190; al-Qalqashandi, *Subh*, 13:117.

2. Copper currency would not be an effective index for comparison. Despite its prominence in fifteenth-century Egypt, copper currency was merely a tertiary (after gold and silver) and petty coinage in Egypt from 1300–1350. Whereas England was able to adhere to the use of silver throughout the period under investigation, copper currency never rose to any prominence in the medieval English economy, and the scarcity of gold coin in England in the early fourteenth century makes the use of silver as a comparative measure all the more important.

3. For the 1300–1350 price series, see al-'Ayni, *'Iqd al-Juman*, 4:72; al-Maqrizi, *Suluk*, 1:898, 908, 949; 2:17, 39, 55, 278, 300, 394, 398, 401, 424, 437, 456, 522, 592, 719; Eliyahu Ashtor, *Histoire des prix et des salaries dans l'Orient medieval* (Paris: SEVPEN, 1969), 284–285. For the 1440–1490 price series, see Boaz Shoshan, "Money Supply and Grain Prices in Fifteenth-Century Egypt," *Economic History Review*, 2nd ser., 36 (1983), 65–67. The values for silver are based on a dirham nuqra of F2/3 silver weighing 2.97 grams and a nisf fidda (half a dirham) of 1.5 grams of ninety percent silver (exchanged for gold ashrafi dinars at a rate of 25 to 1). The values for gold are based on a dinar mithqal of pure gold weighing 4.25 grams and a dinar ashrafi of pure gold weighing 3.45 grams. The ardabb used here is equal to 165 liters of grain.

4. The prices for wheat, barley, and peas for both periods are from David Farmer, "Prices and Wages, 1350–1500," in *The Agrarian History of England and Wales, Vol. III: 1348–1500*, ed. Edward Miller (Cambridge: Cambridge Univ. Press, 1991), 444. The values for gold and silver are from Spufford, *Handbook of Exchange*, lix, lxi.

5. See, for example, Dyer's comment on conditions during the early fourteenth-century famine (*Living Standards*, 268).

6. The studies would bring us into the wider arena of lengthy disputes between historians who see "real" factors (such as population decline and structural changes within the domestic economies) as the driving force behind economic events of the late medieval period and other historians who focus more heavily on monetary flows and long-distance trade. See, for example, Michael Postan, "Medieval Agrarian Society in Its Prime: England," *Cambridge Economic History of Europe from the Decline of the Roman Empire, Vol. 1: Agrarian Life of the Middle Ages*, 2nd ed., (Cambridge: Cambridge Univ. Press, 1966), 560–570; Postan, "The Economic Foundations of Medieval Society," in *Essays on Medieval Agriculture and General Problems of the Medieval Economy* (Cambridge: Cambridge Univ. Press, 1973); Hilton, introduction to *Landlords, Peasants, and Politics*, 1–5; Hilton, "Capitalism: What's in a Name?" in *The Transition from Feudalism to Capitalism*, ed. R. Hilton (London: New Left Books, 1976), 145–158; Hatcher, *Plague, Population, and the English Economy*; Hatcher, "English Serfdom," 247–284; David Herlihy, *Medieval and Renaissance Pistoia: The Social History of an Italian Town, 1200–1430* (New Haven, Conn.: Yale Univ.

Press, 1967); C. C. Paterson, "Silver Stocks and Losses in Ancient and Medieval Times," *Economic History Review*, 2nd. ser., 25 (1972), 205–235; Nicholas Mayhew, "Numismatic Evidence and Falling Prices in the Fourteenth Century," *Economic History Review*, 2nd ser., 27 (1974), 1–15.

7. The precise level of Egyptian monetary stocks during the fourteenth and fifteenth centuries remains unknown. Boaz Shoshan has advanced an interesting theory, albeit cautiously, that Egyptian grain-price inflation in the latter part of the fifteenth century was due to a substantial increase in copper imports ("Money Supply and Prices," 47–67). Shoshan's evidence for increased imports of copper seems well grounded, and it logically dovetails with the end of the silver famine. However, his use of Fisher's equation to attribute rising prices solely to monetary factors (e.g., an increase in copper imports) remains a doubtful proposition. Grain transactions were not conducted solely in copper (as Shoshan maintains). Mamluk sources quote grain prices in both gold and silver, especially during the late fifteenth century. Given the low value of copper relative to gold and silver during the late fifteenth century, gold and silver stocks must have increased as well in order for Shoshan's monetary explanation to work. There is no concrete evidence of an increase in either gold or silver stocks in the late fifteenth century; tentative explorations of the subject have suggested the opposite, that gold and silver were being drained from Egypt to pay for imports from the East; see Abraham Udovitch, Robert Lopez, and Harry Miskimin, "England to Egypt, 1350–1500: Long Term Trends and Long Distance Trade," in *Studies in the Economic History of the Middle East*, ed. Michael Cook, 93–128 (London: Oxford Univ. Press, 1970). Without more concrete evidence to the contrary, this study remains focused upon real factors in the Egyptian economy.

8. Farmer, "Prices and Wages," 480.

9. Spufford, *Money and Its Use*.

10. Ibid., 357.

11. Ibid., 351, 357. See also Pamela Nightingale, "Monetary Contraction and Mercantile Credit in Later Medieval England," *Economic History Review*, 2nd ser., 43, no. 4 (1990), 573. Nightingale demonstrates that credit was ill equipped to take the place of specie during prolonged bullion famines, although she focuses her study more specifically on the late fourteenth century, and her comments on mid-fifteenth-century monetary developments are more exploratory in nature ("Monetary Contraction," 574).

12. Spufford, *Money and Its Use*, 420.

13. This rather obvious point has not gone unnoticed by historians of the late-medieval period; see, for example, Harry Miskimin, *Money, Prices, and Foreign Exchange in Fourteenth-Century France*, Yale Studies in Economics 5 (New Haven, Conn.: Yale Univ. Press, 1963), 53–71.

14. Mayhew, "Money Supply," 238–257.

15. Ibid., 244.

16. Ibid., 239. For an in-depth discussion of mint output and the rate of monetary contraction due to annual losses from wear and tear, hoarding, shipwrecks, and other factors, see John Munro, "Bullion Flows and Monetary Contraction in Late-Medieval England and the Low Countries," in *Precious Metals in the Later*

Medieval and Early Modern Worlds, ed. John F. Richards (Durham, N.C.: Carolina Academic Press, 1983), 97–158. See also Mayhew, "Numismatic Evidence," 1–15. For silver stocks, it should be noted that the normal loss rate of coinage (7 tons per decade = 6,350 kilograms per decade) minus the average output of silver per decade (roughly 3,000 kilograms) equals a total loss of 43,550 kilograms of over some 13 decades from the 1330s to the 1460s. This loss rate does not account for the total drop in silver mint stocks over this period. The loss in silver coinage from the 1330s to the 1460s, computed from silver mint stocks (without factoring in gold), is approximately 193,243 kilograms (Spufford, *Money and Its Use,* 420). For the rate of silver loss and production, see Munro, "Bullion Flows," 101, 156.

17. For the wages of the custodian see Ashtor, "Prix et salaires à l'époque mamlouke: Une étude sur l'état economique de l'Égypte et de la Syrie à la fin du Moyen Âge," *Revue des études islamiques,* 17 (1949), 77, for 1303; *Waqfiyya Raqam 532,* WA, for 1331; *Waqfiyya Raqam 759,* WA, for 1461; *Waqfiyya Raqam 809,* WA, for 1464; Ashtor, "Prix," 81, for 1466; Ashtor, "Prix," 83, for 1474.

For the wages of the doorkeeper, see Ashtor, "Prix," 65, for 1303; *Waqfiyya Raqam 738,* WA, for 1464; Ashtor, "Prix," 81, for 1466; *Waqfiyya Raqam 886,* WA, for 1474.

For the wages of the water carrier, see Ashtor, "Prix," 77, for 1303; *Waqfiyya Raqam 809,* WA, for 1464; Ashtor, "Prix," 81–82, for 1474.

For the wages of the reader see Ashtor, "Prix," 77, for 1303; *Waqfiyya Raqam 532,* WA, for 1331; *Waqfiyya Raqam 749,* WA, for 1444; *Waqfiyya Raqam 759,* WA, for 1461; *Waqfiyya Raqam 809,* WA, for 1464; Ashtor, "Prix," 81, for 1466; Ashtor, "Prix," 81–82, for 1474.

The values for silver are based on a dirham nuqra of F2/3 silver weighing 2.97 grams and a nisf fidda (half a dirham) of 1.5 grams of ninety percent silver (exchanged for gold ashrafi dinars at a rate of 25 to 1). The values for gold are based on a dinar mithqal of pure gold weighing 4.25 grams and a dinar ashrafi of pure gold weighing 3.45 grams. The wages given in the waqfiyat are given on a monthly basis, and have been converted to annual wages by simply multiplying that figure by 12.

18. For the wages of the carpenter and the slater-tiler, see Farmer, "Prices and Wages," 471. For the wages of the thatcher and thatcher's mate, see Dyer, *Living Standards,* 215. The values for gold and silver are from Spufford, *Handbook of Exchange,* lix, lxi. Christopher Dyer has kindly provided me with the basis for converting the daily wages into annual wages based on the following subtractions: 52 Sundays, 40–50 saints days, as well as a few days for illness and bad weather. The approximation used here is therefore 250 working days per year.

CHAPTER 7

1. Robert Brenner, "Agrarian Class Structure," 21.
2. Ibid., 23.
3. Ibid., 41–43.

4. Daniel Crecelius, "The Waqfiyyah of Muhammad Bey Abu al-Dhahab," *Journal of the American Research Center in Egypt*, 15 (1978), 83–146.

5. See Janet Abu-Lughod's discussion of these industries in *Before European Hegemony*, 230–244.

6. Brenner, "Agrarian Class Structure," 42–43.

SELECT BIBLIOGRAPHY

PART 1: EGYPT AND THE MIDDLE EAST

Primary Sources

al-'Asadi, Muhammad ibn Khalil (d. 855/1451). *Kitab al-taysir wa'l-i' tibar.* Edited by Ahmad Tulaymat. Cairo, 1968.

al-'Ayni, Mahmud Ibn Ahmad (d. 855/1451). *'Iqd al-juman fi ta'rikh ahl al-zaman.* Edited by Muhammad Muhammad Amin. Vols. I–IV: 648/1250 to 707/1308. Cairo: al-Hay'at al-Misriyya al-'Amma l'il-Kitab, 1987–1992.

Ibn Duqmaq (d. 809/1406). *Kitab al-intisar li-wasitat 'iqd al-amsar.* Beirut, 1960.

Ibn Fadl Allah al-'Umari (d. 749/1349). *Masalik al-Absar fi Mamalik al-Amsar* (Routes toward Insight into the Capital Empires). 27 vols. Edited by Fuat Sezgin, A. Jokhosha, and E. Neubauer. Frankfurt am Main: Institute for the History of Arabic-Islamic Science at the Johann Wolfgang Goethe University, 1988.

Ibn Hajar al-'Asqalani (d. 852/1448). *'Inba' al-ghumr bi-anba' al-'umr.* Edited by Hassan Habashi. 3 vols. Cairo: al-Majlis al-'Ali, 1969–1972.

———. *al-Durar al-kamina.* 6 vols. Cairo, 1929–1932.

Ibn Humam, Kamal al-Din Muhammad (d. 861/1459). *Sharh fath al-qadir.* 8 vols. Cairo, 1970.

Ibn Iyas (d. 930/1523–1524). *Bada'i' al-zuhur fi-waqa'i' al-duhur.* Edited by Mustafa Muhammad. 5 vols. Cairo: al-Hay'at al-Misriyya al-'Amma li'l-Kitab, 1982.

———. *Nuzhat al-umam fi'l-'aja'ib wa'l-hukm.* Edited by Muhammad Zaynham Muhammad 'Azab. Cairo: Maktab Madbuli, 1995.

Ibn al-Ji'an (d. 885/1480). *Kitab al-tuhfa al-saniyya.* Edited by Mortiz. Cairo, 1898.

———. *Al-qawl al-mustazraf fi safar mawlana al-malik al-ashraf.* Translated by Henriette Devonshire. *Institut français d'archéologie orientale bulletin* 20 (1922): 2–40.

Ibn Mammati, al-As'ad (d. 656/1209). *Kitab al-qawanin al-dawanin.* Edited by Aziz Suryal Atiya. Cairo, 1943.

Ibn Taghri-Birdi (d. 857/1453). *Hawadith al-duhur fi mada al-ayyam wa'l-shuhur.* 8 vols. Edited by William Popper. Berkeley and Los Angeles: Univ. of California Press, 1930–1931.

———. *Al-Nujum al-zahira fi muluk Misr wa'l-Qahira.* 16 vols. Cairo: Dar al-Kutub al-Misriyya. Translated by William Popper as *History of Egypt, 1382–1469* (Univ. of California Publications in Semitic Philology, Vols. 13, 14, and 17). Berkeley and Los Angeles: Univ. of California Press, 1954–1957.

———. *Al-Manhal al-safi.* Edited by Muhammad Muhammad Amin. Vols. 1–7. Cairo, 1985–1994.

Ibn al-Ukhuwwa (d. 729/1329). *al-Ma'alim al-qurba fi ahkam al-hisba.* Translated by Reuben Levy. Cambridge: Cambridge Univ. Press, 1938.

Ibn Zahir (d. 874/1470). *Kitab rawdat al-adib.* Vol. 3. Cairo, 1970.

al-Makhzumi, Abi Yasin 'Ali ibn 'Uthman (d. 575/1189). *Kitab al-minhaj fi 'ilm kharaj misr.* Edited by Claude Cahen. Cairo: Institut français, 1986.

al-Maqrizi, Taqi al-Din (d. 843/1442). *Kitab al-suluk li-ma'arifat duwul al-muluk.* Edited by Sa'id 'Abd al-Fattah 'Ashur. 12 vols. Cairo, 1957–1973.

———. *Kitab al-mawa'iz wa'l-i'tibar bi-dhikr al-khitat wa'l-athar.* 2 vols. Cairo, 1853–1854.

———. *Ighathat al-'Ummah bi-Kashf al-Ghumma.* Cairo, 1957. Translated by Adel Allouche as *Mamluk Economics: A Study and Translation of Al-Maqrizi's Ighathah.* Salt Lake City: Univ. of Utah Press, 1994.

al-Nabalusi, 'Uthman ibn Ibrahim (d. 660/1261). *Kitab ta'rikh al-fayyum wa-biladihi.* Cairo, 1898.

al-Nuwayri, Ahmad ibn 'Abd al-Wahhab (d. 732/1332). *Nihayat al-arab fi funun al-adab.* Vol. 8. Cairo: al-Mu'assasah al-misriyah al-'ammah lil- ta'lif wa'l-tarjamah wa'l-tiba'ah wa'l-nashr, 1964.

al-Qalqashandi, Ahmad ibn 'Ali (d. 821/1418). *Subh al-a'sha' fi-sina'at al-insha'.* 14 vols. Cairo, 1913–1919.

al-Sayrafi, al-Jawhari (fl. 875/1470). *Inba' al-hasr fi abna' al-'asr.* Edited by Hasan Habashi. Cairo, 1970.

al-Sharbini, Yusif bin Muhammad bin Ahmad 'Abd al-Jawad bin Hadar (d. 1101/1690). *Hazz al-quhuf fi sharh qasidat abi shaduf.* Cairo (Bulaq), 1890.

Subki, 'Abd al-Wahhab bin 'Ali (d. 771/1370). *Mu'id al-ni'am wa mubid al-niqam.* Leiden, Neth.: E. J. Brill, 1908.

———. *Tabaqat al-shafi'iyya al-kubra.* 6 vols. Cairo, 1906–1907.

al-Suyuti, 'Abd al-Rahman Ibn Abi Bakr (d. 911/1505). *Husn al-muhadara fi akhbar Misr wa'l-Qahira.* 2 vols. Beirut: Dar al-Kutub al-'Ilmiyya, 1997.

al-Udfuwi (d. 784/1347). *al-Tali' al-sa'id al-jami' li-asma' al-fudala' wa'l-ruh bi-a'la al-sa'id.* Cairo, 1966.

Waqfiyyat. Cairo: Wizarat al-Awqaf (Ministry of Religious Endowments; cited as "WA").

al-Zahiri, Khalil bin Shahin (d. 872/1468). *Kitab zubdat kashf al-mamalik wa bayyan al-turuq wa'l-masalik.* Edited by Paul Ravaisse. Paris: Imprimerie Nationale, 1894.

Secondary Sources

'Abd al-Rahim, 'Abd al-Rahim. "Land Tenure in Egypt and Its Social Effects on Egyptian Society: 1798–1813." In *Land Tenure and Social Transformation in the Middle East*, edited by Tarif Khalidi, 237–247. Beirut: American University of Beirut, 1984.

———. "Financial Burdens on the Peasants under the Aegis of the Iltizam System in Egypt." *Journal of Asian and African Studies* 12 (1976): 122–138.

'Abd al-Raziq, Ahmad. "La hisba et le muhtasib en Égypte au temps des mamluks." *Annales islamologiques* 13 (1977): 116–143.

Abu Zayd, Muhammad Muhammad 'Ali. *Al-Nil wa Misr*. Cairo: Dar al-Hidayat, 1987.

'Afifi, Muhammad. *Al-Awqaf wa'l-Hayat al-Iqtisadiyya fi Misr fi'l-'Asr al-'Uthmani*. Cairo: al-Hay'at al-Misriyya al-'Amma l'il-Kitab, 1991.

Allan, James W. "Sha'ban, Barquq, and the Decline of the Mamluk Metalworking Industry." *Muqarnas* 2 (1984): 85–94.

Amin, Muhammad Muhammad. *Al-Awqaf wa'l-Hayat al-Ijtima'iyya fi Misr*. Cairo: Dar al-Nahda al-'Arabiyya, 1980.

———. *Catalogue des documents d'archives du Caire de 239/853 à 922/1516*. Cairo: Institut d'archéologie orientale, 1981.

———. "Qaytbay's Endowment Deed for a School and Store of Arms at Damietta." [in Arabic] *Egyptian Historical Revue* 22 (1975): 203–244.

———, ed. *Tadhkirat al-Nabih fi Ayyam al-Mansur wa Banihi*. Cairo, 1982.

Ashtor, Eliyahu. "The Diet of the Salaried Classes in the Medieval Near East." *Journal of Asian History* 4 (1970): 1–24.

———. *East-West Trade in the Medieval Mediterranean*. London: Variorum Reprints, 1986.

———. "The Economic Decline of the Middle East in the Later Middle Ages: An Outline." *Asian and African Studies: Journal of the Israel Oriental Society* 15 (1981): 253–286.

———. *Histoire des prix et des salaires dans l'Orient médiéval*. Paris: SEVPEN, 1969.

———. *Levant Trade in the Later Middle Ages*. Princeton, N.J.: Princeton Univ. Press, 1983.

———. "Levantine Sugar Industry in the Later Middle Ages: An Example of Technological Decline." *Israel Oriental Studies* 7 (1977): 226–280.

———. *Les métaux précieux et la balance des payements du Proche-Orient à la basse époque*. Paris, 1971.

———. "Prix et salaires à l'époque mamlouke: Une étude sur l'état économique de l'Égypte et de la Syrie à la fin du Moyen Âge." *Revue des études islamiques* 17 (1949): 49–94.

———. *A Social and Economic History of the Near East in the Middle Ages*. Berkeley and Los Angeles: Univ. of California Press, 1976.

———. *Studies on the Levantine Trade in the Middle Ages*. London: Variorum Reprints, 1978.

———. *Technology, Industry, and Trade: The Levant versus Europe, 1250–1500*. London: Variorum Reprints, 1992.

———. "The Wheat Supply of the Mamluk Kingdom." *Asian and African Studies* 18 (1984): 283–295.

ʿAshur, Saʿid ʿAbd al-Fattah. *Al-Mujtamaʿ al-Misri fi ʿAsr Salatin al-Mamalik.* Cairo: Dar al-Nahda al-ʿArabiyya, 1993.

———. *Al-ʿAsr al-Mamaliki fi Masr waʾl-Sham.* 3rd ed. Cairo, 1994.

Atil, Essin. "Mamluk Painting in the Late Fifteenth Century." *Muqarnas* 2 (1984): 159–172.

———. *Renaissance of Islam: Art of the Mamluks.* Washington, D.C.: Smithsonian Institution Press, 1981.

Ayalon, David. *The Mamluk Military Society: Collected Studies.* London: Variorum Reprints, 1979.

———. "The Plague and Its Effects upon the Mamluk Army." *Journal of the Royal Asiatic Society of Great Britain and Ireland* (1946): 67–73.

———. "Regarding Population Estimates in the Countries of Medieval Islam." *Journal of the Economic and Social History of the Orient* 28 (1985): 1–19.

———. "Studies in al-Jabarti, I. Notes on the Transformation of Mamluk Society in Egypt under the Ottomans." *Journal of the Economic and Social History of the Orient* 3 (1960): 148–174, 275–325.

———. *Studies on the Mamluks of Egypt (1250–1517).* London: Variorum Reprints, 1977.

———. "Studies on the Structure of the Mamluk Army." Part II. *Bulletin of the School of Oriental and African Studies* 15 (1953): 448–476.

———. "Studies on the Structure of the Mamluk Army." Part III. *Bulletin of the School of Oriental and African Studies* 16 (1953): 57–90.

———. "The System of Payment in Mamluk Military Society." *Journal of the Economic and Social History of Orient* 1 (1957–1958): 37–65, 257–296.

Ayrout, Henry Habib. *The Egyptian Peasant.* Translated by John Alden Williams. Boston: Beacon Press, 1963.

Bacharach, Jere. "Circassian Mamluk Historians and their Quantitative Data." *Journal of the American Research Center in Egypt* 12 (1975): 75–87.

———. "Circassian Monetary Policy: Copper." *Journal of the Economic and Social History of the Orient* 19 (1976): 32–47.

———. "Circassian Monetary Policy: Silver." *Numismatic Chronicle* 11 (1971): 267–281.

———. "The Dinar versus the Ducat." *International Journal of Middle East Studies* 4 (1973): 77–96.

———. "Monetary Movements in Medieval Egypt, 1171–1517." In *Precious Metals in the Later Medieval and Early Modern Worlds*, edited by J. F. Richards, 159–181. Durham, N.C.: Carolina Academic Press, 1983.

———. "A Study of the Correlation between Textual Sources and Numismatic Evidence for Mamluk Egypt and Syria, AH 784–872/1382–1468." PhD diss., Univ. of Michigan, 1967.

Bacharach, Jere, and Adon A. Gordus. "Studies on the Fineness of Silver Coins." *Journal of the Economic and Social History of the Orient* 11 (1968): 298–317.

Baer, Gabriel. *Studies in the Social History of Modern Egypt.* Chicago: Univ. of Chicago Press, 1969.

————. "Village and City in Egypt and Syria." In Udovitch, *The Islamic Middle East*, 595–645.

Bagnall, Roger. *Egypt in Late Antiquity*. Princeton, N.J.: Princeton Univ. Press, 1993.

Ball, John. *Contributions to the Geography of Egypt*. Cairo (Bulaq): Government Press, 1939.

Balog, Paul. "Aperçus sur la technique du monnayage musulman au Moyen-Âge." *Bulletin de l'institut égyptien* 31 (1948–1949): 95–105.

————. "The Coinage of the Mamluk Sultans: Additions and Corrections." *American Numismatic Society Museum Notes* 16 (1970): 113–171.

————. *The Coinage of the Mamluk Sultans of Egypt and Syria*. Numismatic Studies 12. New York: American Numismatic Society, 1964.

————. "History of the Dirham in Egypt from the Fatimid Conquest until the Collapse of the Mamluk Empire, 358–922 AH/968–1517 AD." *Revue numismatique*, 6th ser., 3 (1961): 109–146.

Behrens-Abouseif, Doris. *Egypt's Adjustment to Ottoman Rule: Institutions, Waqf, and Architecture in Cairo (16th and 17th Centuries)*. Leiden, Neth.: E. J. Brill, 1994.

Berkey, John. "The Mamluks as Muslims: The Military Elite and the Construction of Islam in Medieval Egypt." In *The Mamluks in Egyptian Politics and Society*, edited by Thomas Philipp and Ulrich Haarmann, 163–173. Cambridge: Cambridge Univ. Press, 1998.

Borsch, Stuart. "Nile Floods and the Irrigation System." *Mamluk Studies Review* 4 (January 2000): 131–145.

Bowman, Alan K. *Egypt after the Pharaohs, 332 BC–AD 642: From Alexander to the Arab Conquest*. London: British Museum Publications, 1986.

Brett, Michael. "The Way of the Peasant." *Bulletin of the School of Oriental and African Studies* 46 (1986): 44–56.

Brown, Robin M. "Late Islamic Ceramic Production and Distribution in the Southern Levant: A Socio-Economic and Political Interpretation." PhD diss., State Univ. of New York at Binghamton, 1992.

Butzer, Karl W. *Early Hydraulic Civilization in Egypt: A Study in Cultural Ecology*. Chicago: Univ. of Chicago Press, 1976.

Cahen, Claude. "Al-Makhzumi et Ibn Mammati sur l'agriculture egyptienne médiévale." *Annales islamologiques* 11 (1972) 141–151.

————. "Contribution à l'étude des impôts dans l'Égypte médiévale." *Journal of the Economic and Social History of the Orient* 5 (1962): 244–275.

————. "Douanes et commerce dans les ports méditerranéens de l'Égypte médiévale d'après le Minhadj d'al-Makhzumi." *Journal of the Economic and Social History of the Orient* 7 (1964): 217–314.

————. "L'évolution de l'Ikta' de IXe au XIIIe siècles." *Annales: Économies, Sociétés, Civilisations* 8 (1953): 25–52.

————. "Nomades et Sédentaires dans le Monde Musulman du Milieu du Moyen Âge." In *Islamic Civilisation*, edited by D. S. Richards, 93–104. London: William Clowes & Sons, 1973.

————. "Notes pour une histoire de l'agriculture dans les pays musulmans médiévaux." *Journal of the Economic and Social History of the Orient* 14 (1971): 63–68.

Chapoutot-Remadi, Mounira. "L'agriculture dans l'empire mamluk au moyen âge." *Les Cahiers de Tunisie* 85–86 (1974): 23–45.

————. "Une Grande Crise à la Fin du XIIIe siècle en Égypte." *Journal of the Economic and Social History of the Orient* 26 (1983), 217–245.

Chaudhuri, K. N. *Asia before Europe: Economy and Civilization of the Indian Ocean from the Rise of Islam to 1750.* Cambridge: Cambridge Univ. Press, 1990.

Conrad, Lawrence. "The Plague in the Early Medieval Near East." PhD diss., Princeton Univ., 1981.

Cook, Michael. "Islam: A Commment." In *Europe and the Rise of Capitalism*, edited by Jean Baechler, John A. Hall, and Michael Mann, 131–135. Oxford: Basil Blackwell, 1988.

Cooper, Richard. "Agriculture in Egypt, 640–1800." In *Handbuch der Orientalistik, Abteilung 1: Der nahe und der mittlere Osten, Band VI: Geschichte der islamischen Lander, Abschnitt 6: Wirtsschaftgeschichte des vorderen Orients in der islamischer Zeit, Teil 1*, edited by Bertold Spuler, 188–204. Leiden and Köln: Brill, 1977.

————. "The Assessment and Collection of Kharaj Tax in Medieval Egypt." *Journal of the American Oriental Society* 96 (1976): 365–382.

————. "Ibn Mammati's Rules for Ministries." PhD diss., Univ. of California, Berkeley, 1973.

————. "Land Classification Terminology and the Assessment of the Kharaj Tax in Medieval Egypt." *Journal of the Economic and Social History of the Orient* 17 (1974): 91–102.

————. "A Note on the Dinar Jayshi." *Journal of the Economic and Social History of the Orient* 16 (1973): 317–318.

Coulson, N. J. *Succession in the Muslim Family.* Cambridge: Cambridge Univ. Press, 1971.

Crecelius, Daniel. "Egypt in the Eighteenth Century." In Daly, *The Cambridge History of Egypt, Vol.2*, 59–86.

————. "Incidents of Waqf Cases in Three Cairo Courts: 1640–1802." *Journal of the Economic and Social History of the Orient* 29 (1986): 176–189.

————. "The Waqfiyyah of Muhammad Bey Abu al-Dhahab." *Journal of the American Research Center in Egypt* 15 (1978): 83–146.

Cuno, Kenneth. "Joint Family Households and Rural Notables in 19th-Century Egypt." *International Journal of Middle East Studies* 27 (1995): 485–502.

————. *The Pasha's Peasants: Land, Society, and Economy in Lower Egypt, 1740–1858.* Cambridge: Cambridge Univ. Press, 1992.

Daly, M. W., ed. *The Cambridge History of Egypt, Vol. 2: Modern Egypt from 1715 to the End of the Twentieth Century.* Cambridge: Cambridge Univ. Press, 1998.

Darrag, Ahmad. *L'Égypte sous le règne de Barsbay, 825–841/1422–1438.* Damascus, 1961.

Day, John. "The Great Bullion Famine of the Fifteenth Century." *Past and Present* 79 (1978): 3–54.

Dols, Michael. *The Black Death in the Middle East.* Princeton, N.J.: Princeton Univ. Press, 1977.

———. "The General Mortality of the Black Death in the Mamluk Empire." In Udovitch, *The Islamic Middle East*, 397–428.

———. "Al-Manbiji's 'Report of the Plague': A Treatise on the Plague of 764–765/1362–1364 in the Middle East." In Williman, *The Black Death*, 65–75.

Ehrenkreutz, Andrew. "Contribution to the Knowledge of the Fiscal Administration of Egypt in the Middle Ages." *Bulletin of the School of Oriental and African Studies* 16 (1954): 502–514.

Escovitch, J. H. *The Office of Qadi al-Qudat in Cairo under the Bahri Mamluks.* Berlin: Carl Schwartz Verlag, 1984.

———. "Vocational Patterns of the Scribes of the Mamluk Chancery." *Arabica* 23 (1976): 42–64.

Fernandez, Leonor. "On Conducting the Affairs of State: A Guideline of the Fourteenth Century." *Annales islamologiques* 24 (1988): 81–91.

Frantz, G. M. "Saving and Investment in Medieval Egypt." PhD diss., Univ. of Michigan, 1978.

Frantz-Murphy, G. M. "A New Interpretation of the Economic History of Medieval Egypt: The Role of the Textile Industry, 254–567/868–1171." *Journal of the Economic and Social History of the Orient* 24 (1981): 274–297.

Garcin, Jean-Claude. *Un centre musulman de la Haute-Égypte médiévale: Qus.* Cairo: Institut français d'archéologie orientale, 1976.

———. *Espaces, pouvoirs, et idéologies de l'Égypte médiévale.* London: Variorum Reprints, 1987.

———. "The Mamluk Military System and the Blocking of Medieval Moslem Society." *Europe and the Rise of Capitalism*, edited by Jean Baechler, John A. Hall, and Michael Mann, 113–130. Oxford: Basil Blackwell, 1988.

———. "Note sur les rapportes entre bédouins et fellahs à l'époque mamluke." *Annales islamologiques* 14 (1978): 147–163.

Garcin, Jean-Claude, and Mustapha Anouar Taher. "Enquête sur le financement d'un waqf égyptien du XVe siecle: Les comptes de Jawhar al-Lala." *Journal of the Economic and Social History of the Orient* 38 (1995): 262–304.

Glick, Thomas. *Islamic and Christian Spain in the early Middle Ages.* Princeton, N.J.: Princeton Univ. Press, 1979.

Greif, Avner. "Reputation and Coalitions in Medieval Trade: Evidence on the Maghribi Traders." *Journal of Economic History* 49, no. 3 (1989): 857–882.

Halm, Heinz. *Agypten nach den mamlukischen Lehensregistern.* 2 vols. Beihefte zum Tubinger Atlas des Vorderen Orients, Reihe B., nr. 38. Wiesbaden: Reichert, 1979; 1982.

Hanna, Nelly. *Making Big Money in 1600: The Life and Times of Isma'il Abu Taqiyya, Egyptian Merchant.* Syracuse, N.Y.: Syracuse Univ. Press, 1998.

Hathaway, Jane. "Egypt in the Seventeenth Century," in Daly, *The Cambridge History of Egypt, Volume 2.*

────. "'Mamluk Households' and 'Mamluk Factions' in Ottoman Egypt: A Reconsideration." *The Cambridge History of Egypt, Vol. 2: Modern Egypt from 1715 to the End of the Twentieth Century*, edited by M. W. Daly, 107–117. Cambridge: Cambridge Univ. Press, 1998.

al-Hayla, Muhammad al-Habib. "al-Nizam al-idariyya bi-Misr fi'l-qarn at-tasi' al-hijri min khilal Kitab rawdat al-abid." In *al-Nadwah al-dawliyah fi-ta'rikh al-Qahirah*, 3:1043–1095. Cairo, 1971.

Hennequin, Gilles. "Mamlouks et metaux precieux à propos de la balance des paiements de l'état syro-egyptienne à la fin du Moyen-Âge: Une question de methode." *Annales islamologiques* 12 (1974): 37–44.

────. "Nouveaux aperçus sur l'histoire monetaire de l'Egypt à la fin du Moyen-Âge." *Annales islamologiques* 13 (1977): 179–215.

────. "Points de vue sur l'histoire monétaire de l'Égypte musulmane au Moyen-Âge." *Annales islamologiques* 12 (1974): 1–36.

────. "Waqf et monnaie dans l'Égypte Mamluke." *Journal of the Economic and Social History of the Orient* 38 (1995): 305–312.

Irwin, Robert. "Factions in Medieval Egypt." *Journal of the Royal Asiatic Society* (1986): 228–246.

────. *The Middle East in the Middle Ages: The Early Mamluk Sultanate, 1250–1382*. London and Sydney: Croom Helm, 1986.

Labib, Subhi. *Handelsgeschichte Ägyptens im Spätmittelalter (1171–1517)*. Weisbaden: Franz Steiner Verlag, 1965.

Lagardere, Vincent. "Moulins d'Occident musulman au moyen âge (IXe au XVe siècles): Al-Andalus." *Al-Qantara* [Madrid] 12 (1991): 59–118.

Lamm, Johan Carl. *Cotton in Medieval Textiles of the Near East*. Paris: Librarie Orientaliste Paul Geuthner, 1937.

Lapidus, Ira. "The Grain Economy of Mamluk Egypt." *Journal of the Economic and Social History of the Orient* 12 (1969): 1–15.

────. *Muslim Cities in the Later Middle Ages*. Cambridge, Mass.: Harvard Univ. Press, 1967.

Larson, Barbara. "The Rural Marketing System of Egypt over the Last Three Hundred Years." *Comparative Studies in Society and History* 27, no. 3 (1985): 494–530.

Levanoni, Amalia. *A Turning Point in Mamluk History: The Third Reign of al-Nasir Muhammad ibn Qalawun, 1310–1341*. Leiden, Neth.: E. J. Brill, 1995.

Lewis, Archibald. "The Islamic World and the Latin West, 1350–1500." *Speculum* 65 (1990): 833–844.

Lindholm, Charles. *The Islamic Middle East: An Historical Anthropology*. Cambridge, Mass.: Blackwell, 1996.

Little, Donald. *History and Historiography of the Mamluks*. London: Variorum Reprints, 1988.

────. *An Introduction to Mamluk Historiography*. Wiesbaden: Franz Steiner, 1970.

Lutfi, Huda. "Coptic Festivals of the Nile: Aberrations of the Past?" In *The Mam-*

luks in Egyptian Politics and Society, edited by Thomas Philipp and Ulrich Haarmann, 254–282. Cambridge: Cambridge Univ. Press, 1998.

MacKenzie, Neil D. *Ayyubid Cairo: A Topographical Study.* Cairo: American University in Cairo Press, 1992.

Mackie, Louise. "Woven Status: Mamluk Silks and Carpets." *Muslim World* 73 (1983): 253–261.

al-Mahdi, Siham Muhammad. "Nuqud Jadida li-Zahir Baybars." *Dirasat 'Athariyya Islamiyya* 4 (1990): 111–125.

Marcus, Abraham. *The Middle East on the Eve of Modernity: Aleppo in the Eighteenth Century.* New York: Columbia Univ. Press, 1989.

Martel-Thoumian, Bernadette. *Les civils et l'administration dans l'état militaire mamluk (IXe–XVe siècle).* Damascus: Institut français de Damas, 1991.

Mayer, Leo. "Lead Coins of Barquq." *Quarterly of the Department of Antiquities in Palestine* 3 (1934): 20–23.

Michel, N. "Les Rizaq Ahbasiyya, terres agricoles en main mort dans l'Égypte mamlouke et ottomane." *Annales islamologiques* 30 (1996): 105–198.

Miller, R. L. "Counting Calories in Egyptian Ration Texts." *Journal of the Economic and Social History of the Orient* 34 (1991): 257–269.

Morimoto, Kosei. "Land Tenure in Egypt during the Early Islamic Period." *Orient: Report of the Society for Near Eastern Studies in Japan* 11 (1975): 109–153.

Mortel, Richard. "Aspects of Mamluk Relations with Jedda during the Fifteenth Century: The Case of Timraz al-Mu'ayyadi." *Journal of Islamic Studies* 6, no. 1 (1995): 1–13.

———. "Prices in Mecca during the Mamluk Period." *Journal of the Economic and Social History of the Orient* 32 (1989): 279–334.

al-Nabarawi, Ra'fat Muhammad. "A Hoard of Mamluk Copper Coins in the American Numismatic Society Museum." *Dirasat 'Athariyya Islamiyya* 4 (1991): 25–54.

———. *al-Sikka al-Islamiya fi Misr: 'Asr Dawlat al-Mamalik al-Jarakisa.* Cairo: Markaz al-Hadara al-'Arabiyya l'il-I'laam wal-Nashr, 1993.

al-Najidi, Hammud ibn Muhammad ibn 'Ali. *al-Nizam al-Naqdi al-Mamluki.* Alexandria: Mu'assasat al-Thaqafa al-Jami'iya, 1993.

Nicol, Norman D., Raf'at Muhammad al-Nabarawi, and Jere Bacharach. *Catalogue of the Coins, Glass Weights, Dies, and Metals in the Egyptian National Library, Cairo.* The American Research Center in Egypt Catalogs. Malibu, Calif.: Undena Press, 1982.

Panzac, Daniel. "The Population of Egypt in the Nineteenth Century." *Asian and African Studies* 21 (1987): 11–32.

Petry, Carl. *The Civilian Elite of Cairo in the Later Middle Ages.* Princeton, N.J.: Princeton Univ. Press, 1981.

———. "A Paradox of Patronage during the Later Mamluk Period." *Muslim World* 73 (1983): 182–207.

———. *Protectors or Praetorians?: The Last Mamluk Sultans and Egypt's Waning as a Great Power.* Albany: State Univ. of New York Press, 1994.

Pipes, Daniel. *Slave Soldiers and Islam: The Genesis of a Military System*. New Haven, Conn.: Yale Univ. Press, 1981.

Poliak, Abraham N., "Some Notes on the Feudal System of the Mamluks." *Journal of the Royal Asiatic Society* (1937): 97–107.

Popper, William. *The Cairo Nilometer: Studies in Ibn Taghri Birdi's Chronicles of Egypt: I*. Univ. of California Publications in Semitic Philology 12. Berkeley and Los Angeles: Univ. of California Press, 1951.

———. *Egypt and Syria under the Circassian Sultans, AD 1382–1468: Systematic Notes to Ibn Taghri Birdi's Chronicles of Egypt*. Univ. of California Publications in Semitic Philology 15–16. Berkeley and Los Angeles: Univ. of California Press, 1955–1957.

Qasim, 'Abd al-Qasim. *al-Nil wa'l-mujtama' al-misri fi 'asr salatin al-mamalik*. Cairo: Dar al-ma'arif, 1978.

Rabie, Hassanein. *The Financial System of Egypt, AH 564–741/AD 1169–1341*. Oxford: Oxford Univ. Press, 1972.

Al-Rahman, 'Abd al-Rahim 'Abd. "The Documents of the Egyptian Religious Courts (al-Mahakim al-Shar'iyya) as a Source for the Study of Ottoman Provincial Administration in Egypt (923/1517–1213/1798)." *Journal of the Economic and Social History of the Orient* 34 (1991): 88–97.

Raymond, Andre. *Cairo*. Translated by Willard Wood. Cambridge, Mass.: Harvard Univ. Press, 2000.

———. "Cairo's Area and Population in the Early 15th Century." *Muqarnas* 2 (1984): 21–31.

Richards, D. S. "A Mamluk Petition and a Report from the Diwan al-Jaysh." *Bulletin of the School of Oriental and African Studies* 40 (1977): 1–15.

Russell, Josiah Cox. "The Population of Medieval Egypt." *Journal of the American Research Center in Egypt* 5 (1966): 69–82.

Sari, Saleh Khaled. "A Note on al-Maqrizi's Remarks Regarding the Silver Coinage of Baybars." *Journal of the Economic and Social History of the Orient* 31 (1988): 298–301.

Sato, Tsugitaka. "The Evolution of the Iqta' System under the Mamluks: An Analysis of al-Rawk al-Husami and al-Rawk al-Nasiri." *Memoirs of the Research Department of the Toyo Bunko (the Oriental Library)* 37 (1979): 99–131.

———. "The Iqta' Policy of Sultan Baybars." *Orient: Report of the Society for Near Eastern Studies in Japan* 22 (1986): 85–104.

———. "Irrigation in Rural Egypt from the 12th to the 14th Centuries." *Orient: Report of the Society for Near Eastern Studies in Japan* 8 (1972): 81–92.

———. "The Proposers and Supervisors of al-Rawk al-Nasiri in Mamluk Egypt." *Mamluk Studies Review* 2 (1998): 73–92.

———. "Rural Society and the Fellahin in Egypt from the 12th to the 14th Centuries." *Memoirs of the Institute of Oriental Culture* 59 (1973): 1–107.

———. *State and Rural Society in Medieval Islam: Sultans, Muqtas, and Fallahun*. Leiden, Neth.: E. J. Brill, 1997.

Schacht, Joseph. *An Introduction to Islamic Law*. Oxford: Oxford Univ. Press, 1964.

Schultz, Warren. "Mamluk Money from Baybars to Barquq: A Study Based on the Literary Evidence and the Numismatic Evidence." PhD diss., Univ. of Chicago, 1995.

———. "The Monetary History of Egypt, 642–1517." *The Cambridge History of Egypt, Volume 1: Islamic Egypt, 640–1517*, edited by Carl Petry, 318–338. Cambridge: Cambridge Univ. Press, 1998.

Serjeant, Robert Bertram. *Islamic Textiles: Material for a History up to the Mongol Conquest*. Beirut: Librarie du Liban, 1972.

Shaw, Stanford J. *The Budget of Ottoman Egypt, 1005–1006/1596–1597*. The Hague: Mouton, 1968.

———. *The Financial and Administrative Organization and Development of Ottoman Egypt, 1517–1798*. Princeton, N.J.: Princeton Univ. Press, 1962.

———. "The Land Law of Ottoman Egypt (960/1553): A Contribution to the Study of Landholding in the Early Years of Ottoman Rule in Egypt." *Der Islam* 38 (1962): 106–137.

Shoshan, Boaz. "Exchange-Rate Policies in Fifteenth-Century Egypt." *Journal of the Economic and Social History of the Orient* 39 (1986): 28–51.

———. "From Silver to Copper: Monetary Changes in 15th-Century Egypt." *Studia Islamica* 56 (1982): 97–116.

———. "Grain Riots and the 'Moral Economy' in Cairo, 1350–1517." *Journal of Interdisciplinary History* 10 (1980): 459–478.

———. "Money, Prices, and Population in Mamluk Egypt." PhD diss., Princeton Univ., 1978.

———. "Money Supply and Grain Prices in Fifteenth-Century Egypt." *Economic History Review*, 2nd ser., 36 (1983): 47–67.

———. "The Politics of Notables in Medieval Islam." *Asian and African Studies* 20 (1986): 179–215.

Staffa, Susan J. *Conquest and Fusion: The Social Evolution of Cairo, AD 642–1850*. Leiden, Neth.: E. J. Brill, 1977.

Tarhkan, Ibrahim 'Ali. *al-Nizam al-Iqta'i fi'l-Sharq al-Awsat fi'l-'Usur al-Wusta*. Cairo: Dar al-Katib al-'Arabi at-Taba'a wa'l-Nashra, 1968.

Thayer, Jennifer M. "Land Politics and Power Networks in Mamluk Egypt." PhD diss., New York Univ., 1993.

Tucker, William F. "Natural Disasters and the Peasantry in Mamluk Egypt." *Journal of the Economic and Social History of the Orient* 24 (1981): 215–224.

Udovitch, Abraham, ed. *The Islamic Middle East, 700–1900: Studies in Social and Economic History*. Princeton, N.J.: Darwin Press, 1981.

Udovitch, Abraham L., Robert Lopez, and Harry Miskimin. "England to Egypt, 1350–1500: Long Term Trends and Long Distance Trade." In *Studies in the Economic History of the Middle East*, edited by Michael Cook, 93–128. London: Oxford Univ. Press, 1970.

Wagstaff, J. Malcolm. *The Evolution of Middle Eastern Landscapes: An Outline to AD 1848*. Totowa, N.J.: Barnes & Noble Books, 1985.

Wakin, Jeanette. *The Function of Documents in Islamic Law: The Chapters on Sales from Tahawi's Kitab al-Shurut al-Kabir*. Albany: State Univ. of New York Press, 1972.

Watson, Andrew. *Agricultural Innovation in the Early Islamic World.* Cambridge: Cambridge Univ. Press, 1983.

Wickham, Chris. "The Uniqueness of the East." *Journal of Peasant Studies* 12 (1985): 166–196.

Willcocks, William. *Egyptian Irrigation.* 2nd ed. London: Spon, 1899.

Winter, Michael. "Ottoman Egypt, 1525–1609." In Daly, *The Cambridge History of Egypt, Volume 2.*

Wittfogel, Karl. "The Hydraulic Civilizations." In *Man's Role in Changing the Face of the Earth* (2 vols.), edited by William L. Thomas, Jr., 152–164. Chicago: Univ. of Chicago Press, 1956.

———. *Oriental Despotism: A Comparative Study of Total Power.* New Haven, Conn.: Yale Univ. Press, 1957.

PART 2: ENGLAND, WESTERN EUROPE, AND WORLD HISTORY

Acheson, Eric. *A Gentry Community: Leicestershire in the Fifteenth Century, c. 1422–c. 1485.* Cambridge: Cambridge Univ. Press, 1992.

Amin, Samir. *Accumulation on a World Scale.* New York: Monthly Review Press, 1974.

———. *Eurocentrism.* New York: Monthly Review Press, 1989.

———. *Unequal Development: An Essay on the Social Formations of Peripheral Capitalism.* New York: Monthly Review Press, 1976.

Astill, Grenville, and Annie Grant, eds. *The Countryside of Medieval England.* Oxford: Blackwell, 1988.

Aston, T. H., ed. *Landlords, Peasants, and Politics in Medieval England.* Cambridge: Cambridge Univ. Press, 1987.

Aston, T. H. and C. H. E. Philpin, eds. *The Brenner Debate: Agrarian Class Structure and Economic Development in Pre-Industrial Europe.* Cambridge: Cambridge Univ. Press, 1985.

Bean, John Malcolm William. "The Black Death: The Crisis and Its Social and Economic Consequences." In Williman, *The Black Death,* 144–188.

———. "Plague, Population, and Economic Decline in England in the Later Middle Ages." *Economic History Review,* 2nd ser., 15 (1963): 423–437.

Biraben, Jean-Noel. *Les hommes et la peste en France et dans les pays européens et méditerranéens.* The Hague: Mouton, 1975.

Blaut, James M. *Eight Eurocentric Historians.* New York: Guilford Press, 2000.

Bowsky, William M., ed. *The Black Death: A Turning Point in History?* New York: Holt, Rinehart, and Winston, 1971. Reprint, Melbourne, Fla.: Krieger, 1978. Page references are to the 1978 edition.

———. "The Impact of the Black Death upon Sienese Government and Society." *Speculum* 39 (1964): 1–34.

Brenner, Robert. "Agrarian Class Structure and Economic Development in Pre-Industrial Europe." In Aston and Philpin, *The Brenner Debate,* 10–63.

————. "The Agrarian Roots of European Capitalism." In Aston and Philpin, *The Brenner Debate*, 213–327.

Bridbury, Anthony R. *Medieval English Clothmaking: An Economic Survey.* London: Heinemann Educational, 1982.

Britnell, Richard H. *The Commercialisation of English Society, 1000–1500.* Cambridge: Cambridge Univ. Press, 1993.

————. "Economic Development." In *A Commercializing Economy: England, 1086 to c. 1300*, edited by Richard Britnell and Bruce Campbell. New York: St. Martin's, 1995.

————. "Feudal Reaction after the Black Death in the Palatinate of Durham." *Past and Present* 128 (August 1990): 28–47.

————. *Growth and Decline in Colchester, 1300–1525.* Cambridge: Cambridge Univ. Press, 1986.

————. "Minor Landlords in England and Medieval Agrarian Capitalism." In Aston, *Landlords, Peasants, and Politics*, 227–246.

Britnell, Richard, and Bruce Campbell, eds. *A Commercializing Economy: England, 1086 to c. 1300.* New York: St. Martin's, 1995.

Caferro, William. "City and Country in Fourteenth-Century Siena: The Second Half of the Fourteenth Century." *Journal of Economic History* 54 (March 1994): 85–103.

Campbell, Bruce. *English Seigniorial Agriculture, 1250–1450.* New York: Cambridge Univ. Press, 2000.

————. "Population Pressure, Inheritance, and the Land Market in a Fourteenth-Century Peasant Community." In *Land, Kinship, and Life-Cycle*, edited by Richard Smith, 87–134. Cambridge: Cambridge Univ. Press, 2002.

Campbell, Bruce, and Mark Overton. "A New Perspective on Medieval and Early Modern Agriculture: Six Centuries of Norfolk Farming, c. 1250–c. 1850." *Past and Present* 141 (November 1993): 38–105.

Cantor, Leonard. *The Changing English Countryside, 1400–1700.* London: Routledge and Kegan Paul, 1987.

Cantor, Norman. *In the Wake of the Plague: The Black Death and the World it Made.* New York: Free Press, 2001.

Carmichael, Ann. *The Plague and the Poor in Renaissance Florence.* Cambridge: Cambridge Univ. Press, 1986.

Childs, Wendy R. "England's Iron Trade in the Fifteenth Century." *Economic History Review*, 2nd ser., 36 (1981): 25–47.

Cipolla, Carlo M. *Before the Industrial Revolution: European Society and Economy, 1000–1700.* New York: Norton, 1980.

————. *Money, Prices, and Civilization in the Mediterranean World, Fifth to Seventeenth Centuries.* New York: Gordian Press, 1967.

Clark, Gregory. "The Economics of Exhaustion, the Postan Study, and the Agricultural Revolution." *Journal of Economic History* 52 (1992): 61–84.

————. "Production Growth without Technical Change in European Agriculture before 1850." *Journal of Economic History* 48 (1987): 419–432.

Coss, Peter R. "The Formation of the English Gentry." *Past and Present* 147 (1995): 38–64.

Deaux, George. *The Black Death, 1347*. New York: Weybright and Talley, 1969.

Dobson, R. Barrie. *Church and Society in the Medieval North of England*. London: Hambledon Press, 1996.

Duncan-Jones, Richard P. "The Impact of the Antonine Plague." *Journal of Roman Archaeology* 9 (1996): 108–136.

Dyer, Christopher. "Changes in Diet in the Late Middle Ages: The Case of Harvest Workers." *Agricultural History Review* 36 (1988): 21–38.

———. "The Economy and Society." In *The Oxford Illustrated History of Medieval England*, edited by Nigel Saul, 137–173. Oxford: Oxford Univ. Press, 1997.

———. " 'The Retreat from Marginal Lands': The Growth and Decline of Medieval Rural Settlements." In *The Rural Settlements of Medieval England*, edited by M. Aston, D. Austin, and C. Dyer, 45–57. Oxford: Blackwell, 1989.

———. "Rural Europe." In *The New Cambridge Medieval History: Vol. VII, c. 1415–c. 1500*, edited by Christopher Allmand, 106–120. Cambridge: Cambridge Univ. Press, 1998.

———. *Standards of Living in the Later Middle Ages: Social Change in England, c. 1200–1520*. Cambridge: Cambridge Univ. Press, 1989.

Epstein, Stephan R. "Cities, Regions, and the late Medieval Crisis: Sicily and Tuscany Compared." *Past and Present* 130 (1991): 3–50.

———. *An Island for Itself: Economic Development and Social Change in Late Medieval Sicily*. Cambridge: Cambridge Univ. Press, 1992.

Farmer, David. "Prices and Wages, 1350–1500." In *The Agrarian History of England and Wales, Vol. III: 1348–1500*, edited by Edward Miller, 431–525. Cambridge: Cambridge Univ. Press, 1991.

Fox-Genovese, Elizabeth. *Fruits of Merchant Capital: Slavery and Bourgeois Property in the Rise and Expansion of Capitalism*. New York: Oxford Univ. Press, 1983.

Frank, Andre Gunder. *World Accumulation, 1492–1789*. New York: Monthly Review Press, 1978.

Fryde, Edmund B. *Peasants and Landlords in Later Medieval England, c. 1380–1525*. New York: St. Martin's, 1996.

Fudge, John. *Cargoes, Embargoes, and Emissaries: The Commercial and Political Interaction of England and the German Hanse, 1450–1510*. Toronto: Univ. of Toronto Press, 1995.

Gatrell, Peter. "Historians and Peasants: Studies of Medieval English Society in a Russian Context." In Aston, *Landlords, Peasants, and Politics*, 394–422.

Goody, Esther N. *From Craft to Industry: The Ethnography of Proto-Industrial Cloth Production*. Cambridge, Cambridge Univ. Press, 1982.

Gould, J. D. "The Price Revolution Reconsidered." *Economic History Review*, 2nd ser., 17 (1964–1965): 249–266.

Grigg, David. "The Nutritional Transition in Western Europe." *Journal of Historical Geography* 21 (1995): 247–261.

Harris, Jonathan. "Two Byzantine Craftsmen in Fifteenth-Century London." *Journal of Medieval History* 21 (1995): 387–403.

Hatcher, John. "English Serfdom and Villeinage: Towards a Reassessment." In Aston, *Landlords, Peasants, and Politics*, 247-284.

———. *Plague, Population, and the English Economy, 1348–1530*. London: Macmillan, 1977.

Herlihy, David. *The Black Death and the Transformation of the West*. Cambridge, Mass.: Harvard Univ. Press, 1997.

Hilton, Rodney. "Capitalism: What's in a Name?" In *The Transition from Feudalism to Capitalism*, edited by Rodney Hilton, 145–158. London: New Left Books, 1976.

———. *Class Conflict and the Crisis of Feudalism: Essays in Medieval Social History*. London: Hambledon Press, 1985.

———. "A Crisis of Feudalism." In *The Brenner Debate*, ed. Aston and Philpin, 119–137.

———. *The Decline of Serfdom in Medieval England*. 2nd ed. London: Macmillan, 1983.

———. *The English Peasantry in the Later Middle Ages*. Oxford: Oxford Univ. Press, 1975.

———. Introduction to Aston, *Landlords, Peasants, and Politics*.

Hodgett, Gerald. *A Social and Economic History of Medieval Europe*. London: Methuen, 1972.

Holderness, B. A. *Pre-Industrial England: Economy and Society, 1500–1750*. London: Dent, 1976.

Hopcroft, Rosemary. *Regions, Institutions, and Agrarian Change in European History*. Ann Arbor: Univ. of Michigan Press, 1999.

Horrox, Rosemary, ed. and trans. *The Black Death*. Manchester: Manchester Univ. Press, 1994.

Kosminskii, Evengii Alekseevich. "The Plague De-emphasized." In Bowsky, *The Black Death*, 38–46.

Kriedte, Peter. *Peasants, Landlords, and Merchant Capitalists: Europe and the World Economy, 1500–1800*. Cambridge: Cambridge Univ. Press, 1983.

Kriedte, Peter, Hans Medick, and Jürgen Schlumbohm. *Industrialization before Industrialization: Rural Industry in the Genesis of Capitalism*. Translated by Beate Schempp. Cambridge: Cambridge Univ. Press, 1981.

Kula, Witold. *An Economic Theory of the Feudal System*. London: Verso, 1987.

Landes, David. *The Wealth and Poverty of Nations: Why Some Are So Rich and Some So Poor*. New York: Norton, 1998.

Lane, Frederic C., and Reinhold C. Mueller. *Money and Banking in Medieval and Renaissance Venice, Vol. 1: Coins and Moneys of Account*. Baltimore: Johns Hopkins Univ. Press, 1985.

Langdon, John. "Lordship and Peasant Consumerism in the Milling Industry of Early Fourteenth-Century England." *Past and Present* 145 (1994): 3–46.

Lerner, Robert E. "The Black Death and Western European Eschatological Mentalities." In Williman, *The Black Death*, 77–105.

Levine, David. *At the Dawn of Modernity: Biology, Culture, and Material Life in Europe after the Year 1000*. Berkeley and Los Angeles: Univ. of California Press, 2001.

Livi Bacci, Massimo. *Population and Nutrition: An Essay on European Demographic History*. Cambridge: Cambridge Univ. Press, 1990.

Lomas, Richard. "A Priory and Its Tenants." In *Daily Life in the Late Middle Ages*, edited by Richard Britnell. Stroud, UK: Sutton, 1998.

Mate, Mavis. "The East Sussex Land Market and Agrarian Class Structure in the Late Middle Ages." *Past and Present* 139 (1993): 46–65.

Mayhew, Nicholas J. "Modelling Medieval Monetisation." In *A Commercialising Economy: England, 1086–1300*, edited by Bruce Campbell and Richard Britnell. Manchester: Manchester Univ. Press, 1995.

———. "Numismatic Evidence and Falling Prices in the Fourteenth Century." *Economic History Review*, 2nd ser., 27 (1974): 1–15.

———. "Population, Money Supply, and the Velocity of Circulation in England, 1300–1700." *Economic History Review*, 2nd ser., 48 (1995): 238–257.

McKendrick, Neil. "Home Demand and Economic Growth." In *Historical Perspectives: Studies of English Thought and Society in Honour of J. H. Plumb*, edited by Neil McKendrick. London: Europa, 1974.

McNeill, William. *Plagues and Peoples*. New York: Doubleday, 1976.

Miller, Edward, ed. *The Agrarian History of England and Wales, Volume III: 1348–1500*. Cambridge: Cambridge Univ. Press, 1991.

Miskimin, Harry. *The Economy of Early Renaissance Europe, 1300–1460*. Cambridge: Cambridge Univ. Press, 1975.

Munro, John. "Bullion Flows and Monetary Contraction in Late-Medieval England and the Low Countries." In *Precious Metals in the Later Medieval and Early Modern Worlds*, edited by John F. Richards, 97–158. Durham, N.C.: Carolina Academic Press, 1983. Reprinted in Munro, *Bullion Flows*.

———. *Bullion Flows and Monetary Policies in England and the Low Countries, 1350–1500*. Variorum Collected Studies 355. Aldershot, UK: Ashgate, 1992.

———. *Textiles, Towns, and Trade: Essays in the Economy of Late-Medieval England and the Low Countries*. Variorum Collected Studies 442. Aldershot, UK: Ashgate, 1994.

Nightingale, Pamela. "Capitalists, Crafts, and Constitutional Change in Late Fourteenth-Century London." *Past and Present* 124 (August 1989): 3–35.

———. "Monetary Contraction and Mercantile Credit in Later Medieval England." *Economic History Review*, 2nd ser., 43 (1990): 560–575.

Norris, John. "East or West? The Geographic Origin of the Black Death." *Bulletin of the History of Medicine* 51 (1977): 1–24.

North, Douglass C. *Structure and Change in Economic History*. New York: Norton, 1981.

North, Douglass C., and Robert Paul Thomas. *The Rise of the Western World: A New Economic History*. Cambridge: Cambridge Univ. Press, 1973.

North, Tim. "Legerwite in the Thirteenth and Fourteenth Centuries." *Past and Present* 111 (May 1986): 3–16.

Ormand, Mark, and Phillip Lindley, eds. *The Black Death in England*. Stamford, UK: Paul Watkins, 1995.

Platt, Colin. *King Death: The Black Death and Its Aftermath in Late Medieval England*. Toronto: Toronto Univ. Press, 1996.

Poos, Larry R. *A Rural Society after the Black Death: Essex, 1350–1525.* Cambridge: Cambridge Univ. Press, 1991.

Pounds, Norman John Greville. *An Historical Geography of Europe.* Cambridge: Cambridge Univ. Press, 1990.

Raftis, James Ambrose. *The Estates of Ramsey Abbey: A Study of Economic Growth and Organisation.* Toronto: Pontifical Institute, 1957.

———. *Tenure and Mobility: Studies in the Social History of the Medieval English Village.* Toronto: Pontifical Institute, 1964.

Razi, Zvi. "Family, Land, and the Village Community in Later Medieval England." In Aston, *Landlords, Peasants, and Politics,* 360–393.

Renouard, Yves. "The Black Death as a Major Event in World History." In Bowsky, *The Black Death,* 25–34.

Robbins, Helen. "A Comparison of the Effects of the Black Death on the Economic Organization of France and England." *Journal of Political Economy* 36 (1928): 447–479.

Russell, Josiah Cox. *Medieval Regions and their Cities.* Bloomington: Indiana Univ. Press, 1972.

———. *Medieval Demography: Essays.* New York: AMS Press, 1987.

Schofield, Phillipp. "Tenurial Developments and the Availability of Customary Land in a Later Medieval Community." *Economic History Review,* 2nd ser., 49, no. 2 (1996): 250–267.

Skwara, Erich Wolfgang. *Plague in Siena.* Translated by Michael Roloff. Riverside, Calif.: Ariadne Press, 1994.

Slicher van Bath, Bernard Hendrik. *The Agrarian History of Western Europe.* London: Edward Arnold, 1963.

Snooks, Graeme. "The Dynamic Role of the Market in the Anglo-Norman Economy and Beyond, 1086–1300." In *A Commercialising Economy,* ed. Britnell and Campbell, 27–54.

Spufford, Peter. *Handbook of Medieval Exchange.* London: Offices of the Royal Historical Society, 1986.

———. *Money and Its Use in Medieval Europe.* Cambridge: Cambridge Univ. Press, 1988.

Stone, David. "Productivity of Hired and Customary Labor: Evidence from Wisbech Barton in the Fourteenth Century." *Economic History Review,* 2nd ser., 50, no. 4 (1997): 640–656.

Veitch, John. "Repudiations and Confiscations by the Medieval State." *Journal of Economic History* 46 (March 1986): 31–36.

Wallerstein, Immanuel. *The Modern World System.* New York: Academic Press, 1974.

Williman, Daniel, ed. *The Black Death: The Impact of the Fourteenth-Century Plague.* Medieval and Renaissance Texts and Studies 13. Binghamton, N.Y.: State Univ. of New York Press (Center for Medieval and Early Renaissance Studies), 1982.

Zell, Michael. "Credit in the Pre-industrial English Woollen Industry." *Economic History Review,* 2nd ser., 49, no. 4 (1996): 667–691.

Ziegler, Philip. *The Black Death.* New York: John Day, 1969.

INDEX

Italic page numbers refer to figures and tables.